Politics and Public Policy in Scotland

Politics and Public Policy in Scotland

Arthur Midwinter

Michael Keating

James Mitchell

First published 1991

Published by
MACMILLAN EDUCATION LTD
Houndmills, Basingstoke, Hampshire RG21 2XS
and London
Companies and representatives
throughout the world

Printed in Hong Kong

British Library Cataloguing in Publication Data
Midwinter, Arthur F.
Politics and public policy in Scotland.
1. Scotland. Politics
I. Title II. Keating, Michael, *1950–* III. Mitchell,
James, *1960–*
320.9411
ISBN 0–333–52265–6 (hardcover)
ISBN 0–333–52266–4 (paperback)

Contents

List of Tables

List of Figures

Preface and Acknowledgements

The title of this book begs a question. Is there such a thing as Scottish politics? The United Kingdom is, after all, a unitary state with a single government and parliament. Our answer is that there is a Scottish politics but that its nature and the position of Scotland within the United Kingdom are widely misunderstood. Some English scholars are in the habit of using the terms Britain and England interchangeably, an error which is almost universal in Europe and North America. Even within Scotland, few people are aware of the details of the distinct governmental arrangements.

Part of the problem lies in the peculiar development of the United Kingdom, a gradual process of territorial consolidation combined with an extraordinary absence of constitutional imagination. There has been neither an attempt to build a uniform state on continental lines, nor an acceptance of the federal principle for recognising and accommodating distinct territories within the state. Parliamentary sovereignty (itself a disputed legacy of the Union of 1707), remains the only firm constitutional principle. Under the unitary Parliament, a wide variety of political and administrative practices have developed in the different parts of the kingdom. Lacking its own source of political authority, Scottish administration has developed piecemeal, without clear organising principles or consistency. This argument, developed in an earlier book (Keating and Midwinter, 1983) was unwittingly confirmed by a critic who commented that 'the clearances apparently did their work only too well, leaving only some agencies here, a complex organisational network there' (Raab, 1983). Intended as a criticism of the book, this serves as a fair, if rather sweeping, portrayal of Scottish government. Until administrative decentralisation is matched with a degree of local political control, Scottish government will remain an untidy patchwork without the clear focal point provided by a representative body.

Our treatment of Scottish politics and government reflects this inconsistency. There is much to be said on the Scottish Office and on local government. The role of the Treasury, the main instruments of economic policy-making, the civil service and, to some degree, the main political parties, are not so distinctive in Scotland and our coverage reflects this. The future of Scottish government is a matter of political controversy and we return at several points to this theme.

The book is a collaborative effort and the order of names simply reflects our practice of rotation in joint publications. We all contributed to Chapter 1. Keating and Mitchell drafted Chapters 2 and 8. Mitchell drafted Chapter 3. Keating drafted Chapter 4 and Midwinter Chapters 5 and 7. Midwinter and Keating drafted Chapter 6 and we all contributed to Chapter 9. The final draft of the whole book was written by Keating.

We have received advice, comments and criticisms from a number of colleagues, including Alan Alexander, David Heald, Richard Parry and Urlan Wannop. Many people in public life have shared their experiences with us and, though discretion and the canons of governmental secrecy prevent our naming them, we are grateful. Any errors of fact or judgement remain our exclusive responsibility.

ARTHUR MIDWINTER
MICHAEL KEATING
JAMES MITCHELL

1
Scottish Politics and Society

Twenty years ago, a book on Scottish politics might have appeared an eccentricity. The 'homogeneity thesis' held that Britain's unitary constitution rested on a uniform political culture in which issues of territory, religion, language and nationality had given way to a politics of class. In the early 1970s, Blondel (1974, p.20) could describe Britain as probably the most homogeneous of industrial nations, while Finer (1974, p.137), conceding that Britain had had its 'nationalities', 'language', 'religious' and 'constitutional' problems, insisted that these were no more. The mid 1970s provided a rude awakening, with the resurgence of Scottish and Welsh nationalism and the renewed conflict in Northern Ireland, reminding us that the United Kingdom is a complex, multinational state. Since then, there has been a considerable body of writing on Scottish politics and government. Much of this has been polemical, advocating or opposing constitutional change, but a number of analytical works have sought to understand and explain institutions and modes of political behaviour neglected while the homogeneity thesis held sway. There has been a strong focus in the recent literature on nationalism, rescuing it from antiquarianism and trivialisation; but scholars have also recognised that there is much more to Scottish politics than nationalism.

Scotland stands out from the rest of Britain in several politically important respects – in institutions, political behaviour and political issues. It has its own legal system, requiring a substantial body of separate Scottish legislation. There is a separate department of central government for Scottish affairs,

1

headed by a Secretary of State. Local government is organised differently from England and bodies such as the Scottish Development Agency and Highlands and Islands Development Board have had no counterparts south of the border. The British political parties are the dominant forces in Scotland, but levels of support for them have frequently diverged from those in England and the Scottish National Party (SNP) provides a distinctive element. The big political issues, such as unemployment, inflation, housing and social services are common to England and Scotland yet their relative importance can differ, while issues of religion, Highland development and Home Rule have historically given Scottish politics a distinctive character.

On the other hand, the United Kingdom remains a unitary state, in which ultimate sovereignty resides in Parliament. This mixture of unity and diversity has been a source of confusion to observers since the Union of England and Scotland in 1707. Described in England as the Act of Union and Scotland as the Treaty, this document abolished the separate parliaments of England and Scotland a century after the crowns had been united. It replaced these with a new Parliament for a state which, until the Union with Ireland in 1800, was called Great Britain. While the Union of 1707 has some claim to be the founding document of the British constitution, however, no provision was made for its enforcement and in practice the new Parliament came to see itself as the continuation of the English one, as though only the Scottish one had been abolished. It arrogated to itself unlimited sovereignty and in 1954 even celebrated its 'seven-hundredth anniversary'.

The position of Scotland within the British polity has, from time to time, sparked a lively academic debate. While there is a 'Scottish politics', its nature and the significance of Scottish differences continue to elude the standard conceptual categories of political science. Kellas (1973, 1984, 1989), in a pioneering work on the subject, wrote of a 'Scottish political system'. Rose (1970, 1985) described it as a culturally distinctive but politically integrated nation in a multinational state. A French observer (Leruez, 1983) wrote of *une nation sans état*. Miller (1981, p.10) claimed that 'a Scottish governmental machine has been constructed complete with Prime Minister, subordinate ministers, its own civil service'. Ross (1981), on the other hand, concludes that the existence of a Secretary of State for Scotland has not reversed the trend to centralisation and standardisation in British government.

The Scottish Political Dimension

Much of the confusion about Scottish politics stems from a failure to distinguish between the state and civil society. The state comprises the institutions of government and in the United Kingdom is based upon the sovereignty of Parliament. Civil society comprises those institutions which operate in the public domain but are not part of government. They include economic institutions, professions and other self-governing social institutions. Religion, too, should be included as part of civil society, though in England and Scotland there are established churches, formally linked to the state. In pre-Union Scotland, civil society was better developed than the state, notably in law, municipal corporations (the royal burghs) and education. The Church, while established, was, under the doctrine of the 'twa king-domes', largely independent of state direction and had wide jurisdiction in education and moral regulation.

Indeed, the persistence of a Scottish national identity after 1707 is also to be explained by the nature of the Union itself. An incorporating but not an assimilating union, it abolished the Scots Parliament but left many of the institutions of civil society intact. The most important of these were the legal system, the established Church, the educational system and the royal burghs. In turn, they served as carriers of Scottish identity and as a focus for a distinctive Scottish politics after the Union. Elements of a distinct Scottish civil society survived through the eighteenth and nineteenth centuries (Nairn, 1982; Harvie, 1977) and, despite breaches of the Union such as the restoration of patronage in the Kirk, replacing the practice of allowing parishioners a direct say in who should be their minister, these retained a degree of informal autonomy. From the mid nineteenth century assimilationist trends in the economy and the rise of the interventionist state put this at risk. A key test was the Education Act of 1870, initially intended to apply to the whole of Britain, which sparked off a campaign to preserve Scotland's distinctive educational heritage. In turn, the protest against assimilation was a factor in the Home Rule campaigns of the late nineteenth century.

The response, however, was not a change in the constitutional order to reflect the diverse societal conditions in Scotland (or Wales and Ireland) but an adaptation of the institutions of the British state on lines already pioneered after the Union. A Secretary for Scotland was appointed as a member of the central government and a Scottish Office gradually developed. This was not a devolution of political power or a transformation of the state but it was a safeguard against continuing assimilation of Scottish civil institutions. Assimilationist trends were not completely halted and in the economic sphere became more pronounced in the twentieth century; but the Scottish Office provided a focus for distinctive Scottish interests and helped to preserve and strengthen Scottish identity. The tension between assimilation and differentiation has characterised Scottish history since the Union, with each predominating at various times. The result is a society and culture which remains, in important respects, 'different'.

Even the most ardent Unionist accepts that Scotland differs from the rest of Britain. To a large degree, this is a matter of identity and self-perception, visible in fields such as sport and both popular and 'highbrow' culture; but it does have a political dimension. Almost three hundred years after the Union the persistence of a Scottish *political* identity can be explained by the symbiotic relationship between the extant Scottish institutions and a distinct culture. The acceptance of a distinctive Scottish political dimension leant weight to the case for Scotland being treated differently and the development of peculiarly Scottish institutions which, in turn, fed the belief that Scotland was politically distinct. As one writer commenting on an earlier work on Scottish politics remarked:

> there is at least a degree of mutual support between the plain Scotman's culture and the great institutions which survived the Union. Neither, probably, could have survived without the other. Each gives the other a point, and after all the Lord President and Paw Broon are brothers beneath the wig (or bunnet, as the case may be).
>
> (MacCormick, 1973)

Yet, while it is known that people *feel* Scottish, it is more difficult to assess the real meaning and significance of this. Survey research is of limited help. When asked whether they consider themselves to be Scottish or British the majority of people living in Scotland consistently reply that they consider themselves to be Scots. The 1979 Scottish Election study found 53 per cent of respondents felt they were Scots compared with 35 per cent British, 2 per cent English, 1 per cent Irish and 8 per cent who could not answer the question (Brand, 1984, p.5). The implication of this is not, of course, that 53 per cent of Scots are political nationalists. Scottish identity appears to be based on the simple cirteria of place of birth, residence or some emotional attachment to Scotland.

Nor, despite the invitation to do so posed in the 1979 survey, do most Scots regard Scottish and British identities as incompatible. On the contrary, most manage very well with a dual identity, also spanning the fields of culture, society and politics. Most manage to reconcile national identities with other attachments, such as religion and class. Even amongst SNP voters in the 1979 survey, class was seen as important. Indeed, only slightly more of those who voted for the Scottish National Party (SNP) and who perceived themselves to be Scots thought they had more in common with fellow Scots of a different class than with English people of the same social class (Brand, 1984, pp. 7, 11). The consistent support for a measure of self-government since the beginning of modern opinion polling taps a politically relevant measure of identity, though one that has only sporadically been a major priority for Scottish voters, preoccupied as these are with their other class or partisan identities.

Like other national identities, Scotland's relies partly on myths, beliefs about themselves or their society which people hold but whose power and significance is independent of their truth. Myths have been described thus:

> a story that people tell about themselves, and tell for two purposes. These purposes are, first, to explain the world, and, second, to celebrate identity and to express values. To what extent these explanations are true, and to what extent expressed values are realised in practice, are questions that we shall for the moment leave open.
>
> (Gray, McPherson and Raffe, 1983, p. 39)

Some of these myths are historical, others contemporary. The experience of independent statehood before 1707 and the struggles against English dominance in the centuries preceding it are a powerful myth, replete with heroes and villains and stirring adventures. The dynastic struggles of the seventeenth and eighteenth centuries have also been pressed into service, with the Jacobite leaders (supporters of the deposed Stuart dynasty in Scotland and England) being romanticised and, against the strict evidence, portrayed as Scottish national heroes. The 'kailyard school' of popular literature in the late nineteenth and early twentieth centuries portrayed another mythical Scotland, a wholesome, moral, small town life untainted by the ugliness and class conflict of industrial society. Other historical experiences which have helped mould contemporary Scottish culture are the Highland clearances, Red Clydeside and the democratic intellect. All are myths told by Scots about themselves which 'celebrate identity and express values.' Each has a basis in historical fact, though the extent of this is disputed by historians.

The Highland clearances have been a potent myth, given the close association between land and identity. Emigrants leaving Scotland in late twentieth century are regarded as the linear descendants of the Highlanders who were forced off the land in the nineteenth century. The Scottish diaspora has an important place in Scottish folklore. Community values are paramount in this myth along with the celebration of Gaelic identity. Though Gaelic is now spoken or read by only 82,620 Scots (1.6 per cent of total population), mainly in the Highlands and western coastal regions (1981 census), the clearances still evoke a sense of outrage throughout Scotland.

Red Clydeside, based on the rent strikes and industrial militancy during the First World War, is a myth which is both historically and geographically specific:

> The myth was that the Clydeside workers, led by SLP (Scottish Labour Party) shop stewards, enlightened by Marxists evening classes held by [John] MacLean, and fired by the examples of the Bolsheviks, had come within an ace of revolution.
>
> (Smout, 1986, p 259)

Like other myths, this has been subject to conflicting interpretations. For some, Clydeside became the 'synonym for "revolutionary agitation" during the war, the myth of the "canny Scot" was shattered by the spontaneous mass militancy and anti—militarism of the Scottish working class' (Young, 1979, p. 189). For others, the Clydeside episode was the consequence of unusual circumstances with rapacious landlords taking advantage and a highly sensitive and not too well-informed government reacting precipitously and unwisely (MacLean, 1983). Whatever the truth of the matter, the legend has provided a heroic and radical reference point for a Labour movement whose practice has been altogether more conservative. Equally significant, from the perspective of contemporary politics, is the comment made by Harvie:

> The heroics of the Red Clyde, faithfully retailed by further generations of activists, masked a fundamental defeat.
>
> (Harvie, 1981, p. 23)

The celebration of glorious defeats often seems part of the national psyche, with 'Argentina' referring to events in 1978, when the national football team suffered an inglorious exit from the World Cup, rather than the British victory in the Falklands War of 1982. It is almost as if Scots have never known victory.

It was Walter Elliot, a senior Conservative politician writing in 1932, who coined the expression 'democratic intellectualism'. Elliott (1932, p. 59) maintained that a 'fierce egalitarianism, and a respect for intellectual pre-eminence, and a lust for argument on abstract issues' were the traditions of Scotland. These ideas were later developed into a sophisticated thesis embodying epistemology, university and social history, as well as cultural and intellectual history, by George Davie in *The Democratic Intellect* (1961) and later developed in *The Crisis of the Democratic Intellect* (1986). While accounts of university history in nineteenth-century Scotland have challenged part of Davie's argument (Anderson, 1983), the coherence and depth which he provided to what has been a popular notion is widely recognised.

The popular articulation of the 'democratic' component of the myth is expressed in the 'lad o' pairts'. With roots in the nostalgic sentimentality of the kailyard school of Scottish literature, the 'lad o' pairts' refers to the openness of access to higher education afforded to Scots of all backgrounds. Though the myth exaggerates the actual extent of access, the 'lad o' pairts' did exist, albeit 'drawn from the middle rather than the lower ranks: the children of ministers, teachers, farmers, shopkeepers, and artisans enjoyed opportunities, especially for entry to the professions, which long had no equivalent in other countries' (Anderson, 1985, p. 100). But the importance of the 'lad o' pairts' lies in the fact that it is a story Scots tell about themselves. The Secretary and Senior Chief Inspector of the

Scottish Education Department in their evidence to the Royal Commission on the Constitution in 1969 made reference to the broad-based curriculum and egalitarian national identity based in Scottish historial tradition (McPherson and Raab, 1988, pp. 406–7). Attempts to change the fundamentals of Scottish education have provoked fierce resistance. The Educational Institute of Scotland's (the main teaching union) press advertisements asking 'Is Scottish education still *Scottish*?' exemplify the potency of the myth of Scottish educational distinctiveness (*The Scotsman* and *Glasgow Herald,* 10 October 1988).

Political views are formed in the context of a political culture which draws upon its myths and values,

> 'political traditions and folk heroes, the spirit of public institutions, political passions of the citizenry, goals articulated by the political ideology, and both formal and informal rules of the political game.'
>   (Dawson and Prewitt, 1969, p. 26)

Yet there is disagreement on the political implications of Scotland's culture. Conservative commentators have argued that Scots have become dependent on a bureaucratic state and consequently the latent entrepreneurial talents of Scotland have been stifled (Fry, 1987). The Chancellor of the Exchequer's view that Scots 'exhibit the culture of dependence rather than that of enterprise' (*The Scotsman,* 24 November 1987) was his explanation for the lack of support for his party in Scotland. Others credit Scotland with a strong radical or socialist tradition (Young, 1979). Scotland is sometimes thought to be more open, democratic and egalitarian. Yet, it has suffered from religious sectarianism, access to higher education is extremely limited compared with West European norms, England apart, and wealth is distributed in a grossly inequitable way. Conflicting myths are not unusual but the idea that Scotland is, in MacDiarmid's words, 'whaur extremes meet' has become a central theme in both the literature and politics of the country. Earlier this century, Gregor Smith (1919) coined the tortured expression, 'Caledonian antisyzygy' to describe these contradictions. Nairn (1981, p. 150) interprets it as 'an anguished examination of conscience and consciousness, a troubled subjective posturing, to which Scots intellectuals have been especially prone'. Davie (1986, p. 115) views it more positively as the 'inevitability of endless struggle'. However interpreted, this theme persistently appears in twentieth-century commentaries on Scottish politics and society.

Of the institutions of civil society which have maintained Scottish identity and the idea of a distinctly Scottish public domain, four critical ones are religion, law, education and the media. In addition, the economy and social conditions have become the focus of a distinctly Scottish debate.

Religion

After the Union of 1707 'religion remained one of the few facets of Scottish civil life in which a collective identity could survive' (Brown, 1987, p. 6) and the religious structure of Scotland continues to mark it out from the rest of the UK. Most of the population belongs, at least nominally, to the Church of Scotland whose influence on Scottish values and practices has been immense. A Presbyterian church heavily influenced by Calvinist doctrines, it became the established Church after the Scottish reformation of the sixteenth century, a privileged position which was retained under the Treaty of Union. A major split occurred in 1843, known as the Disruption, the secessionists under Thomas Chalmers setting up the Free Church of Scotland. Chalmers and his followers objected to state interference and the diminution of the democratic component in Church governance. A series of disputes followed regarding the custodianship of estates and several attempts were made to heal the rift in some of which the state, through the offices of the Secretary for Scotland, was involved. A reunion occurred in 1929 though a small United Free Church continued to exist together with some fundamentalist offshoots (the 'wee frees'). Up to the last war, the Churches played a significant part in both the secular and religious life in Scotland. The structure of local government grew out of the Kirk parishes and its social and political values were important. The social ethics of the Kirk were particularly significant in the development of the poor law and education. The harsh Scottish poor law, with the refusal of relief to the able-bodied unemployed was a distinguishing feature which, according to one historian, inculcated a disposition to save amongst the Scottish working class (Smout, 1986, p.241). George Davie (1961, 1986) has argues that a 'Presbyterian inheritance' in education was the basis for the democratic intellect which he argues has been under assault particularly during the course of the twentieth century.

Another important element in Scottish life is the large Catholic population, especially in the west. In 1985, 13.2 per cent of marriages in Scotland took place in Catholic churches, compared with 7.3 per cent in England and Wales. Many of the Catholics are descended from nineteenth-and twentieth-century Irish immigrants and sectarian tensions have been an important element in Scottish politics. Catholics were long excluded from the skilled trades in the heavy industries, while in the professions they formed their own partnerships and supportive networks. Much of the discrimination has now disappeared and the elimination of the old skilled trades and urban renewal have greatly reduced occupational and residential segregation. Sectarianism, however, still exists within the society and Scottish politicians, aware of its political potential, have made efforts to prevent the Northern Ireland troubles from spreading to Scotland. In contrast to Northern Ireland, the Labour Party in Scotland has largely managed to span the sectarian divide and to defuse religious tensions. The issue of separate Catholic schools, a key element in the Scottish religious settlement, remains, however, a troublesome one.

Presbyterian and Catholic influences have converged to make Scotland less of a 'permissive society' than England. For many years, this was reflected in legislation on social issues, in which MPs are allowed a free vote. Opposition from Scottish members prevented the reform of Scotland's divorce laws until the 1970s, several years after England. The 1966 bill to legalise homosexual relations was amended to exclude Scotland after opposition from Scots MPs had prevented its passage (Keating, 1975). There were demands to exclude Scotland from the legalisation of abortion in 1967 but practical considerations and the fact that its sponsor was a Scottish MP led to a British-wide bill. By the 1980s, Scottish social legislation had largely been brought into line with England but practice continues to differ. The Scottish divorce rate remains lower than the English as does the rate of abortions.

Law

The Scottish legal tradition has retained a degree of autonomy despite a shared legislature. It requires the passage of separate legislation for Scotland on many matters even when the policy content is identical to English legislation. It allows the law on a variety of matters to differ from that of England; and it is linked to a separate judicial system allowing for the development of a distinctive case law. The Treaty of Union made a distinction between matters of 'public right, policy and civil government', for which uniform provision was to be made throughout Great Britain, and 'private right', in which the law was to be changed only 'for the evident utility of the subjects within Scotland'. In practice, the distinction is impossible to make and there are no hard and fast rules as to which matters should be dealt with by Scottish law and which by UK legislation. Generally speaking, matters subject to administrative decentralisation to the Scottish office are legislated for separately, as are many matters of private law and morality. The law on industrial, economic and commercial matters is usually the same throughout the UK as are laws on newer areas of state responsibility such as race relations or consumer protection.

A distinct jurisprudence based on Roman law rather than the common law of England, remains. Some Scots lawyers have deplored a tendency to convergence of the Scottish and English legal systems and the consequent threat to some traditional principles of Scots law. On the other hand, the trend is for separate Scottish legislation to be used increasingly for the translation of UK policy into legal form. Confusion remains about the status of Scots law and the Treaty of Union. While pre-Union Scottish statutes continue to be the law of Scotland, the courts have accepted that some of them can be deemed to have lapsed (Lock, 1989). In 1953, the Scottish nationalist John MacCormick sought to challenge the use of the title Queen Elizabeth II in Scotland. The court declared, in effect, that the Treaty of Union had been breached but that they were powerless to do anything about it. The judge in the case, Lord Cooper, made the radical claim that the 'principle of the unlimited sovereignty of Parliament is a distinctively English principle which has no counterpart in Scottish constitutional law' but that in the absence of any mechanism for judicial review,

the Scots principle was incapable of being invoked in practice
(Session Cases, 1953)

The situation is thus as confusing as that of the relationship of
Scottish politics and government to the wider British political
system. Essentially, a British legal system exists with a distinctive Scottish dimension within which a degree of practical
autonomy may be available. This parallels the political situation
of Scotland.

Education

Education is equally problematic. It is generally felt that there is
a strong Scottish basis to education despite the fact that the
major changes have paralleled those south of the border. The
received wisdom that Scotland has a better, more open, more
generalist tradition may owe more to myth than reality but the
myth itself is important for the political culture. As one
educational historian has stated:

> Much more than in England, a certain view of the educational
> past has underlain current controversies, a view which may be
> called 'mythical' not because it was necessarily untrue, but
> because it idealized and simplified the facts and had an
> inspirational or creative function which took on a life of its
> own.
>
> (Anderson, 1985, pp. 82–3)

MacPherson and Raab (1988, p. 476) demonstrate that the
Scottish myth in education 'sustained a common sense of
identity both within the policy community, and between it and
the wider world of education'.

The Scotch (sic) Education Department (SED) was established in 1872, pre-dating the Scottish Office by thirteen years.
The view that the early SED advanced the Knoxian ideal of
egalitarian educational provision is suggested in histories published early this century (Morgan, 1927, 1929; Steward, 1927)
though Davie (1961, 1986) argues that the SED, and the SED
Secretary in particular, set about anglicising Scottish education.
Changes in Scottish education in recent years have been strongly
resisted because they run contrary to Scottish educational
traditions.

The existence of the SED and the Scottish educational policy community (Raab, 1982; MacPherson and Raab, 1988) has ensured that Scottish education has retained an appearance in Scotland as a distinctively Scottish commodity. Peculiarly Scottish institutions exist. The General Teaching Council advises government on the training and supply of teachers, and registers teachers. The Scottish Certification of Education Examination Board is the sole examining centre for schools and is 'perhaps the most visible' feature of Scottish education for the average family (MacBeth, 1983, p. 169).

In 1985, the Scottish Tertiary Education Advisory Committee listed nine distinctive features of Scottish education:

(*i*) A secondary school system which has traditionally been characterised by a broad curriculum and an avoidance of early specialisation.

(*ii*) A similarly broadly-based examination system, the Scottish Certificate of Education, which is commonly taken at the Higher grade in the fifth year of secondary education and which provides the basic qualifications for entry to higher education.

(*iii*) A consequent tendency (particularly noticeable in the west of Scotland) for school-leavers to enter higher education at the relatively early age of 17–18.

(*iv*) Consistent with early entry to higher education, a four-year Honours degree course in most subjects.

(*v*) The existence, in parallel with Honours degree courses, of broadly-based three-year Ordinary degree courses, taken by almost half of the Scottish higher education students and leading to a distinct form of qualification which is valued and respected in its own right.

(*vi*) Traditionally high participation rates in higher education.

(*vii*) Universities which admit large numbers of students from outside Scotland.

(*viii*) Consistent with (*vi*) and (*vii*), a higher education system which produces a share of graduates exceeding the proportion of Scots to the overall population of the UK.

(*ix*) A non-university sector which is for the most part funded, and in which the range of course is controlled, by central government is essentially complementary with that of the universities (e.g. liberal arts courses are provided only in the universities and, where the same subjects are offered in both the university and the non-university sectors, the approach is different).

(Cmnd. 9676, 1985, p. 5)

Much of what STEAC identified as distinctive can be summed up in the term of the 'democratic intellect', an openness and generalism in subject matter with particular encouragement given to speculative philosophy and an openness and accessibility of educational provision for all, regardless of background.

Other differences are institutional. Traditionally, Scotland has had a much smaller independent sector than England. However, there was a doubling in the number of pupils on registers of 'independent' schools between 1984/85 and 1985/86 from 15,400 to 31,900, representing 4 per cent of Scottish pupils (*Scottish Abstract of Statistics* No. 16, 1987). The major explanation is the Education (Scotland) Act, 1981 which restored state assistance for private schools (MacPherson and Raab, 1988). Universities are separated administratively from other branches of education in Scotland and proposals to transfer universities to the Scottish Office by the Scottish Tertiary Education Advisory Council (STEAC) in 1985 were not taken up. Controversy has continued, however, over the extent to which the UK Department of Education and Science and Universities Funding Council can accommodate Scotland's distinctive needs and traditions, and over the administrative separation of Scottish universities from other parts of the educational system.

Media

Distinctive Scottish media cater for all social classes. The readership of the quality *Glasgow Herald* and *The Scotsman* constitutes 12 per cent, while the popular *Daily Record* commands 43 per cent of the Scottish market. Newspapers published in England have about a third of the market, mostly accounted for by the *Express*, which abandoned its Scottish base in the 1970s but still produces a 'Scottish edition' and the *Sun* which has established a Scottish printing facility in Glasgow. Until recently, it might have been expected that the Scottish middle class became British on Sundays inasmuch as there was no quality Scottish Sunday paper. The *Sunday Standard* made an abortive attempt to fill this market from April 1981 to July

1983. The launch of *Scotland on Sunday* from *The Scotsman* stable in 1987 not only provided a quality Scottish Sunday but provoked *The Sunday Times* and *The Observer* to introduce Scottish supplements. A notable consequence of this has been the reduction in the coverage of Scottish issues in the English editions of the London press, further accentuating the divide between 'UK' and 'Scottish' affairs which has been a marked feature of post-war politics.

Table 1.1 Sales of newspapers in the UK and Scotland, 1985–6

UK	thousands	per cent	SCOTLAND	thousands	per cent
Sun	4000	27	Record	758	43
Mirror	3300	22	Sun	210	12
Express	1990	14	Express	178	10
Mail	1800	12	Courier	130	7
Star	1400	10	Herald	119	7
Telegraph	1200	8	Press & Journal	112	6
Guardian	500	3	Scotsman	96	5
Times	500	3	Star	94	5
			Mail	36	2
			Mirror	25	1
			Telegraph	24	1
			Guardian	14	1
			Times	15	1

Source: Punnett, 1987; Hutchison, 1987.

Television and radio also have a Scottish dimension. Scottish Television serves most of Scotland including the heavily populated Central belt. Grampian Television serves the North-East and Highlands and Islands while Border Television serves the South-West and the Borders. BBC Scotland's output is small and as with independent channels, the bulk of the output, including current affairs, is network material from London. Local radio stations supplement BBC network radio and Radio Scotland. Scottish affairs are covered as an adjunct to British news on the broadcasting media. This is most obvious in the daily news bulletins where the Scottish output is generally a poor supplement to the network news.

The political slant of the Scottish media is rather different from that of the English media. In Scotland, the pro-

Conservative popular papers have a fraction of the coverage which they have in England while the pro-Labour *Daily Record* attracts some 40 per cent of the market compared with 22 per cent in the UK as a whole for its English sister paper, the *Daily Mirror*. While nearly 75 per cent of English readers take a pro–Conservative newspaper, this is true of less than 45 per cent of Scots. Following the 1987 General Election when the Conservatives were reduced to ten Scottish MPs, an internal party report commented on the role of the media. It noted the antagonism towards the party of the Scottish quality press, the *Glasgow Herald* and *The Scotsman* but was more concerned about the *Daily Record* and its dominant place in the Scottish market (*Glasgow Herald*, 10 September 1987). It has been suggested that the failure of the Scots to show increased support for the Conservatives in the immediate aftermath of the South Atlantic conflict was due to a media consensus which, though supportive of the action, was critical of the Prime Minister (Miller, 1983). Whether the Scottish media were following Scottish opinion or were leading it is unclear but, once more, a symbiosis between Scottish institutions and Scottish attitudes existed to maintain something distinctively Scottish.

The Economic and Social Context

Scottish economic development has been similar to that of the rest of the UK. The industrial revolution produced a considerable shift from agriculture to industry but left a legacy of outdated industrial structure and poor housing which were to plague Scotland in the twentieth century (Levitt, 1983). Scotland's position in the British Empire in the heyday of free trade provided the basis for the rise of the heavy industries (Kendrick, 1983) but rendered it vulnerable to the loss of imperial markets and the growth of protectionism in the 1930s (Harvie, 1981). After the First World War, the separate Scottish capitalism which had been an important force in the nineteenth century died out as Scottish firms moved their headquarters south or were absorbed by British conglomerates (Scott and Hughes, 1980), with the trade union movement following suit. Further centralisation was introduced by the nationalisations under the Labour government after the Second World War. By mid century, most economists rejected the notion of a 'Scottish economy' as a useful unit of analysis.

At first glance, the economic statistics do not give a consistently distinctive profile of Scotland. Draper and McNicoll (1979) found that 23 per cent of Scottish output was exported, of which 15 per cent was to the rest of the UK. There are slightly more people in agriculture and fishing than elsewhere in the UK, at 2.2 per cent of the workforce, against an average of 1.7 per cent, but these numbers are in both cases very small. Manufacturing industry employs 25 per cent of the workforce, against 28 per cent of the UK as a whole. On the other hand, there are some important differences within industrial sectors. Scotland in the twentieth century has had a large proportion of industries in declining markets and some of these, such as shipbuilding, have taken on great political significance as symbols of Scotland's whole economy. Strathclyde region, in particular, has suffered from an unbalanced industrial structure (RSA, 1983) and, to the occasional exasperation of MPs from other parts of Scotland, its problems have often been presented as *the* Scottish problem. Of direct political relevance is the higher level of public employment. Although the proportion of public employment in Scotland, at 29.8 per cent, was only slightly higher in the early 1980s than the UK average of 27.5 per cent, it was exceeded only by Northern Ireland, Wales and Northern England (Parry, 1985).

Gross Domestic Product per head is close to the UK average, at between 95 per cent and 98 per cent since the mid 1970s. While wages are above the UK average, so is unemployment, so that disposable income per head is about the average and has been since at least the early 1950s (Lythe and Majmudar, 1982). Scottish unemployment has exceeded the UK average since the 1930s and tends to be more prolonged (Davies and Sinfield, 1983), though the margin of difference has varied. In times of recession, the differential tends to narrow but in boom periods Scotland has never been able to attain the full employment enjoyed in the south. Nationalists point to this as the price of the Union, noting that national deflationary policies are introduced to curb overheating and inflation in the south at the peak of its business cycle, when Scotland still has idle capacity.

The combination of high wage levels and high unemployment suggests considerable social division within Scotland between the employed and the unemployed. Among the employed, too, there is a high incidence of low pay. Twine (1983) claims that, with the 10.6 per cent of all male and 11.5 per cent of female low-paid workers in Britain, Scotland had a larger share of low pay than any other region. Low-paid occupations such as unskilled labourers, porters and cleaners appear to have persisted in Scotland to a greater extent than in England (Payne and Ford, 1983).

Scotland's economic problems are therefore more extreme manifestations of British problems rather than being substantively different. These economic problems have social consequences. By all the available evidence, Scotland has higher levels of social deprivation than the rest of the UK. Official statistics show that the number of households living in poverty has grown in the 1980s. Half of these are elderly, single-parent families or the sick and disabled, with the remainder unemployed or low paid (Norris, 1983).

The gross figures on social conditions often mask considerable regional variation within Scotland. In terms of health, Scotland compares rather poorly with England and Wales, with a lower life-expectancy and particularly high rates of heart disease and lung cancer, attributable in large part to smoking, alcohol and poor diet (Brooks, 1983). On the other hand, the perinatal mortality rate is almost identical to that of the UK as a whole but in the Central Region is double that of Dumfries and Galloway. Welfare dependence is higher in Scotland, with proportionately more people drawing the major social benefits. In the field of housing, Scotland does stand out, with a tradition of poorer housing, low rents and, since the Second World War, a large proportion of publicly rented housing. Despite the right-to-buy policy, public sector tenancies still accounted in 1987 for 49.2 per cent of Scottish households, against 24.2 per cent in England; and the gap was widening, since only 9.6 per cent of the Scottish public sector stock had been sold off, compared with 16.6 per cent in England (Parry, 1987). Other differences are visible in Scotland's cities. As a result of the pattern of redevelopment since the war, these lack the run-down inner city neighbourhoods characteristic of the older English cities but have, instead, large areas of deprivation around the periphery in the public housing schemes. In this respect, the contemporary Scottish city, like that of previous ages, has more in common with its French than its English counterpart.

Government economic strategy in the 1980s had important implications for Scotland. With higher unemployment and poverty, higher levels of public employment and public housing tenure and an outdated industrial structure, Scotland was affected by the reduction in intervention, subsidy and many categories of social expenditure. Changes in welfare benefits had a direct effect on Scotland's households. The failure to increase many benefits in line with average earnings excluded many from the increased national prosperity of the late 1980s. Increasingly, these issues have come to be seen as territorial, rather than in purely class or sectoral terms, strengthening the sense of Scottish identity and its political significance.

Despite the difficulties of modelling a Scottish economy, economic issues have come to be seen in specifically Scottish terms since the 1960s when Britain, like other Western Europen counties, adopted policies of regional planning as part of national economic planning (Keating, 1988b). In Scotland, this involved an expansion in the economic role of the Scottish Office and the assumption by the Secretary of State of responsibility for the health of the Scottish economy. Thus the economic debate came to focus on Scottish themes while expectations were raised which were to prove impossible to fulfill. It is in this political context that the discussion of North Sea oil as a Scottish economic resource must be understood. In the 1980s, the territorial focus of economic debate was again strengthened, this time in a series of struggles over industrial closings. Ironically, many of the plants involved, such as the steel works at Ravenscraig, the aluminium smelter at Invergordon and the vehicle plants at Linwood and Bathgate, were brought to Scotland by the regional policy measures of the 1960s. Their closure provoked broad coalitions of defence encompassing both sides of industry, local government, the churches and politicians of all persuasions. This served to strengthen the Scottish identity as the gap between the global logic of national and multinational business and the spatial logic of communities was exposed (Keating, 1989b). Developments in the growth areas of the Scottish economy, such as new technology and oil, have sparked a debate on the absence of Scottish control. High technology industries are to a large degree under American control while studies have shown that 40 per cent of direct employment by oil companies comes from outside Scotland.

Scotland, as we shall argue in the conclusion, had a large investment in the economic and social consensus of the 1945–79 period, with its emphasis on planning, active government, high

public spending and a collectivist approach to welfare services.
It was thus particularly challenged by the new Conservatism
after 1979 (Fry, 1987).

Conclusion

Scotland's distinctiveness is thus not simply a hangover from the
Union in 1707 but reaches into areas of contemporary social and
economic life. Since the Second World War, despite trends to
assimilation in the economy and tendencies to centralisation in
government, Scottish identity has in critical respects been
strengthened (Brand, 1978). Some of these are politically
relevant, others not. Yet others have the potential to become
politically relevant.This strengthening of Scottish civil society
and identity has put increasing strain on the unitary state and
the arrangements for managing Scottish affairs within it. The
remainder of this book is concerned with the political and
administrative mechanisms through which public policy is made
in Scotland. Kellas (1988) has argued that Scotland's distinctive
culture, institutions and procedures amount to a political system
in their own right. We are dubious of this argument and address
it more formally later. First, we examine Scottish political
behaviour and the role of political parties. Then we analyse the
institutions of Scottish government and their ability to produce
distinct policies, to lobby for Scotland and to manage Scottish
business within the unitary state. These general chapters are
followed by an analysis of policy making in key areas and the
increasing tensions which we discern in Scottish politics. In the
concluding chapter, we assess the extent to which the arrangements for governing Scotland as part of the unitary British
political system are coping with stress, and the ways in which
the system can maintain itself.

2

Parties and Elections

Patterns of Party Competition

The Scottish party system is, like other elements of Scottish
politics, an integral part of the British political system. Yet
there are distinctive features. Scotland in the 1980s has been
characterised by four-party competition, while the relative
fortunes of the British parties in Scotland have often diverged
from those south of the border. The national political parties
play a vital role in integrating Scotland into the British political
system. Dedicated to winning national majorities, they focus
attention on Westminster politics but at the same time need to
cater for distinctively Scottish demands. The territorial dimension in political conflict is subordinated to the logic of class and
ideological competition but it is never completely suppressed
and the parties have always had to preserve some capacity to
represent territorial interests. This has frequently created tensions within them. For the SNP the issues are reversed. Its very
raison d'etre is a territorial demand-for Scottish independence-
but it confronts a society in which class, sectoral and ideological
divisions are marked and must seek either to suppress or
accommodate the resulting demands. In this chapter, we
examine the ideologies, organisation and structure of the parties
in Scotland and assess their electoral performance.

Conservatives

The Conservative Party in Scotland dropped 'Conservative' from
its name between 1912 and 1965, preferring to be called the

Scottish Unionist Party. The Union referred to was not the Anglo–Scottish Union but that with Ireland. The recovery in Conservative fortunes in Scotland towards the end of the nineteenth century was largely due to the split in the Liberal Party over Home Rule and changing the party's name was an attempt to capitalise on the realignment taking place in Scottish politics.

Unionism has been central to Scottish Conservative ideology and has a number of facets. In constitutional terms it means the sovereignty of Parliament at Westminster and opposition to measures of Home Rule, whether Irish or Scottish, though accepting the need for some institutional mechanisms to provide for Scottish distinctiveness. Indeed, the functions and responsibilities of the Scottish Office developed under the Conservatives more than any other party. Under Heath, the party went further and uncharacteristically supported a limited measure of legislative devolution. This, however, was not enacted when Heath became Prime Minister and was rejected by the party's Scottish conference in 1973. When Margaret Thatcher became leader, the traditional opposition to Home Rule was reinstated.

The ideology of Unionism goes further than the expression of a constitutional order. Although a secular party, it was influenced in the twentieth century by ideas which, while not strictly religious, were rooted in the 'presbyterian inheritance' (Davie, 1961). The democratic intellect (see Chapter 1) and even the idea of a property-owning democracy were rooted in Presbyterian social philosophy which stressed individualism. This same philosophy which allowed the Liberals to dominate nineteenth-century politics was, in a more secular form, to help the Conservatives for much of the twentieth century.

The progressive element of Unionism may have been swamped at times by sectarianism but important figures in Conservative politics in the inter-war years including Walter Elliot, Noel Skelton and John Buchan articulated a progressive form of Unionism. It was Skelton who coined the phrase a 'property owning democracy' (Skelton, 1924) not, it must be stressed, as a reversal of public involvement in housing but as a genuine attempt to allow individuals the opportunity to gain a degree of personal freedom. Both Skelton and Elliot stressed in their writings and in their work as ministers the importance of the state's contribution to their goals. Major developments in public-sector housing occurred during their terms as Scottish

Office ministers, including the establishment of the Scottish Special Housing Association in 1937 when Elliot was Secretary of State. This was not seen as conflicting with their individualist beliefs which allowed a role for the state as facilitator whenever the private sector failed.

The working-class Protestant vote was the principal target of Unionist electoral politics. The heightened denominational tensions of the 1920s (Brown, 1987) coincided with party realignment and important changes in Scottish voting behaviour. The decline of the Liberals and rise of the Labour Party did not simply involve a straightforward movement of opinion from one to the other. The Liberals' hegemony in nineteenth-century Scottish politics has been partly attributed to their association with Presbyterianism (Kellas, 1961). During the twentieth century the Unionists strived to pick up this mantle with a fair degree of success while Labour became closely associated with the immigrant Irish population.

A significant feature of Scottish Conservative propaganda in the immediate post-war period was their anti-nationalisation campaigns. Responding to the Attlee Government's nationalisation programme, Scottish Conservatives argued forcefully that nationalisation would take control of industries away from Scotland. Their 1949 publication *Scottish Control of Scottish Affairs* aimed to tap both anti-nationalisation and . pro—nationalist sentiment at the time of the Scottish Covenant Association. Playing the Scottish card was very much part of the Conservative strategy in elections in the late 1940s and early 1950s and might partly explain their electoral successes around this time.

During the post-war period, the Conservatives reached a peak of electoral success in 1955 but have declined fairly steadily ever since. The erosion of their support in urban areas left the party with a 'grouse moor image' more marked than south of the border (Keating, 1975). Their Parliamentary ranks were increasingly dominated by landowners and military men, with a larger proportion of English public school products than among English Conservative MPs (Keating, 1975). These might be Scots by birth and ancestry but they talked in the accents of the Home Counties, giving the party an increasingly anglicised image. There were few Scottish Conservative politicians of the stature or intellect of A. J. Balfour, Walter Elliot or John Buchan of the previous fifty years. Electoral defeat and perception that the party was failing to meet new challenges led to a number of changes in the mid 1960s. 'Conservative' returned to the party's official name, a major reorganisation took place and strenuous efforts were made to encourage party members to contest local elections as Conservatives rather than as Independents, Progressives or Ratepayers. Though the party achieved a mild recovery in 1979, largely due to the fall in SNP support, recovery to the 1955 level or to being the largest of Scotland's minorities has eluded the Conservatives.

The Thatcher years may have given the Scottish Conservatives control of the Scottish Office but simultaneously this period has seen their support erode further. The Scottish Office has traditionally not been an innovative department and few, if any, of the policies distinctively associated with the period from 1979 have originated from Dover House. In the field of local government, the Scottish Office has certainly been ahead of the Department of the Environment in its measures to curb local authority spending and the poll tax originated as a response to rates revaluation in Scotland. But the poll tax apart, these measures have been means to ends determined by Treasury constraints rather than Scottish Office initiatives. The poll tax remains the outstanding example of the Scottish Office leading the way in terms of a 'Thatcherite' policy but that was the result of a reaction to middle-class outrage at the 1985 revaluation rather than part of a coherent ideological or electorally strategic process. Essentially, Scottish Conservatives in the post-war period-and no less so since 1979-have contributed little to the formation of ideas and policies but have generally gone along with whatever has been proposed for England.

Organisationally, the Scottish Unionist Party was organised into two divisions, Eastern and Western. The reforms in the 1960s included a merger of the divisions and an upgrading of central office in Scotland. The late 1970s also saw a major overhaul of the party's organisation following the defeats of 1974. A series of recommendations by Russell Fairgrieve, an MP and former Scottish chairman, had the effect of merging aspects of the organisation with central office in London. Ironically, this was taking place at a time when the party was advocating a measure of legislative devolution. The weakness of the party in Scotland which necessitated greater reliance on London was itself partly attributable to the demise of Scottish indigenous capitalism, which had led to the drying-up of industrial contributions to the Scottish party's funds. Further reforms occurred following the 1987 election when the party adapted its central office and a number of constituency offices to take advantage of sophisticated information technology.

Margaret Thatcher's dominance of her party was a slow process which was far from complete at the time of her election as Prime Minister. Tory Party loyalty to their leader is an ingrained tradition which makes identifying opposition difficult to detect. However, it is clear that Mrs Thatcher had few staunch supporters amongst the Scottish Tory MPs elected in 1979. The Scottish Office under George Younger gained a reputation as the 'wettest Department in Whitehall' for its unwillingness to apply Thatcherite policies and Younger operated more in the old patrician style than that of the new model Thatcherites such as Norman Tebbit. Few of the backbenchers would be termed as Thatcherite and a number were associated with views critical of the Prime Minister including Ian Lang, Peter Fraser and Michael Ancram − all of whom later became Government Ministers and loyal supporters of the Prime Minister.

One staunch Thatcherite elected in 1979 but who initially failed to be offered a Government post was Iain Sproat. Sproat's anti-devolution, free-market views were far closer to the Prime Minister's than were those of other Scottish MPs but he had so antagonised others in the leadership-Willie Whitelaw particularly-that he had to wait until September 1981 before being offered a junior Ministerial post in the Department of Trade. Sproat's decision to swap constituencies in 1983 at the time of boundary changes resulted in him losing the Borders seat he moved to while his former South Aberdeen seat was retained by the Tories. However, the election of Michael Forsyth in Stirling in 1983 introduced, in Thatcherite terms 'One of Us'. A number of right-wing backbenchers such as Bill Walker had been around but Forsyth provided the intellect and ideas to back up Thatcherite prejudices. His appointment as a junior Scottish Office Minister in 1987 confirmed the Prime Minister's diagnosis that Tory electoral failure in Scotland was accounted for by the lack of Thatcherite rigour in the Scottish Office rather than its surplus. This was further confirmed by his appointment as Scottish Party Chairman in 1989. A new image for the Scottish Office was developed after 1987, aided considerably by the publicity-conscious Forsyth, which projected an image more in keeping with that which Mrs Thatcher preferred. Malcolm Rifkind, as Scottish Secretary, abandoned his support for legislative devolution which had led to his resignation from the front bench in the previous decade and adopted the mantle which Younger had avoided.

Attempts to revivify the party in Scotland in line with the developments in the Scottish Office were set in motion. Ross Harper, a leading Glasgow lawyer, became president and assumed a more prominent role than previous incumbents who viewed this post as an internal office rather than a public office. Harper was another prominent pro-devolutionist from the 1970s who changed his mind in the 1980s. This dependence on Tories who in the 1970s were closely associated with Heath's views but who gradually came to accept the Thatcherite line was significantly more marked in Scotland than in England.

Since 1987, concerted efforts have been made to build up support for the Conservatives in the Scottish business community. The Scottish Business Group, formed in 1987, was chaired by James Gulliver, former head of the Argyll group and included a number of well-known businessmen such as Bill Hughes of Grampian Holdings, Sir Hector Laing of United Biscuits, Sir Ian MacGregor, formerly of British Steel and the National Coal Board, Lord Weir of Weir Pumps, and Angus Grossart, the merchant banker. The group meets ministers periodically and has established local groups in a few constituencies to help raise funds and mobilise local businessmen in support of the Tories.

Labour

The Labour Party had separate origins in Scotland in the late-nineteenth-century alliances between radical Liberals, land reformers in the Highlands, trade unions frustrated with the old Lab–Lib formula for accommodating working-class interests, and socialists. The electoral and organisational weakness of the Scottish movement at the turn of the century, however, led to its becoming part of the wider British movement and in 1909, the Scottish Workers' Representation Committee, a separate Scottish body seeking parliamentary representation for the working class, was wound up. Continued weakness in Scotland led to the formation of a Scottish Advisory Committee in 1915 and, despite the protests from those who had wanted something more substantial (Harvie, 1988a), this was incorporated in the 1918 Constitution as a mere 'regional council' equivalent to those in the English provinces. The Scottish Council of the Labour Party, as it is known, holds an annual conference but, until the 1970s, was limited to strictly Scottish subjects. Described as 'neither prestigious nor influential' in the 1940s (Harvie, 1988b, p. 68), the Scottish Council lost the privilege of having its minutes tabled at meetings of the NEC in 1942. In 1957, party leader Gaitskell, in Scotland for a meeting of the Scottish Trades Union Congress (the STUC), did not bother to take in the Scottish Labour conference sitting at the same time. Now it is allowed to debate UK and international affairs, which has enlivened the proceedings, but it has no policy-making powers.

Labour Party organisation remains centralised. There is an office in Glasgow responsible not to the Scottish Executive elected by the conference but to the National Executive Committee (NEC) in London. Suggestions that, in line with its commitment to parliamentary devolution, Labour should practise it within its own organisation have consistently been rejected by the NEC and items of Scottish policy still require the endorsement of the national conference before being officially adopted.

Scotland has been critical to the Labour Party's electoral fortunes at various times-and in 1922-3, in 1964 and in 1974. Since 1979, it has provided a substantial part of the party's parliamentary presence. Yet there has rarely been a distinctively Scottish input to Labour's policy and campaigning style. Even after 1979, there has been only sporadic interest south of the border in Labour's success in Scotland and how it might be reproduced more generally. Nor is there a stable and recognisable Scottish faction within the party, extracting policy commitments and providing a power base for leading party figures. This is most striking in comparison with other western countries, where territory forms an important element of the power basis of political leaders. There are several reasons for it.

Labour generally has tended to de-emphasise the politics of territory within the party. Representation in its decision-making bodies is on a corporate basis, with provision for trade unions, constituency parties, socialist societies and women-but not territorial interests. In policy debates, ideological considerations, notably the entrenched divisions between right and left, over-ride territory and both sides have usually been committed to centralised social and economic strategies (see below).

Scottish influence has also been reduced by the perennial weakness of party organisation. We have referred to the weakness at the turn of the century. In the 1920s and 1930s, most constituency organisation consisted of branches of the Independent Labour Party and was devastated by the ILP disaffiliation in 1932. By the early 1940s, only seven constituency parties really functioned and the Glasgow burgh party had to be disaffiliated by the NEC (Harvie, 1988b). The situation was little better in the 1950s and 1960s, with Scotland accounting for between 7.5 and 8.5 per cent of Labour membership, well short of its share of the vote (Keating, 1988c). In 1968, the Glasgow city party was again dissolved by the NEC. Low membership and lack of participation were associated in the cities with machine politics, a tradition inherited from the Irish ward bosses who went over to Labour after the Irish settlement of 1922. In the postwar years, the municipal patronage machine was fed with council tenancies, jobs, especially for teachers and manual workers, and political and trade-union positions. These were traded for votes and for support for the bosses within their ward and constituency parties. In some areas, the distinction between union branches, Labour Party branches and tenants' associations was hazy and many individuals were credited with party membership without being aware of it. The machines mainly died out in the 1970s under the impact of urban renewal, which was breaking up the old working-class communities, and electoral defeats, mainly at the hands of the SNP, which swept away many of the old generation.

Another reason for the lack of impact of Scottish Labour is the pattern of recruitment of political leaders. Two of the party's founding figures, Keir Hardie and Ramsay MacDonald, were Scots but they made their political careers in the South. The first Scottish Parliamentary breakthrough, in 1922, brought in some charismatic figures, the famous Clydesiders, but of these only John Wheatley was to make a major impact on the party or in Government. Jimmie Maxton and the others drifted out of the party mainstream, finally breaking with Labour altogether in 1932 when the ILP disaffiliated. From the 1930s, there developed a marked tendency to choose as Parliamentary candidates middle-aged, male municipal councillors. Labour MPs serving between 1945 and 1970, 53 per cent were former councillors (Keating, 1975), against 43.4 per cent in England and Wales (Mellors, 1977). Scottish Labour MPs also tended to be older on first election, perhaps reflecting the need for a local government apprenticeship. These tendencies are even more pronounced in the case of Glasgow, no less than 83 per cent (24 out of 29) of whose Labour MPs in these years were former councillors. Between 1945 and 1987, 76 per cent of Glasgow Labour MPs were former councillors, suggesting that the pattern may be beginning to change (Keating *et al.*, 1989). In 1987, seven out of the eleven Glasgow Labour MPs were former councillors, just 63 per cent. On the other hand, of those elected for the first time in 1987, four out of five were councillors. The reason for this trend seems to be the great difficulty of non-councillors in gaining nomination for safe seats in Glasgow. Of the non-councillors elected to Parliament from Glasgow since 1959, three (Bruce Millan, John Maxton and George Galloway) won the seats from other parties, two (Donald Dewar and Michael Watson) were selected when Labour was under intense pressure from the SNP, and the other, the widow of the former MP, served briefly after a by-election. The safe seats selecting candidates for the last thirty years have always chosen local councillors. So non-councillors have normally been able to come in only when seats have changed party control.

Another post-war trend was the decline in the number of non-Scots representing Scottish constituencies. Before and just after the war, it was not uncommon to find non-Scottish candidates winning Scottish seats; John Strachey, Emrys Hughes and Willie Hamilton are examples. From the 1950s onwards, this became more unusual; and the home-bred Scots MPs became less inclined to play roles on the UK stage (Keating, 1975). To this extent, there was an undercurrent against assimilation, though not in favour of Home Rule or independent Scottish initiative. It was, rather, a retreat into a dependent or secondary role, a parochialism in which attention was focussed on local and constituency matters, with most members entering the UK political arena only where there was a local material interest at stake (Keating, 1975).

The promotion patterns of Scottish MPs reflect this. Only a handful have achieved Cabinet office in the three Labour Governments since 1945. The same was long true of the Shadow Cabinet in opposition. Of 32 MPs elected to it between 1951 and 1964, only one, Tom Fraser, represented a Scottish constituency. On several occasions in the 1950s, Scottish MPs were unable to get the Shadow Scottish Secretary into the Shadow Cabinet. Again, Glasgow stands out. The city has produced just one Labour Cabinet Minister since the war, the Secretary of State for Scotland. It is significant that both he and the only Glasgow MP to make it to the Shadow Cabinet were among the handful of Glasgow Labour MPs who were not former councillors. Since 1979, the number of Scots in the Shadow Cabinet has steadily increased, peaking at five out of fifteen. This somewhat over-represents their presence in the parliamentary party and is a dramatic change from the former position. Some tendency does also appear to be developing for Scottish MPs to vote for their own in Shadow Cabinet elections, though the long-term significance of this is hard to assess.

One of the enduring myths of the Scottish Labour movement is that of its own radicalism. The legend of Red Clydeside is nurtured to present the party as a crusading movement, well to the left of the party in England. There is little evidence, the rhetoric aside, to support this view. Labour implanted itself in the urban areas of Scotland on a trade-union base, expanded and developed through class appeals, control of local government, expansion of public services and has been sustained for much of its history by patronage and ward-heeling. Its policies where it has controlled local government have been, at least until recently, orthodox, based on central guidance, and heavily conditioned by a tradition of municipal paternalism. In the last few years, a new generation of local leaders has emerged with fresh ideas, especially on housing and the decentralisation of local services. There has, however, been little evidence of the 'new urban left' which has been so important in some English cities (Gyford, 1985), with its agenda for local socialism. Outside the urban and industrial areas, Labour's presence has steadily shrunk and the radical potential of the land reform movements in the Highlands has been tapped by other anti–Conservative forces.

There is some evidence, albeit fragmentary, that Labour representatives are closer to their electoral class base than their counterparts in England. Scottish MPs in the 1945–70 period were more likely to be from working-class backgrounds than Labour MPs as a whole (Keating, 1975). In Glasgow, a survey in 1986 found that no less than 76 per cent of Labour councillors came from working-class backgrounds. Indeed 63 per cent of them had started their own careers in manual occupations, though nearly all had moved into white-collar jobs following a period of adult education (Keating *et al.*, 1989).

Labour has throughout its history been torn between the two traditions of centralisation and decentralisation. The early Labour Party in Scotland inherited the Home Rule traditions of radical Liberalism and from its inception the Scottish Council of the party was committed to self-government. During and after the First World War, this developed into a strident nationalism, with calls for Home Rule and even dominion status coming regularly from both the party and the Scottish Trades Union Congress (Keating and Bleiman, 1979). In practice, the commitment was a dead letter after the early 1920s. The first generation of Scottish Labour MPs had opted for a strategy of UK-wide advance. The collapse of Scottish industry in the recession destroyed the self-confidence of the Scottish labour movement and the belief that Scotland could go it alone. In the longer term, amalgamations of Scottish trade unions with their English counterparts removed an important independent element. From the 1930s, the party as a whole was committed to a policy of centralised state planning and nationalisation and this, rather than constitutional reform, was the priority of the Attlee Government after 1945. The Home Rule policy remained officially in place until 1958 when, after a determined campaign by the party's Scottish leadership, it was dropped from the programme. In its place was a commitment to the vigorous promotion of Scottish interests within the UK. By the 1960s, spokesmen were deriding the idea of a devolved assembly for Scotland while the left of the party insisted that the devolution would merely divide the working class and distract attention from the 'real' conflict in society.

Home Rule sentiment, however, never died out completely and, from the late 1960s, began to revive. In the early 1970s, unease about the threat from the SNP, frustration at Labour's impotence in the face of the Heath government's housing legislation, North Sea oil and the as-yet uncertain implications of EEC membership caused a reawakening of interest. This coincided with a general move on the European left, away from the centralised model of state planning and back to the earlier socialist ideas of local and community based action (Keating, 1988b). The pace of the issue was forced by the SNP

breakthrough in 1974. A panicking Labour leadership, faced
with opinion poll evidence on the danger to Labour seats,
forced the Scottish executive to reconvene the Scottish conference between the two elections of 1974. Proposals for an
elected legislative assembly were adopted with little dissent.
While political expediency was undoubtedly the leadership's
motive for the change of line, opinion in the party was already
moving in that direction and, as in the 1940s and 1950s,
devolutionary feeling was stronger among the rank and file than
at the summit. It was some years, however, before the party as
a whole was able to convince itself of the merits of its revived
policy. A strident minority continued to oppose the policy
publicly and to campaign for a NO vote in the 1979 referendum.
It is indicative of the relative lack of importance of the issue to
the party that none of these suffered a political penalty for their
defiance of party policy or, indeed, for the role which their
actions on devolution played in the fall of the Labour
government. Indeed, a prominent anti-devolution campaigner,
Brian Wilson, was even appointed spokesman on Scottish affairs
after the 1987 elections. The British party, which was not even
asked to endorse devolution until 1976, following the introduction of the legislation, has never really been converted and most
English MPs in the 1974–9 parliament saw it as a disagreeable
necessity to contain the SNP.

After 1979, the commitment to devolution was reaffirmed but
a rift opened up in the Scottish party. On one side were those
who wished to use the repeal of the Scotland Act, after it had
received majority support in the referendum, and the Conservatives poor electoral performance to deny the legitimacy of the
Thatcher government in Scotland. On the other side were the
leadership and the majority of the Scottish parliamentary group,
committed to the principles of constitutionalism and parliamentary sovereignty, who argued that Labour's priority was to seek a
UK majority which could then be used to legislate the party
programme, including a devolved assembly. The Parliamentary
leadership had to hold the party together on this issue, while
resisting nationalist taunts at Labour's inability to protect
Scotland against the new Conservatism and convincing the
Scottish electorate of its ability to win a UK majority. This was
to impose severe strains on the party and bring into some doubt
its ability to act as an integrative force within the British
political system.

Scottish National Party

The Scottish National Party was formed after the merger of the National Party of Scotland and the Scottish (Self-Government) Party in 1934. The NPS had been set up in 1928 by a number of Labour Party members who were disappointed to see a series of Home Rule Bills presented in the 1920s voted down in Parliament, and tended to be hardline on the constitutional question favouring independence. The Scottish Party was set up in 1932 and consisted mainly of Liberals and a few Conservatives who were generally moderates favouring a limited measure of Home Rule. The fundamentalist-gradualist tension has been the major source of conflict throughout the SNP's history.

Despite the original association of the left with fundamentalism and the right with gradualism, the tendency in recent times has been for the left to be seen as gradualist and the right as fundamentalist. Part of the explanation lies in a debate which came to a head in 1969 over whether the party ought to project itself simply as a movement for Scottish self—government or as a political party with a coherent socio-economic ideology. The victory of Billy Wolfe in the election of chairman of the party over Arthur Donaldson that year saw the SNP beginning to adopt a series of policies on social and economic issues.

The rapid growth in SNP support and membership in the 1960s and dramatic fluctuations reflecting its level of support saw the party's organisation develop in response. A large number of senior office-bearers are elected each year including the convenership (in 1988 the term 'chairman' was replaced by 'convener'), senior vice-convener, five executive vice-conveners, national secretary, national treasurer, president, three vice-presidents, and ten ordinary executive members. These office bearers plus ten ordinary members, MPs, an MEP and youth representatives form the party's executive. A notable feature of the SNP has been the way the chairman/convener has traditionally assumed a role chairing rather than leading the party. The party's best known and most influential figures do not always hold the most senior office. Figures such as Winnie Ewing, Margo MacDonald and Jim Sillars have been far better known than Arthur Donaldson, Billy Wolfe or Gordon Wilson over the last twenty years. This feature is not peculiar to the SNP. There is an absence of charismatic leadership in Scottish politics generally and some of the most flamboyant Scots in the twentieth century have made their names outside Scotland.

The SNP failed to make a serious impact in parliamentary elections until the 1960s. Prior to then the party had won a by-election in 1945 in Motherwell but this was in the unusual circumstances of the wartime coalition when Labour and Conservative Parties would not contest by-elections in seats they did not hold. A series of by-elections and local elections from the early 1960s saw the SNP gaining respectable votes. The Hamilton by-election in November 1967 saw the party's first major breakthrough with the election of Winnie Ewing. Though Ewing lost the seat at the subsequent General Election the party won the Western Isles, its first seat won at a General Election. The 1974 elections brought the party its best results to date, winning seven seats in February and eleven in October. Only two of these were held in 1979 when the party suffered a major setback following the referendum.

The consequence of defeat in 1979 was a period of introspection and division. The socialist republican' 79 Group was set up and attracted into its membership, and thereby into the SNP, the former Labour MP Jim Sillars. At the party conference in 1982 the SNP supported its chairman Gordon Wilson who, in exasperation at the prospect of the party tearing itself apart, moved that all groups be disbanded. Failure to comply with the terms of the resolution led to the expulsion of seven party members later that year. The fall in electoral support at the 1983 Election and dramatic fall in membership forced the party to unite or face further collapse and the period between 1983 and 1987 saw the development of a consensus around a 'moderate left of centre', gradualist position (Mitchell, 1990).

The introduction of the poll tax in Scotland a year earlier than south of the border offered the SNP a propaganda weapon which allowed it to attack both the Labour Party-for its inability to stop it-and the Conservatives-for imposing it against Scottish wishes. At its 1988 conference the party voted to support a campaign of non-payment of the poll tax. The near unanimity on such a controversial matter was a remarkable achievement in a party which six years before had been on the verge of civil war. The SNP's high profile campaign against the poll tax was an important backdrop to the Govan by-election in November 1988. The party's image as strongly anti-Conservative, demonstrated by its position on the poll tax, proved popular, particularly when articulated by Jim Sillars.

Another important policy development in the aftermath of the 1987 election was the SNP's explicitly pro-European Community position. At their 1984 conference, the SNP changed its position on European Community membership. The party had campaigned for withdrawal from the Community in the 1975 referendum and subsequently had generally adopted a hostile attitude. From 1984, but more explicitly from 1988, the SNP refined its constitutional goal as 'Independence In Europe'. The short-lived Scottish Labour Party of Jim Sillars had supported this option in the 1970s and Sillars was instrumental in having the change accepted. With strong support from Winnie Ewing, Gordon Wilson and Alex Salmond, the pro-Europe position found support across the spectrum of SNP views.

The rationale behind the European dimension was manifold. The heightened interest and media coverage of European Community affairs in the lead up to '1992' gave the SNP's distinctive polity a modern appeal. The increasing importance of the European dimension demanded that all the parties would be required to explain how Scotland would fit into the emerging European policy. The Nationalists alone would be arguing that Scotland could only hope to have influence as an independent state with representation in the Council of Ministers, the key decision-making forum of the Community. The European dimension was also perceived by the SNP as a means of gaining independence from London as part of a wider, more progressive 'Common Market'-a position similar to that achieved by the Republic of Ireland. Environmental issues, control over multinational corporations and coping with fluctuations in the international economy are perceived as more realistically achievable through an entity such as the Community. This assessment of the role of the EEC in affecting Scottish society requires, in the SNP's eyes, direct Scottish representation.

In 1988, a think tank, the Scottish Centre for Economic and Social Research (SCESR), was established which set out to consider various policy options for a self-governing Scotland. It is vaguely associatd with the SNP though contributors to its discussion papers have included a wider range of people. Part of the remit of the SCESR has been a series of papers on the European dimension:'1992 Series'.

Over the period of its existence the SNP has developed into a conventional political party rather than the movement for self—government which it was initially. Accepting that dual membership with other parties was unacceptable during the last war was the first stage. In the late 1960s the SNP came to accept the need to develop policies on a range of subjects, and this was set in motion in the 1970s. That decade involved the party coming to terms with identifying its position on the conventional left—right axis. The February 1974 election included a reference to social democracy in its manifesto but the debate was only really concluded in the early 1980s when the 'left of centre' label gained consensus. The late 1980s have seen the SNP modernise its image and up-date its policies, taking particular account of the increasing importance of the European dimension. There appears to have been a fair degree of consistency and consensus within the party in these developments unlike the major tension which has always existed in the SNP-that between its gradualist and fundamentalist wings.

During the 1980s, Gordon Wilson had gained support in the SNP for the idea of a constitutional convention to 'repatriate the Scottish constitution'. Opposition from fundamentalists to a scheme which seemed likely to result in a mere devolutionary settlement was eventually overcome. The idea was also adopted by the Alliance and the cross-party Campaign for a Scottish Assembly (CSA). In 1988, a committee established by the CSA produced 'A Claim of Right for Scotland', including proposals for a constitutional convention. While the Conservatives refused to have anything to do with the convention, Labour overcame its early suspicions and agreed to participate. The SNP then reversed its own position and decided to boycott the proceedings, producing considerable internal controversy only two months after its Govan by-election success.

The debates on the Constitutional Convention exemplify the difficulties the party has always had in this respect. While Nationalists such as Gordon Wilson and Jim Sillars were early advocates of a Convention-elected by proportional representation and thereby recognised as embodying sovereign powers-the SNP found it impossible to be part of the unelected Convention of the Campaign for a Scottish Assembly. The tension over this matter in early 1989 was well-contained by the SNP in the post-Govan mood of optimism. However, the debate within the party and the continuing support for the idea of a Convention demonstrates that the strategy of accepting a measure short of independence or going straight for independence is a perennial source of internal tension.

Liberals, SDP and Democrats

The Scottish Liberal Party has never come close to achieving the level of support it enjoyed during the nineteenth century. The splits in the party in the 1930s were particularly damaging in Scotland and by 1945 the Liberals had lost all their Scottish seats, though a few MPs continued until the 1960s to sit as National Liberals, in practice indistinguishable from the Conservatives with whom they sat in Parliament. In the 1960s, their fortunes began to revive at the Conservatives' expense in the Highland, Island and Border regions which have produced two of the party's postwar leaders. Elsewhere, however, it has struggled to win support since the Second World War and even during its revival in England in the mid 1970s failed to contest many seats in Scotland. The Social Democratic Party which broke away from the Labour Party in 1981 included only two Scottish MPs, Robert MacLennan and Dickson Mabon, soon joined by Roy Jenkins at Glasgow Hillhead. The formation of the Alliance allowed all seats in Scotland to be contested in 1983, with further successes in the Highlands and Borders.

The Liberals' distinctive contribution to Scottish post-war politics was their consistent advocacy of Home Rule at a time when the two major parties were opposed. Their official policy, indeed, was Home Rule All Round in a federal United Kingdom and from time to time there were discussions on a possible tactical alliance with the SNP. Despite its antiquity (dating back to the late nineteenth century), however, this policy was never clearly defined. Scottish and English Liberals failed to agree on whether England or the English regions should constitute the units of the new federation and, when the Labour government asked them for their devolution proposals under the Lib–Lab pact of the late 1970s, the party leadership had to borrow a ready-made scheme from the Outer Circle Policy Unit. The Social Democrats were from the outset committed to decentralisation and devolution within the United Kingdom but there were powerful centralist elements within the party and the schemes which emerged from the Alliance were almost indistinguishable from the Labour Party's devolution proposals.

The Alliance in general worked rather more smoothly in Scotland than in England with few serious arguments over the allocation of seats and little personality conflict. The 1987 election saw further advances at the Conservatives' expense around the Scottish periphery but a breakthrough in urban central Scotland continued to elude them. Both SDP MPs joined the merged Democrat party in 1988 and the continuing Social Democrats of David Owen are a tiny group. The new party, however, owes more to the Liberals than the old SDP.

The Parties as a Centralising Force

The two major British parties in Scotland serve not only to integrate Scotland into the British political system but to centralise the policy process. While both have in recent years published Scottish manifestos, these consist mainly of synopses of policies adopted for the UK as a whole, with a few Scottish items added on. In neither case does the Scottish Conference have the authority to make policy independently while both parties' full-time officials are appointed from London. In the Labour Party, an additional centralising force is provided by the trade unions, which tend not to have autonomous wings and so adopt lines at the Scottish Labour conference in conformity with their UK policy. Neither party has produced dominant Scottish leaders able to use Scotland as a power base for influence in the party or to force concessions to Scottish interests. This reflects those values in Scottish society which de-emphasise personal leadership and which we have already noted in the SNP. It also reflects the structure of the parties and career patterns in British politics. Politicians are often forced to choose between Scottish and UK careers and those opting for the UK arena will maintain a certain distance from Scottish affairs, partly because of lack of time, partly to avoid the appearance of 'parochialism' (Keating, 1975). At the Scottish level, Secretaries of State and their shadows are appointed by the party leaders and do not need an independent political base within Scotland. A proposal some time ago that the Scottish Labour conference should elect the party's Scottish spokesman, just as the electoral college at the national conference elects the party leader, received short shrift. The Parliamentary parties have Scottish committees which discuss purely Scottish business and put pressure on the front benches but they are not major influences.

The major British parties in Scotland thus reinforce the centralist bias of government while serving to manage Scottish particularity by channeling demands to the UK level, where they can be resolved by overall UK policies or the discrete concessions available through the Scottish Office (Chapter 4). Their overall objective remains that of securing parliamentary majorities, and territorial interests will necessarily be subordinated to this. Yet, electoral trends within Scotland in recent years, diverging increasingly from those in England, have created increasing tensions between their role in reflecting Scottish opinion and the imperative to command UK majorities.

Voting and Elections in Scotland

In the 1987 General Election, Labour took 50 of Scotland's 72 Parliamentary seats. With the Alliance parties taking 9 and the SNP 3, the governing Conservatives were reduced to 10 – despite a majority of nearly 100 in the UK as a whole. This confirmed a trend which had been apparent throughout the 1980s. In 1979 the gap between the Conservative lead over Labour in Scotland and England rose to a record 21 per cent (Miller, 1981), only to increase further, to 26 per cent in 1983 and to 35 per cent in 1987. To some observers, this confirmed that there was substance in the long-standing myth of Scotland's anti-Conservatism. To others, it was evidence of Labour's continuing strength in a traditional heartland. In fact, the picture is more complicated. The relationship between seats won and shares of the popular vote is, in Scotland as elsewhere, often quite arbitrary. Labour's best share of the popular vote in Scotland was in 1966, when it gained over 49 per cent, against just 42 per cent in 1987. The picture has been further complicated in recent years by the four-party system, with the fluctuating fortunes of the SNP and Alliance reducing the support for the major parties and further complicating the relationship between vote share and seats. In 1987, the Conservative and Labour parties gained just 66 per cent of the Scottish vote between them, against 73 per cent in the UK as a whole.

Figure 2.1 % Vote, General Elections in Scotland, 1900–87

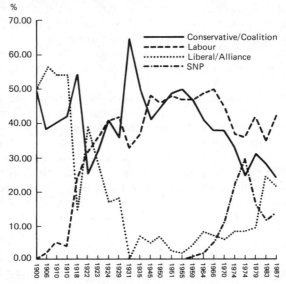

Source: F.W.S. Craig (1989) *British Electoral Facts, 1832–1987* (5th ed) (Aldershot: Gower).

Figure 2.2 % Vote, General Elections in UK, 1900–87

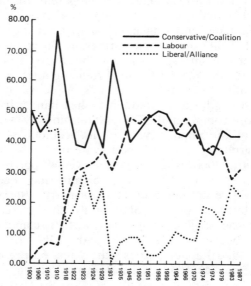

Source: F.W.S. Craig (1989) *British Electoral Facts, 1832–1987* (5th ed) (Aldershot: Gower).

Table 2.1 Seats won in the UK and Scotland since 1900

	UK				SCOTLAND				
	Cons	Lab	Lib	Coalition	Cons	Lab	Lib	SNP	Coalition
1900	402	2	184		36	0	34		
1906	157	30	400		10	2	58		
1910 Feb	273	40	275		9	2	59		
1910 Dec	272	42	272		9	3	58		
1918	50	58	36	473	2	6	8		54
1922	344	142	62		13	29	27		
1923	258	191	158		14	34	22		
1924	412	151	40		36	26	8		
1929	260	287	59		20	36	13		
1931		52	4	554		7	–	–	64
1935		154	21	429		37	3	–	43
1945	210	393	12		27	37	–	–	
1950	298	315	9		31	37	2	–	
1951	321	295	6		35	35	1	–	
1955	345	277	6		36	34	1	–	
1959	365	258	6		31	38	1	–	
1964	304	317	9		24	43	4	–	
1966	253	364	12		20	46	5	–	
1970	330	288	6		23	44	3	1	
1974 Feb	297	301	14		21	40	3	7	
1974 Oct	276	319	13		16	41	3	11	
1979	339	269	11		22	44	3	2	
1983	397	209	23		21	41	8	2	
1987	376	229	22		10	50	9	3	

Source: F.W.S. Craig, *British Electoral Facts, 1832–1987*, 5th edn (Aldershot: Gower).

Taking a longer historical perspective, we can see that Conservative support in Scotland was relatively weak in the early part of the century, to the advantage, first of the Liberal Party and then of Labour. From the mid 1930s this began to change and by 1945 the Conservatives were doing slighly better in Scotland than in England. The improvement in Conservative fortunes continued until 1955 when they won an overall majority of the Scottish vote. In 1959 their vote started a slide which was to continue to 1987, interrupted only briefly by their recovery of support from the SNP in 1979.

With the Conservative retreat, Labour's share of the vote continued to rise until 1966. Thereafter, it has fluctuated considerably in response to the counter-attractions of the SNP and Alliance-in contrast to England where it has fairly steadily declined. SNP and Alliance performances have been less consistent. In the 1950s and 1960s, the Liberals tended to do rather worse in Scotland than elsewhere, but the concentration of their vote in the Scottish periphery enabled them to pick up relatively more seats. In the 1970s, they were largely eclipsed by the rise of the SNP and did not experience the revival which occurred south of the border under the Heath government. The Liberal/SDP Alliance, on the other hand, performed just as well in Scotland as in England in the mid 1980s, to the surprise of some who had written it off as a purely English formation.

Since the early 1960s, then, Labour has consistently led in Scotland, though not equalling the Liberal dominance of the early part of the century. Three other party formations have vied for second and third place. One result is that the Conservative governments elected in 1970, 1979, 1983 and 1987 lacked a plurality either of Scottish votes or seats. This is not quite unprecedented. It happened in the one-year parliament of 1922, while in 1959 the Conservatives, though slightly ahead in the Scottish vote, gained fewer seats than Labour. For a party to govern for a decade without a plurality of Scottish votes or seats, however, is unprecedented since the advent of universal suffrage. We explore the constitutional implications of this later (Chapter 9).

Examination of the results on a regional basis helps to put Labour's lead in perspective. As figure 2.3 shows, Labour's support in the 1983 and 1987 General Elections was concentrated in the regions of the industrial Central belt. In these four regions (Fife, Lothian, Central and Strathclyde), Labour won

Figure 2.3 % Vote by region in General Elections, 1983–87

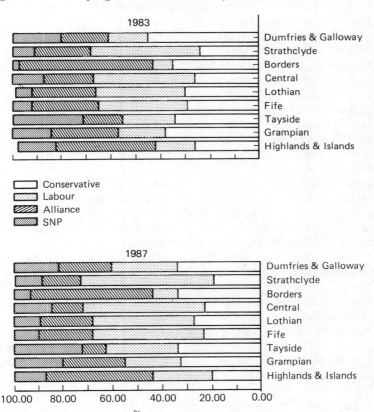

over 40 per cent of the vote. In no other region was its support as much as 30 per cent. Conservative support, on the other hand, was weak everywhere in the 1980s and nowhere reached as much as 35 per cent in 1987. The performance of the Alliance and SNP was also uneven, with the Alliance dominant in the Highlands and the Borders but notably weak in Central and Tayside. For its part, the SNP did relatively well in Tayside and Grampian. This suggests a relationship between the SNP and Alliance votes. Where the SNP has an advantage, the Alliance do poorly and vice versa. This effect, while visible from the regional figures in figure 2.3, is even more pronounced at constituency level. So in the two Grampian constituencies won by the SNP in 1987, the Alliance vote was down to about 10 per cent, while in the Grampian constituency won by the Alliance the SNP was reduced to 7 per cent.

This spatial polarisation of the vote within Scotland is a relatively new phenomenon. It is difficult to compare results from the 1950s with those from the 1980s because of the four—party competition in the later period. It is nevertheless notable that while Labour scored almost precisely the same percentage of the vote in Strathclyde in 1987 as it had in 1955, the Conservatives had been reduced from 47 per cent to 19 per cent. In Grampian, conversely, the rise of third and fourth parties has hurt both major parties, the Conservatives falling from 53 per cent in 1955 to 33 per cent in 1987 and Labour from 47 per cent to 23 per cent in the same period. In 1955, indeed, there were only seventeen Scottish seats in which Labour failed to gain a third of the vote, and two of these were in Glasgow. It was in that year that the Conservatives won seven of Glasgow's fifteen seats, including Pollok, Scotstoun and Cathcart (the latter with 73 per cent of the vote) and failed to win Provan by just 180 votes. In 1983 they held no seats at all in the city. The four constituencies just mentioned had become the location of Glasgow's four great peripheral housing schemes (see Chapter 8) and the Conservative vote had sunk to negligible proportions. Yet, in contrast to some English cities where the outward movement of the middle class has helped Labour in the city but aided the Conservatives in the suburbs, all but one of Glasgow's suburban seats were in Labour hands by 1987.

Explaining the widening gap between Scottish and English voting behaviour is not easy. There is little agreement in the literature on the territorial dimension of voting behaviour. Some would argue that major divergences of voting patterns and swings in different parts of the country, are merely a function of other differences and not significant in themselves. So it might be thought that Scottish voting behaviour reflects the socio—economic composition of Scotland and is no more significant as a *Scottish* vote than the tendency of the North-East of England to vote Labour against the general British trend. For a long time, psephologists saw voting behaviour largely as a matter of socialisation. People voted according to their social background and upbringing. In most cases, this meant voting according to social class, though other factors such as religion and gender were seen as independently important. More recently, the importance of housing tenure in voting has been recognised (Rose and McAllister, 1986), with a strong tendency for council tenants to vote Labour, while owner-occupiers are more inclined to vote Conservative.

McAllister and Rose (1984) found that most of the gap between Scottish and English voting behaviour could indeed be explained by factors such as socio-economic status and the proportions of council housing. Interestingly, they found that in 1983 the Labour vote in Scotland was *below* that which would be predicted on the basis of socio-economic structure, but, given the four-party competition which does not exist in England, this was also true of the Conservatives. Miller (1981), however, maintains that in the 1940s and 1950s Labour did worse in Scotland than might be predicted purely on class grounds but by 1979 was doing better than in England even after taking account of the socio-economic composition of the electorate.

The Conservatives' success in Scotland in the 1950s has been attributed to a number of factors-the residual Protestant working-class vote supporting the Unionists, the weakness of the Liberals, the Conservatives' strong identification with Scottish issues and the fortuitous ending of rationing and apparent economic expansion of the early 1950s under Conservative Governments (Mitchell, 1990). Most of these factors, however, apply equally in England. One which does not, except in a few English regions, is religion. Surveys in the west of Scotland in the 1950s and 1960s found a strong link between religion and voting (Budge and Urwin, 1966; Budge *et al.*, 1972). A Glasgow survey in the late 1960s found 60 per cent of middle-class Protestants voting Conservative and 22 per cent voting Labour, while for middle-class Catholics the proportions were almost exactly reversed, at 23–61. Among all categories of the working class there was majority support for Labour but in the case of Catholics the ratio was 78–6, while among Protestants it was just 52–33 (Budge *et al.*, 1972). Labour's improvement in Scotland could thus be a result of the decline of religious attachments allowing class politics to become more generalised as Butler and Stokes (1969) argued had earlier happened in Britain as a whole.

This would not, however, explain how Labour has in recent years performed *better* than would be expected on class grounds. Heath *et al.* (1985) conclude that, at the 1983 Election, the *hypothetical* difference between Conservative support in Scotland and the south of England, on the basis of class and housing, was 11 per cent but the *actual* difference was 31 per cent. Again at the 1987 General Election the electorate throughout Britain 'did not cast a nationwide verdict', but, instead, showed considerable regional variation, particularly in the Labour vote (Curtice and Steed, 1988).

Of course, simply talking in terms of working-class and middle-class voters is a gross simplification, given the changes at work in the British class system. Crewe (1987) divides the working class into 'traditional' and 'new' and observes significant differences in voting behaviour between the two. The distinction is based on region of residence, housing tenure, union membership and whether an individual works in the public or private sector. Major differences in the voting behaviour of the two groups were observed, with Labour support much stronger among the traditional working class. Scotland, as we have seen (Chapter 1), has a relatively large public sector and a low rate of owner occupation, particularly in the industrial central belt and this, it is generally agreed, explains part of Labour's advantage there. Changes in the composition of the working class could also help to account for changing territorial patterns of voting over time. However, it is notable that, on the basis of Crewe's figures, the difference between Labour and Consvervative is greater when working-class voters are categorised according to region rather than on the basis of any one of the other classifications, suggesting that territory is an independent factor.

Territorial differences in voting behaviour have often been attributed to the 'milieu effect', the tendency for people in constituencies dominated by one party to vote for that party even when it is not the one normally associated with their socio−economic class. The casual mechanism whereby this happens has never been adequately specified but there is evidence of some such effect. Miller (1984) showed that in 1983, while class differences had a diminished impact on individual voting behaviour, the class composition of constituencies contined to be a reliable predictor of election outcomes. So Labour's vote held up better in its traditional, working-class constituencies. Johnston and Pattie (1988) confirm this 'party strength effect' for changes in the vote between 1979 and 1987. They also discern an additional, regional effect, albeit less visible in the case of flows of support between the Conservatives and the Alliance than in other cases.

The failure over the years to appreciate and measure territorial differences in voting behaviour has both intellectual and practical causes. Behavioural approaches to political science have systematically downplayed territory in their efforts to generate social background variables which could be measured and compared over time. Modernisation theories of political development prevalent in the 1960s and 1970s predicted the demise of such 'premodern' bases of alignment such as territory, religion and ethnicity and their exponents were resistent to suggestions that these might be of continuing importance in modern, industrial societies (Keating, 1988b). With the dominant paradigm in electoral studies having no place for territory, the questions which might have explored its importance have simply not been included in surveys. At the same time, few surveys have a sufficiently large sample to be able to break electors down into regional and local samples. Even for Scotland, whose politics have been a considerable general interest since the 1970s, there are very few usable electoral surveys. So it has been necessary to rely on ecological analysis, comparing the social characteristics of whole constituencies with electoral outcomes.

Recently, some scholars have sought to rescue territory as an independent element in politics (Agnew, 1987). The assumption of most studies of voting behaviour has been that background variables such as class, religion and housing tenure have a similar effect everywhere and that spatial variations in voting can be attributed to the differential incidence of these variables. Even studies which recognise the significance of territory treat it for purposes of analysis and measurement as a residual. That is, variations in party support which cannot be accounted for by the differing incidence of socio-economic factors are assumed to represent the true but mysterious purely territorial element in voting choice. It may be, however, that the meaning and experience of the standard background factors themselves differ territorially. It is obvious, for instance, that the significance of being a Catholic in Northern Ireland is very different from that of being a Catholic in England. In the west of Scotland, the historical experience of sectarian politics has given religion a significance it lacks in most regions south of the border. Housing, too, has a different significance in Scottish political traditions, particularly in the west. It is likely, too, that class perceptions and class solidarities will differ from place to place. Johnston and Pattie (1989) suggest that class attachments remain stronger in Scotland. SNP voting has proved impervious to all attempts to reduce it to class interest or mere protest. It remains largely an expression of a territorial interest, cutting across class identities, though differing in force in the various parts of Scotland. Agnew's (1987) place-centred social science breaks with the assumptions that political behaviour is the product of national trends, with occasional local variations from the norm, and sees it as intrinsically geographical. Political expression in Scotland is thus 'the product of political behaviour structured by the historically constituted places in which people live their lives' (Agnew, 1987, p. 108). We would argue that territory may be an intervening variable moulding the way in which the standard social and economic categories are experienced and perceived. Unfortunately, survey evidence on this is very sparse, given the dominant paradigm of electoral studies.

The cultural element in Scottish political behaviour may also be important. Unfortunately, most attempts to examine and measure this (such as Hechter, 1975) have been based on the nebulous concept of ethnicity, which has never been adequately specified as an independent explanatory variable, or have used measures such as religion which are themselves of declining political significance in mainland Britain. It may be, though, that there are elements in modern Scottish political culture which are antithetic to the values of contemporary Conservatism. We have referred (Chapter 1) to the belief among Conservatives that Scotland has developed a 'dependency culture'. Their opponents put the same point in a less pejorative way, claiming that Scots have more generally retained the collectivist, welfare values which formed an important part of the post-war British consensus. Miller (1981) shows some evidence for this in the 1970s. In Chapter 9 we show more evidence for its continued importance in the 1980s. Clearly, the cultural environment in which Scottish politics operates is distinct, and equally clearly Scots perceive there to be a distinct Scottish dimension. The belief in the existence of a Scottish *political* identity may create problems for the Conservatives in so far as they have allowed themselves to be portrayed as anti-Scottish.

Recent studies have shown that the traditional social-class variables are of diminishing importance (Franklin, 1985). It may be, therefore, that voters are increasingly 'beginning to choose' (Rose and McAllister, 1986) between the parties on the basis of policy and self-interest. In that case, territorial interests are likely to be a consideration. Samuel Beer commented in 1958 that the 'regions of England, and of the United Kingdom, have different interests ... if only they would think that way' (Beer, 1980, p.5). It would appear that the regions and nations making up the United Kingdom have now taken note of his comments. If voters are increasingly identifying themselves in territorial as well as purely class terms, then parties able to identify themselves with the promotion of Scottish interests may have an advantage. This is certainly something which the Labour Party has consistently striven to achieve since the early 1960s, first through promises of regional development aid for Scotland and later through the promise of constitutional reform. With the existence of a significant nationalist competitor, Scottish political debate has continued to focus on specifically Scottish issues and on which party is most capable of promoting Scottish interests. In Chapter 9, we present evidence that voters are able to distinguish government's record generally from its record in Scotland, with substantial numbers of voters found to think that Mrs. Thatcher was a good Prime Minister for the United Kingdom but bad for Scotland. Johnston and Pattie (1989) found that fewer people in Scotland in 1987 thought that things had improved or would improve under the Conservatives. Even among those who thought things had improved, Scots were less likely than English to vote Conservative.

Following the 1987 General Election there was much speculation in Scotland on the extent to which 'tactical voting' took place. Organisations with the sole purpose of encouraging voters to identify the candidate most likely to defeat the Conservative existed throughout Britain but in Scotland there was evidence of greater impact being made in the media. The existence of a peculiarly Scottish organisation 'Tactical Voting' 87, allied with the much-discussed idea of the 'Doomsday Scenario', of the Tories winning the General Election but reduced to a rump in Scotland, may have been a factor in the results though considerable differences exist as to the extent of Scottish tactical voting (Bochel and Denver, 1988; Lawson, 1988). Organisational factors, too, may be important. In parts of west central Scotland, the Conservatives effectively gave up in national and local contests in the 1980s, presenting only token opposition to Labour or using elections there to test candidates destined for better prospects in the south. They lacked effective urban-based leaders of the calibre of the populist Teddy Taylor who held Cathcart against the odds until 1979.

Scottish voting behaviour remains an under-researched area and our conclusions here must necessarily be tentative. Nevertheless, it does appear that there is a historic tendency for Scottish voters to be less sympathetic to the Conservative Party, though this was broken in the 1950s and could change again in the future. Labour is solidly established only in the industrial belt but local and by-election results since the late 1960s have shown that, even there, its dominance is vulnerable to attack from the nationalists. Elsewhere in Scotland, there are complex patterns of four-party competition. The resulting electoral turbulence has created severe problems for the main British parties and their ability to manage Scottish affairs within the United Kingdom. We return to this theme in the final chapter.

3

The Structure of Government in Scotland

The Development of the Scottish Office

Prior to the establishment of the Scottish Office in 1885, Scottish central administration consisted of a disparate collection of boards in Edinburgh responsible for lunacy, fisheries, manufactures, prisons and poor law. The patronage associated with these boards brought them into disrepute and in England the Northcote-Trevelyan reforms had begun to professionalise the public sector after 1854. Scotland lagged behind England and many of the boards continued to operate even after the establishment of the Scottish Office, in some cases until 1939. In Parliament, Scottish affairs were theoretically the responsibility of the Home Secretary but in practice they devolved upon the Lord Advocate. Successive Lord Advocates exercised considerable power and patronage, though none had the influence of an early nineteenth-century Scottish manager such as the infamous and corrupt Henry Dundas.

It was dissatisfaction within Scotland and a feeling that Scottish affairs were being neglected in Westminster and Whitehall in the latter half of the last century which led to agitation for a Secretary of State for Scotland. As cross-party demands for this post reached a high point in the 1880s, the Liberal Government under Gladstone introduced legislation to establish special administrative apparatus for Scotland. There was no clear idea as to what shape this apparatus should take; nor was there a clear idea what functions and responsibilities it should have. Eventually the bill completed its passage through

51

Parliament under Lord Salisbury after Gladstone's Ministry fell in 1885. The Secretaryship for Scotland was, therefore, a product of bipartisan consensus which began its legislative passage under the Liberals and finished as a Conservative measure.

Argument as to what the principal responsibilities of the Scottish Office ought to be revolved around education and law and order. Neither educationalists nor lawyers wanted their respective concerns to come under the Scottish Office. Educationalists, including the teachers' organisation, the Educational Institute of Scotland, campaigned for a British Ministry of Education. They lost the argument and so education became the Scottish Office's principal responsibility at its inception. However within two years law and order was added, partly because of lobbying by A. J. Balfour, the only Scottish Secretary to date to make it eventually to 10 Downing Street. The first Scottish Secretary, the Duke of Richmond and Gordon, had privately opposed the establishment of the Office as he could not imagine what the Secretary for Scotland would actually have to do. But he accepted the Office at Salisbury's insistence because, as Salisbury maintained, it was necessary that a figure of prominence in Scottish society be appointed since, as Salisbury put it in a letter to the Duke, 'the whole object of the move is to redress the wounded dignities of the Scotch people-or a section of them-who think that enough is not made of Scotland' (quoted in Hanham, 1965).

The Duke's view that the Office was merely a showpiece to appease Scottish sentiments was markedly different from later Scottish Secretaries who became responsible for a wide and growing range of matters and a substantial bureaucracy. Robert Munro (Scottish Secretary, 1916–22) remarked after demitting Office on the impossibility of a Scottish Secretary dealing adequately with all his responsibilities (Munro, 1930). Based in Dover House in Whitehall, the Scottish Secretary had outreaches in Edinburgh where a series of Boards were responsible for a range of matters from fisheries and prisons to local government and lunacy. Although the Scottish Secretary was the political head of these Boards, they were, in strict legal terms, separate from the Scottish Office.

The functions of the Scottish Office increased incrementally. It gained responsibility for law and order in 1887 following agitation in the Highlands, when A.J. Balfour appealed to his uncle, Prime Minister Lord Salisbury, for the powers to deal with the situation (Gibson, 1985). Agriculture, with the exception of animal health, became a Scottish Office responsibility in 1912. Following the First World War, health, which essentially meant housing, was added, followed by a steady accumulation of responsibilities reflecting the increase in state intervention during the twentieth century.

The rather messy set-up over which the Scottish Secretary presided by the inter-war period included the Scottish Office in London and the disparate Boards scattered throughout Edinburgh. Administrative efficacy was at a minimum and was made more difficult as responsibilities grew (MacDonnell 1915, p.77). Each year saw new powers and responsibilities added in areas such as education and housing and the pressure for some rationalisation of the central administration of Scottish affairs mounted. In 1935, an Edinburgh office of the Scottish Office was opened, headed by David Milne who became Permanent Secretary from 1946 to 1959. Before this, arrangements in Edinburgh had been rather *ad hoc*. This was followed by a far more ambitious plan to consolidate the Scottish central administration.

Plans to bring all the various officials for whom the Scottish Secretary was responsible under one roof in Edinburgh had been under consideration from the early 1930s. Ramsay MacDonald backed the idea of building a prestigious new headquarters to house the disparate bodies responsible for Scottish administration in Scotland. In 1936 a committee was set up under Sir John Gilmour, a former Scottish Secretary, to investigate the duties of the Scottish Office and allied administrative agencies and make recommendations, 'keeping in view the prospective concentration of Departments in one building in Edinburgh'. The Gilmour Committee reported the next year recommending a consolidation of the administrative agencies in a new organisation (Mitchell, 1989).

The Reorganisation of Offices (Scotland) Act, 1939 brought the modern Scottish Office into being. The Boards disappeared, with minor exceptions, and a consolidated Scottish administration was organised functionally into four departments: the Department of Agriculture for Scotland, the Scottish Education Department, the Department of Health for Scotland, and the

Scottish Home Department. A Permanent Secretary overseeing the four departments had the crucial task of ensuring coordination.

According to Hanham (1969), the opening of St. Andrew's House on Calton Hill in Edinburgh in 1939 'gave Scotland for the first time since the eighteenth century a seat of government'. This was true only in the sense that the new building and the consolidated Scottish Office focused attention on an institution which previously had been a disparate collection of public agencies scattered around Edinburgh. Though some staff were transferred from Dover House, the 1939 reforms mainly involved bringing together civil servants administering a range of functions already in Edinburgh. The perception of a transfer of power and responsibility from London was certainly conveyed, as was intended, but this was inaccurate.

The Modern Scottish Office

The intention of housing all the staff of the Edinburgh offices under one roof was never realised. By the time St. Andrew's House opened in 1939 the staff had grown and many officials of the Department of Health were based outside the Calton Hill headquarters. As post-war developments in the welfare state increased the number of civil servants, the Scottish Office was soon beginning to resemble the old structure. Not only was the staff not centralised but new quasi-autonomous agencies, not directly part of the Scottish Office, developed, resembling in many respects the old Boards.

A number of relatively minor accretions to Scottish Office responsibilities followed the recommendations of the Royal Commission on Scottish Affairs (Balfour, 1954). These included appointment of Justices of the Peace, animal health, roads, bridges and ferries, electricity in southern Scotland, and the school milk scheme. They were important in establishing a Scottish Office role in economic development but the establishment of more comprehensive economic responsibilities came later, in the 1960s.

An enquiry into the Scottish economy conducted under the auspices of the Scottish Council (Development and Industry) with Scottish Office support (Toothill, 1961) proposed that sections of the Home and Health Departments should be brought together in one department. Under the provisions of the 1939 Act, this did not require new legislation, and in 1962 two departments were merged to form the Scottish Home and Health Department and a Scottish Development Department (SDD) was set up in line with the dominant thinking of that time to enhance the role of economic planning. The SDD had responsibility for local government, the environment, and planning. Prior to 1962 there were no economists employed by the Scottish Office. From then the economic functions and number of economists in the Scottish office grew.

In 1964 a Scottish Economic Planning Board consisting of officials from relevant Scottish and UK departments was established under Scottish Office tutelage, as part of the Labour Government's scheme for regional planning (Lindley, 1982). Its role was to cordinate government policies on economic planning and development in Scotland. A further major overhaul came with the creation of the Scottish Economic Planning Department (SEPD) in 1973 resulting in the demise of the Planning Board. Regional policy as it affected Scotland and industry policy, including responsibility for the Scottish Development Agency set up in 1975 became SEPD responsibilities. In conformity with the Thatcher Government's dislike of the term 'planning' and its implications, the SEPD was renamed the Industry Department for Scotland in 1983. The Department and their responsibilities as of 1989 are as follows:

Department of Agriculture and Fisheries for Scotland: agriculture and fisheries, including crofting.

Scottish Development Department: housing, local government, planning, roads and transport.

Industry Department for Scotland: regional economic policy, industrial development, new towns, electricity, the Scottish Development Agency and the Highlands and Islands Development Board.

Scottish Education Department: Scottish education except the universities; social work services.

Scottish Home and Health Department: police, prisons, crime, the Scottish health service.

Additionally, a central services group in charge of personnel and finance exists in Edinburgh. The small staff in the Dover House 'Liaison Division' in London perform a vital function. The Treasury, Cabinet and Parliament and most other Departments are based in London which gives the London office of the Scottish Office an importance which its small staff might not suggest. Most senior Scottish Office civil servants will spend a considerable amount of time in London and it is almost a prerequisite for promotion to the senior positions-principal and above-for civil servants to have spent a period based in Dover House. In the past, the separation of the London office from Edinburgh by four hundred miles caused serious practical problems but modern information technology now allows all parts of the Office to be in immediate contact.

Current Powers and Responsibilities of the Scottish Office

Shortly after taking up office as Secretary of State for Scotland in 1986, Malcolm Rifkind described his role as similar to that of Governor-General. In respect of the multitudinous responsibilities in his remit, Rifkind certainly had a point. It has been estimated that he is responsible for the equivalent of eleven different Whitehall ministries. The Welsh and Northern Ireland Offices are responsible for the equivalent of eight and thirteen respectively (Rose, 1982). Of course, this is an imprecise figure as the responsibilities of these territorial departments are not congruent with other Whitehall departments. Immigration, nationality and broadcasting as they affect Scotland are the responsibility of the Home Office and not the SHHD. The Department of Education and Science has responsibility for the universities throughout Britain, despite the contrary recommendation of the Scottish Tertiary Education Advisory Committee (STEAC, 1985).

The range of *responsibilities* should not be equated with the *powers* of the Scottish Office. Though much has been expected of the Scottish Office throughout its existence, there has often been an appreciable failure to recognise its limitations. Salisbury's comment in 1885 that, measured by the expectations of the Scottish people, the Scottish Secretary was 'approaching the

Archangelic' prompted a latter-day Scottish Secretary to adopt the title when writing of his experiences (Ross, 1978). The tendency to credit the Scottish Office with greater powers and responsibilities than those strictly allocated to it was noted in the Gilmour Report in 1937 where reference was made to the 'penumbral' duties of the Scottish Secretary and the popular perception of him as Scotland's Minister:

> 'our evidence shows that there is an increasing tendency to appeal to him on all matters which have a Scottish aspect, even if on a strict view they are outside the province of his duties as statutorily defined'.
>
> (Gilmour, 1937 p.19)

Kellas (1989) states that the Scottish Secretary has been called Scotland's Prime Minister. The reality is that a great deal is expected in Scotland of a relatively junior British Cabinet Minister with limited powers of innovation. If Ministerial power is measured by the extent to which a Minister can initiate and implement a policy, then the Scottish Office works within tight constraints (see Chapter 4). It was never intended to be an innovatory department and performs best in articulating and defending Scotland's interests. Though exaggerated, Fry's description of the Scottish Office's affect on British politics has some truth in it:

> 'The true accomplishment was to make Scotland herself the biggest pressure group in Britain. Reaching domestic consensus on an issue was easy because of the establishment's small compass and the countless channels through which its members regularly met. Once arrived at, it could be represented by the civil service as Scotland's national view, and carry much greater weight than was possible for any single sectional interest.'
>
> (Fry, 1987, p.239)

Defending Scottish interests rather than progressing Scottish wishes has been the major function of the Scottish Office. Those few occasions when it has initiated policies have been exceptional or within strict parameters.

Scottish Office Ministers

The campaign in the 1880s had been for a Secretary of State but the Act of 1885 provided for the establishment of a Secretary for Scotland. The Secretaryship of State is an antiquated term dating back to times when the monarch's secretary had political and administratrive responsibilities. In style only, the modern Secretaries of State are the successors of these regal appointees. In strict legal terminology there is only one Secretary of State, which is why legislation traditionally-though not always-referred only to the Secretary of State rather than any particular Secretary of State. The term also tends to be used in contemporary legislation to allow for the possibility that Departments might merge, disappear or change their name.

In practice, the distinction between a Secretary and a Secretary of State proved negligible. Scottish Secretaries were continuously Cabinet members from 1892 with the exception of the small War Cabinets during the First and Second World Wars-from which most government ministers were excluded. The convention of Scottish Secretaries being in the Cabinet had been established by 1918 so that the one positive attribute usually associated with a Secretaryship of State had already been achieved by the time the office was up-graded in 1926. The other feature of holding a Secretaryship of State is the right to direct communication with the monarch, though this appears to have fallen into abeyance.

Nonetheless, the announcement that the office was to become a Secretaryship of State was greeted with what reads today as excessive euphoria. The Conservatives who provided the concession presented it as 'giving the country a status unknown since the '45'(*The Scotsman,* 6 March 1926). The increase in status did not, however, bring an increase in salary commensurate with other Secretaries of State. That had to wait until 1937. Once more, the relevance of Salisbury's cynical, but fairly accurate, words about the Office redressing 'the wounded dignities of the Scotch' is notable. Style as much as substance has been important throughout the history of the Scottish Office.

Since its establishment to Malcolm Rifkind's incumbency there have been 33 Scottish Secretaries, all men. On average Scottish Secretaries served for little more than three years though Lord Balfour of Burleigh was in office for eight years four months before being sacked for his rather secretive maneouvrings on free trade against the Prime Minister, A.J. Balfour-himself a previous holder of the office. Burleigh therefore has the distinction of holding the record for number of years and being the only Scottish Secretary to be dismissed over a matter of policy or principle, albeit not one directly related to his departmental responsibilities. The only Scottish Secretary to have resigned because of a policy difference was Sir Archibald Sinclair in 1932. Notably the issue concerned an international trade agreement, the Ottawa Agreement, and had no direct bearing on his responsibilities.

A striking picture emerges from a review of the educational backgrounds of past Scottish Secretaries. Only five were educated at Scottish state schools while nine attended Eton, nine more went to other English fee-paying schools, two were privately educated and eight went to Scottish fee-paying schools. Only eight were educated at a Scottish university, and twelve attended Oxbridge, four went to Sandhurst and one to London University. The heavy bias towards Eton and Oxbridge reflects the preponderance of English public school and Oxbridge products until recently in the ranks of the Scottish Conservatives (Keating, 1975).

The Scottish Office was seen by many holders of the post as the pinnacle of their ambitions. For the most part these were politicians whose entry to the Cabinet could only be made through the Scottish Office. Often the office has been filled by some harmless and loyal supporter of the Prime Minister, though occasionally, ambitious and highly able politicians have been appointed. The former tended to limit their contributions in Cabinet to peculiarly Scottish affairs with the latter taking a wider view of their role as members of the Cabinet. It is widely believed, though, that where Scottish ministers and officials do not restrict themselves purely to the Scottish aspects of issues but try to contribute to the development of policy as a whole, their influence and hence their ability to advance Scottish interests is enhanced. Recent history shows that the Scottish Office is something of a career peak for its holders, though whether this is because of the demands of the office and the difficulty of making a mark in government as a whole or because of the individuals who have been appointed is impossible to determine. George Younger's move to Defence in 1986 was the first occasion that a Scottish Secretary moved directly from the Scottish Office to a more senior Cabinet rank since Walter Elliot moved to the Ministry of Health in 1938, though Michael Noble became President of the Board of Trade in 1970 having been Scottish Secretary from 1962–64.

As the Office's responsibilities grew so did the demand for assistance in the shape of junior ministers. An Under Secretary was appointed in 1919 with particular responsibility for health. Another was added in 1940 and a third in 1952, together with a Minister of State. Since then there have been occasions when a second Minister of State, a more senior post, replaced one of the Under Secretaries. Since 1952 a Minister of State has generally been appointed from the Lords, or else a defeated MP has been sent to the Lords and appointed Minister of State as happened in 1959 when J. Nixon Browne became Lord Craigton and in 1983 when Hamish Gray became Lord Gray. Unlike Secretaries of State, junior ministers do routinely move onto UK departments from the Scottish Office, though under recent Conservative governments the need to man the Scottish Office with a limited pool of MPs has reduced the opportunities for this.

The disposition, though not the appointment, of the junior ministers is entirely up to the Secretary of State. Given the wide range of functions under the purview of the Secretary of State, it is necessary to delegate a lot of work to junior ministers. They all have assigned responsibilities but these do not always correspond to the departments in the Scottish Office. There are rarely enough junior Ministers to make this possible and political considerations often require particular allocations of responsibilities. So under a Labour government, a junior minister may be given the coveted housing portfolio along with the less desirable agriculture one. As DAFS and SDD are in different buildings in Edinburgh and such a minister will also have to attend to business in Parliament and in the European Community, in addition to his constituency duties, his time in any one place is bound to be limited. The result is that Scottish ministers, when not taking their lead from Whitehall departments, may be more dependent on civil service advice than their counterparts in England who are more specialised and less geographically mobile.

Administrative Devolution?

The term 'administrative devolution' was invented by a civil servant proposing reforms aimed as a response to agitation for Scottish Home Rule in the early 1930s. The term deliberately conveyed the idea that the Scottish Office represented a form of self-government. This has been a theme throughout the history of the Office. Proposals which amounted to no change in terms of devolving power to Scotland were described as 'Scottish Control of Scottish Affairs' by Conservatives aiming to harness Home Rule support and to embarrass the Attlee government in the late 1940s. George Younger's assertion in 1967 that the Scottish Secretary was 'controlled absolutely by Scottish Ministers who are Scots MPs backed by the 71 Scottish members of Parliament' conforms with this style of presenting the Scottish Office as some kind of self-government (*The Scotsman,* 15th December 1967).

In reality the Scottish Office is neither an example of devolution, which would involve a capacity to take authoritative decisions and responsibility to a Scottish constituency, nor merely a form of field administration for UK departments. Rather, it is an example of territorial division of administrative responsibilities, existing alongside the more familiar functional one. So, while there are separate education and housing departments for the four parts of the United Kingdom, they are part of the same government, just as the Department of Defence and the Department of Trade and Industry are part of the same government. The unity of Cabinet government and accountability to the unitary Parliament are in no way affected by this. Despite the rhetoric in which it was establised and subsequently developed, it was never intended as a measure of Home Rule. Nevertheless, its very existence has provided for a distinct pattern of administration and a focus for peculiarly Scottish grievances. In this way, the sense of Scottish political identity has been strengthened, as has the view that the Scottish Office *should* be responsible to a Scottish legislative assembly.

Other Central Departments in Scotland

While we have concentrated on the Scottish Office, it would be wrong to omit mention of other central government departments in Scotland. The vast bulk of civil servants in Scotland do not work for the Scottish Office. Under 10,000 are Scottish Office employees. The remaining 52,000 work in departments such as the Department of Social Security, Department of Trade and Industry and the Ministry of Defence. The Scottish Office, however, remains distinct in the number of senior civil servants located in Edinburgh. Though four-fifths of civil service jobs are based outside London, the senior posts of the UK departments are generally concentrated there.

Plans to disperse many of the jobs in London to other areas have often been proposed. The territorial dimension of public employment has been seen as doubly important – as a measure of provision of public services and as an influence upon employment opportunities in a region (Parry, 1980a). Deliberate dispersal was government policy during the last war as part of the evacuation needs, and following the war the question was raised as to which offices should return to London. The Admiralty Department remained in Bath and the reorganised Ministry of National Insurance was established in Newcastle. Between 1945 and 1963, 25,000 jobs were moved out of London. In 1963 an internal enquiry by Sir Gilbert Fleming recommended that 24,000 posts should be dispersed from London. The Government's response was to announce its intention to move about 13,500 (Parry, 1980b; Written Evidence from Civil Service Department to R. Comm. on Constitution, 1970). A further enquiry was commissioned, this time chaired by Sir Henry Hardman, and reported in 1973 (Hardman, 1973). It recommended the dispersal of 31,000 jobs from London but, significantly, also proposed that dispersal of jobs from the Scottish Office in Edinburgh to Glasgow should be considered. This ran contrary to the view put by the Gilmour Committee in their report in 1937 that the Scottish Office ought to be concentrated under one roof.

The siting of the Post Office Savings Bank in Glasgow in March 1964 was a significant, though rare example of the moves which occured after Fleming's report. But even here there was a shortfall of about 3,000 in the target of 7,500 jobs originally intended. There was also a dispersal of jobs in the Ministry of Defence and Overseas Development Agency to Glasgow and East Kilbridge, but, again, this fell short of the original target. Inevitably, pork-barrel politics came into play with Scottish and Welsh Secretaries arguing for dispersal to their respective fiefdoms. An example of this was recorded by Richard Crossman in his diaries when the Welsh Secretary successfully argued for the siting of the new Royal Mint in the Rhondda Valley (Crossman, 1976).

Initially, the rationale behind these proposals related to high costs in London. Later, particularly from the early 1960s, regional policy considerations became more important. This created some conflict of purpose, as government sought to reconcile the principles of minimal disruption to the civil service and maximum benefit to the receiving locations. Combined with resistance on the part of many of the civil servants involved, this has slowed down implementation of the dispersal policy.

Ad Hoc Agencies

As we have noted, part of the rationale for establishing the Scottish Office in the last century was to rationalise the untidy array of boards and agencies responsible for much of Scottish administration. In practice, the process was a lengthy one and largely completed only on the eve of the Second World War. Similar considerations were at work in the reorganisation of local government in the 1970s. There was some success in both cases. The existence of the Scottish Office in Edinburgh has eliminated the need for some of the *ad hoc* agencies and committees which have been created in the English regions in health, higher education and planning (Hogwood and Keating, 1982). The creation of large regional councils in 1975 allowed the water function to be given to local government in Scotland when in England it had gone to *ad hoc* authorities. Yet special agencies have continued to proliferate in Scotland. In some cases, these have been a response to pressing issues and a need to demonstrate a government response. So, in the 1950s a new Crofting Commission was set up, followed in 1965 by the Highlands and Islands Development Board, as an expression of government concern for the Highlands. The Scottish Development Agency in the 1970s followed proposals dating from the 1930s when the Scottish Trades Union Congress called for a special development agency for Scotland, and more recent suggestions in the West Central Scotland Plan (1974) and from the Scottish Council of the Labour Party. The idea reached the political agenda, however, as a result of the rise of the SNP in the elections of 1974.

Governments have also seen agencies as a way of implementing programmes without increasing the power of local government. So the SDA was given the lead responsibility for the GEAR programme in 1976 because of Scottish Office distrust of Glasgow's local politicians. Similarly, the Highlands and Islands Development Board was seen by its Labour sponsors partly as a means of circumventing Conservative politicians in the Highlands who were resistant to change. The Scottish Special Housing Association, set up in the 1930s to build houses in development areas, was kept in existence in the post-war period because of the overwhelming housing crisis but outlasted local government reform, continuing to build houses in areas where the local councils were not doing so.

In the late 1980s, government proposals for the Scottish Homes agency are seen as a way of reducing local government involvement in the housing market. The Scottish Enterprise proposals involving a transformation of the SDA and the transfer of some economic functions from local authorities to new local enterprise boards tend in the same direction. As we show later (Chapter 8), centrally controlled agencies have emerged as a central element of Government's urban policy in recent years. Appointed by central government but with representation from the business community, they allow policy to be shifted in the direction desired by the centre but without central government having to become involved in detailed issues of implementation. On the other hand, critics have raised serious questions about the potential for centralisation involved, about the large scope for ministerial patronage in appointments to boards and about control and accountability of agencies.

Scotland in Parliament

Scotland's representation in Parliament has been determined in several different ways since the union of 1707. Initially, it was given 45 members in the new Parliament of Great Britain, a number which was seen as reflecting its relative wealth. This was raised to 53 by the 1832 Reform Act and 60 in 1867, reaching 74 by the end of the nineteenth century to reflect the more democratic criterion of Scotland's population share. With the abolition of the university seats after the Second World War, the number fell to 71 but was increased to 72 in 1983. The only rule now governing Scottish representation is the instruction to the Scottish Parliamentary Boundary Commission that there should be a minimum of 71 constituencies in Scotland. As the number of English constituencies has not grown to reflect England's growing share of UK population, this has resulted in Scotland being relatively over-represented. In 1986, the average number of electors per constituency in Scotland was 55,370, compared with 69,137 in England. In recent years, this has provided an advantage to the Labour and Alliance parties and occasionally there are complaints from Conservatives about the inequities of the system. In general, though, all parties in Scotland defend the over-representation as part of the price of keeping Scotland in the United Kingdom. By a reversal of the argument used to justify the under-representation of Northern Ireland while the Stormont regime existed, it is argued that generous representation is needed at Westminster to compensate for the lack of an elected Scottish Assembly. There is also a fear that, were the special provisions for Scottish representation in Parliament successfully attacked, the more important provision for guaranteed representation in Cabinet might be vulnerable.

The arrangements for handling Scottish business in Parliament parallel the 'administrative devolution' of the executive branch. The necessity for special procedures for dealing with Scottish business in Parliament stems from the existence of a separate Scottish legal system, with its requirement for Scottish legislation. In some cases, this is accommodated in UK legislation containing separate clauses applicable only in Scotland or in Scottish modifications of UK legislation but, since the report of the Renton (1975) committee, there has been a policy of using separate Scottish bills or clauses rather than the cumbersome adaptation clauses to be read in conjunction with the relevant England and Wales legislation. Over the years, demands for greater devolution for Scotland and the need to scrutinise the work of a growing Scottish administration led to an expansion of the number and scope of Scottish institutions within Parliament.

The earliest Scottish committees were the Grand Committees set up in the sessions of 1894 and 1895 in response to demands for more time to debate Scottish affairs. In 1907, the Scottish Grand Committee became a permanent feature, consisting of all

Scottish MPs plus ten to fifteen non-Scottish members added to reflect the party balance in the whole House. The original function was to take the committee stages of Scottish bills and, on occasion, to debate matters of concern to Scotland. In 1945, the first suggestion was made that second readings of Scottish bills might be taken in the Grand Committee but, at the time, was widely considered a threat to the unity of Parliament. The Speaker commented:

'It may be a good thing to have a Parliament in Edinburgh but, if they are going to have a Second Reading off the floor of the House, why meet here at all?' (*Third Report* from the Select Committee on Procedure, HC 1898, 1945–6)

By 1948, attitudes had changed as a result of growing pressure for devolution and, equally important, Parliamentary congestion. Following the recommendations in the White Paper on Scottish Affairs (Cmnd. 7308), three categories of bill could be referred to the Grand Committee for second reading: bills of a technical character relating only to Scotland; certain bills which make for Scotland provision similar to that already made or proposed for England and Wales; certain bills of purely Scottish interest for which time could not be found under existing arrangements. Where a bill is certified by the Speaker as applying exclusively to Scotland, a minister can move that it be referred to the Grand Committee for consideration of principle. The motion can be rejected by ten members objecting. On its return, the bill can be 'deemed' to have been read a second time unless six members put down an amendment, in which case a full second reading debate takes place on the floor of the House. At the same time, extra provision was made for estimates debates in the Grand Committee. A provision for taking the Report stage of Scottish bills in Grand Committee exists but is not used.

The next major reform came in 1957, again as a result of parliamentary congestion and the burden on Scottish members imposed by the need to attend the Grand Committee. A Scottish Standing Committee was established with a minimum of thirty members to take the committee stage of Scottish bills. In 1971, because of the difficulty of the Conservative government in finding a majority among its Scottish members, the minimum was reduced to sixteen members. The procedure for dealing with Scottish legislation is set out on page 68.)

None of these changes represented a real devolution of power or a change in the power balance, since decisions continued to be taken in accordance with the party balance in the House of Commons as a whole. In 1980 the non-Scottish members were dropped from the Grand Committee, an easy concession to make since the government elected in 1979 would have lacked a majority on the committee even with the maximum of added non-Scottish members. Votes, however, were always rare in the Grand Committee and since the government lost its majority there, have been non−existent. Another reform in 1980 was equally symbolic. This was to allow the Grand Committee to meet in Edinburgh. While this does generate some publicity and provide an opportunity for demonstrations and lobbies, it takes the Scottish members away from the centre of influence in London.

Between 1968 and 1972 and between 1979 and 1987, there was a Select Committee on Scottish Affairs, an investigative committee with power to scrutinise administration and question ministers and civil servants. The second committee was the fruit of the St John Stevas reforms which produced specialised committees to shadow the main departments of the state though, coming after the repeal of the Scotland Act, it was inevitably seen, at least initially, as a substitute for devolution. This produced expectations, particularly in media still high with the excitement of the late 1970s, which it could not deliver. Like all select committees, it had a majority of government MPs, though the chairmanship was conceded to the Labour Party. It was thus no more representative of Scotland than the other committees and could hope to make an impact only by seeking interparty consensus behind agreed reports. In the aftermath of the repeal of the Scotland Act and with the increasing partisan divide in Scotland, this was no easy task. After its first chairman had been lured away to the Labour front bench, the committee languished. It was abandoned altogether in 1987 since the government and could not muster enough Scottish backbenchers to provide a majority on it. Some Conservatives had also expressed the fear that it would be used to attack the government for being out of touch with majority Scottish opinion.

The Scottish committees and institutions of Parliament are now as follows:

Grand Committee
Membership   —All Scottish MPs
Responsibilities —Second Reading debate on Scottish bills
                         —Report stage of Scottish bills considered in grand committee at second reading stage
                         —Scottish Estimates
                         —Scottish Matters
First Scottish Standing Committee
Membership   —16-50 MPs. At least 16 of these must be Scottish MPs
Responsibilities —Committee stage of Scottish bills
Second Scottish Standing Committee
Membership   —16-50 MPs
Responsibilities — Committee stage of Scottish (usually private members') bills
Select Committee on Scottish Affairs (1968–72 and 1979–87)
Membership   —13 Scottish MPs
Responsibilities —Investigating Scottish administration.
Floor of House
Responsibilities —Second reading debate on some Scottish bills
                         —Report stage of Scottish bills
                         —Third reading of Scottish bills
                         —Secretary of State's question time

Between the end of the Second World War and the late 1980s, Scottish activity in Parliament became increasingly self-contained. Non-Scottish MPs effectively disappeared from the standing committees in 1964 and the committees were reduced in size by the 1970–4 Conservative government to permit this to continue. Scottish MPs, in turn, had increasingly to concentrate on Scottish affairs in order to manage the volume of legislation and debate (Keating, 1975). This, in turn, forced a role choice onto MPs, who had to decide whether to make their careers in the Scottish political arena or to strike out into UK affairs. A detailed examination of their activities over thirty years (Keating, 1975) showed that most of them confined themselves to a role paralleling that of the Scottish Office, immersing themselves in the work of Scottish committees and only venturing into the UK arena on matters where obvious Scottish material interests were at stake. In contrast, a small group of self-consciously 'UK-oriented' MPs made their careers in UK affairs and were marked by their lack of involvement in the Scottish work of the House of Commons. This increased differentiation of Scottish work in Parliament, as in the executive, did not, it must be emphasised, necessarily represent a transfer of power to Scotland but it did have important political implications. The idea of a distinct Scottish sphere of public policy was reinforced and policies were increasingly presented in a Scottish framework. This was to be a factor in shaping the demands for devolution in the 1970s and 1980s, though much of the initial resistance to devolution was to come from precisely the Scottish–oriented MPs, whose role would be most affected by the transfer of their work to an assembly.

Scottish MPs can be very jealous of their rights in relation to Scottish legislation. Richard Crossman (1977, p 48) records that, on his way to sit in on the second reading debate on the Social Work (Scotland) Bill of 1968, he changed his mind, fearing that 'the Scots would suspect some poisonous English conspiracy, so we would have to keep out, come what may'. He added that '(Secretary of State) Willie Ross and his friends accuse the Scot. Nats. of separatism but what Willie Ross himself actually likes is to keep Scottish business absolutely privy from English business' (Crossman, 1977, p. 48). In 1973, an anti-devolution Labour MP argued that only Scottish MPs be allowed to vote on proposals to change Scottish divorce law. In the same debate, an equally anti-devolution Conservative joined the filibuster to block the reform, though he had himself recently used his English domicile to obtain a divorce under the reformed English law. In 1971, Willie Ross, at that time opposition spokesman and no devolutionist, complained that Scottish housing law was being assimilated to that of England and that 'the whole tradition of Scottish housing finance which it should have been the Secretary of State's responsibility to safeguard, has gone' (*Hansard*, 827, 16 Dec. 1971). This type of complaint, however is the product of the partisan tradition of the House of Commons and hardly reflects a nationalist commitment on the part of oppositions who make them. In the 1940s, the Conservatives used the Scottish stick to beat the Labour government, complaining that for Scotland nationalisation meant denationalisation (in the form of control from London).

While parliamentary control over the executive in British government is notoriously weak, given the disciplined party system, it is particularly weak in the case of Scotland. This is because a revolt by Scottish backbenchers will rarely be enough to foil a piece of legislation and English members are unlikely to risk the displeasure of the leadership for the sake of a Scottish issues which they tend to regard as marginal. It is thus easy for governments to use their overall majorities to legislate for Scotland on matters which might cause some trouble in England. Occasionally, governments will defer to Scottish parliamentary opinion on matters not central to the government's programme, such as the creation of a new region in the local government reform bill (Keating, 1975) but this is not the norm. Executive government in Scotland is further strengthened by the difficulty which the limited number of available MPs has in scrutinising the wide range of Scottish office activity.

While there is no constitutional necessity for a government to have a majority of Scottish MPs or, indeed, any representation in Scotland at all, the conventions which have grown up around the Scottish committees do require, as a practical matter, that the governing party have MPs available to man the committees. With the governing Conservatives reduced to ten Scottish members in the election of 1987, severe problems have arisen. The Select Committee on Scottish Affairs had to be abandoned because of the lack of willing backbenchers. The difficulties of manning the standing committee has led the government to include Scottish clauses in English bills rather than having separate Scottish legislation on a number of issues. In 1989, the refusal of two Scottish Conservative backbenchers to serve on the Scottish Standing Committee considering the new education bill required English MPs to be drafted onto it in their place, reviving a practice which had disappeared in the early 1960s. The Second Standing Committee has not functioned for several years. While all of this has generated the expected Opposition complaints, it does not amount to a constitutional crisis. It does, however, place further strain on the mechanisms of discrete accommodation by which Scotland has been managed within the United Kingdom.

4

Making Policy

Channels of Influence in Policy-making

After a history alternating between assimilation and differentiation, Scotland has preserved its own legal system and distinct forms in local government and education, while the scope of administrative devolution has been expanded greatly. We have emphasised that in the absence of a written constitution, of any mechanism for preserving the terms of the Treaty of 1707 or of any restraints on the sovereignty of Parliament, the UK remains a unitary state, with no federal element. Yet a unitary state need not necessarily be a *centralised* one and even a unitary and centralised state need not be a *uniform* one. Studies of unitary states (e.g. Grémion, 1976) have shown that they can generate specific forms of local power, based on the ability of local elites to manipulate the mechanisms of central power. Rhodes (1981) has shown how, in the UK, the complexity of Government can generate power for individuals throughout the system. It is possible, then, that the institutions of Scottish Government, while constitutionally part of the unitary state, may be capable of bending public policies in significant ways in response to distinctly Scottish pressures. A unitary Cabinet could permit differentiated policies for different parts of the state; Scottish pressures could influence the overall content of UK policy; and policy in Scotland could be more or less subtly altered in the course of implementation.

It is these questions that we examine in the present chapter, using the device of a policy network, in which the various elements of government interact in the making of policy. At the centre of the policy network (figure 4.1) is Cabinet. Of course, scholars have long recognised that the full Cabinet is not where the major decisions are taken and that power has retreated into Cabinet committees, inter-departmental bargaining and the office of the Prime Minister. So, in practice, Cabinet itself is a decision-making network. We shall unpack this in due course, to examine the role of the Scottish Office in Cabinet committees and inter-departmental bargaining. For the present, we use the term Cabinet as a short-hand for the decision-making system which focusses on it. The Scottish Office is an integral part of this, since its Minister sits in Cabinet and its civil servants are in regular communication with their counterparts in other departments. The other elements of the UK policy network are the individual departments, with their Ministers and civil servants, Parliament, interest groups, local government and the European Community. In the lower part of the diagram, we indicate a distinct Scottish policy network, focused on the Scottish Office and including Scottish interest groups, Scottish MPs and Scottish local authorities. While it is easy to separate these two networks diagrammatically, they are in practice inter-related at several

Figure 4.1 The policy network

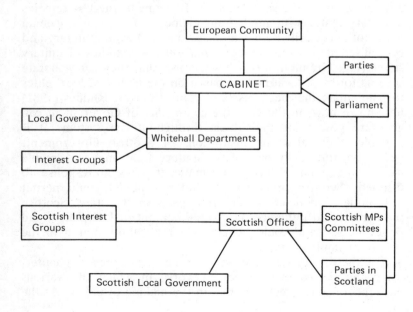

points. Most obviously, the Scottish Office is an element of both. In addition, the political parties, with the obvious exception of the Scottish National Party, operate at both levels, with a greater or lesser leeway allowed to their Scottish wings. Some interest groups are organised on a uniform UK basis; others have Scottish branches; others have independent Scottish affiliates; and others are organised quite separately in Scotland from the rest of the UK. Scottish MPs have their own committees but also participate in the wider business of Parliament.

The network is thus complex and allows access to government at different points by different interests. The major economic interest groups are organised at both Scottish and UK levels and can pursue both with the economic departments in London and through the Scottish Office. Groups organised separately in Scotland, such as teachers, can deal only with the Scottish Office. The most clearly differentiated element is local government, since Scottish local authorities are confined in their dealings with central government almost entirely to the Scottish Office. Alliances can be shifting, with the Scottish Office coming into conflict with interest groups on policy matters within Scotland but cultivating their support when lobbying for Scotland within government. This whole set of procedures for handling Scottish affairs within the unitary state is governed by a series of unwritten understandings or 'rules of the game' which have developed over the years and which reflect the mixture of uniformity and differentiation which characterises Scotland's position within the state.

The Rules of the Game

The basic rule of the game is adherence to the principle of parliamentary sovereignty, under which unlimited authority is given to Parliament and thus, under normal circumstances, the party with a majority in the House of Commons. The simple plurality electoral system serves most of the time to produce majority governments and polarise politics on two party lines. Even where they win seats, third parties have little influence in a system where the executive controls not only the policy-making process but, except in the rare event of a hung Parliament, the procedures of the House of Commons itself.

The scope for distinct parties representing Scottish and other territorial interests is thus much reduced, and the politics of territory must be conducted within the framework of the two party system.

Given the understanding that, while there is a distinct Scottish political arena, governments are responsible to Parliament as a whole, Oppositions do not question the legitimacy of governments ruling Scotland without a Scottish majority. In recent years, the Labour Party has, while complaining about the unrepresentativeness of the Thatcher administration, at its Scottish conference, passed a resolution stating that the Conservatives have 'no Scottish mandate'. Yet, in practice it has accepted Conservative rule, just as the Conservatives have accepted the legitimacy of Labour rule in England when their majority has depended on Scottish votes. Labour's parliamentary leadership has rejected the tactics used by Irish members before 1922, whether the parliamentary disruption of the Parnellites in the late nineteenth century or the abstentionism of Sinn Fein after 1918. On the other hand, there is a firm convention that the Secretary of State should be a Scottish MP and his junior ministers Scottish MPs or peers. So Scottish ministers must have a political base in Scotland though they do not need to represent the majority. The delicacy of this position has sometimes led Secretaries of State to act with considerable discretion in pushing policy initiatives of their own except where a clear Scottish consensus exists. It has not, however, prevented them applying their (UK) party's programme in Scotland.

Another important understanding is that there is a common interest among all actors in the Scottish network in promoting Scotland's material interests. Again, this does not attenuate partisan or sectional loyalties but is an extra dimension to politics. Few Scottish politicians quarrel with Scotland's over-representation in Parliament-72 seats when its population would indicate less than 60-or with the privileged access to Cabinet represented by the Secretary of State. Scottish lobbying tends to be discrete, conducted behind closed doors in Cabinet or in inter-departmental discussions. This allows governments and MPs to maintain partisan solidarity and civil servants to adhere to the canons of bureaucratic neutrality, while pressing their case strongly in private. It has long been understood, especially in the Labour Party, that this privileged access to the centre is an explicit *quid pro quo* for accepting the centralised regime, that there is a trade-off between autonomy and access such that more of the former would mean less of the latter (Jones and Keating, 1985). This is a common feature of centralised regimes, that mechanisms for access to central decision-making are developed and nurtured. Such a system places a great burden on the territorial intermediaries, who must reconcile local demands with central policies, maintaining their credibility at both levels. Success can enormously enhance their status but failure may threaten the whole system. Such is the problem of Secretaries of State for Scotland and their officials, mediating between the Scottish and UK levels of government. Hitherto, the role has been manageable underpinned, as it is, buy the two-party alternation in government which has given both parties a stake in the constitutional *status quo* and the practices and assumptions of parliamentary government.

Parties and Interest Groups

There are two models of the British policy process presented in the literature. The traditional, 'responsible party government' model shows parties contesting elections on the basis of policy promises and perceived competence and, on winning a Parliamentary majority, putting their programme into effect. The other model de-emphasises the role of parties and parliamentary majorities and focuses on the outside interests and pressures brought to bear on any government (Richardson and Jordan, 1979). Both of these models offer valuable insights into the way in which policy is made in British government, with the relative importance of party policy and group pressure differing according to the time and the circumstances. From a territorial politics perspective, however, the critical point is that both are concentrated on the institutions of central government in London and provide relatively little scope for territorial interests.

As we have seen, the major parties themselves have become an important factor in political integration, while having to manage Scotland's distinct characteristics and accommodate territorial issues within their own organisations. Both Conservative and Labour parties are British organisations in which policy-making is centralised, in the case of the Conservatives in the leader, in that of Labour in the party conference.

The parties in Scotland thus reinforce the centralist bias of government, while serving to manage Scottish particularity by channeling demands to the UK level, where they can be resolved by overall UK policies or the discreet concessions available through the Scottish office. Their overall objective remains that of securing parliamentary majorities, and territorial interests will necessarily be subordinated to this.

Scotland stands out within the UK in possessing a wide range of interest groups which pursue their own policy agendas within Scotland while contributing to the wider Scottish lobby within British government. Some of these operate in areas where Scotland has traditionally organised separately from the rest of the UK, for example in education, law and housing. Others have grown up in response to the presence of the Scottish Office which provides a point of access to government and is assumed to be more responsive to Scottish interests. In turn, the Scottish Office may favour the emergence of Scottish interests groups as allies in its battles with Whitehall or in order to provide evidence to Cabinet of the pressure it is under and the need for policy concessions.

In general, the main producer interest groups are organised on a UK basis, reflecting the centralisation of most economic and industrial policy and the decline of a distinct Scottish economy. The main employers' organisations, the Confederation of British Industry, has a Scottish 'regional' council and an office in Glasgow. While matters of national importance are dealt with in London, the Glasgow office has close links with the Scottish Office departments, both in formal meetings and in continuous informal contacts. On trade union side, there is a Scottish Trades Union Congress, quite separate from the British TUC, though its origins in the last century had less to do with Scottish identity than with the exclusion of trades councils from the British TUC. The major Scottish unions were absorbed within UK unions in the course of this century, though most of the latter have a Scottish level of organisation and affiliate both to the TUC and the STUC. Only the miners, however, have a Scottish policy-making conference so that the STUC is the sole focus of a distinct Scottish trade unionism. Its fortunes have fluctuated greatly over the years but in the 1960s and 1970s it grew in stature and was consulted regularly by the Scottish Office on policy matters and nominations to agencies such as the Manpower Services Commission and the Scottish Development Agency. In recent years, it has strongly supported the establishment of a Scottish Assembly with economic powers, though at the same time insisting on the economic unity of the UK, a position which has caused some confusion but which stems from its desire to strengthen the Scottish industrial lobby within a unified economy. Both employers and unions thus have the opportunity to operate at both Scottish and UK levels, depending on the matter under consideration and their changes of a favourable response. Farming and fishing interests, which differ significantly from those in England, are organised separately and work exclusively through the Scottish Office, which must pursue their interests not only in London but through the European Community.

The existence of Scottish interest groups or Scottish sections of UK groups cuts across the functional division of interest group activity just as the Scottish Office cuts across functional divisions in government. Occasionally, this can give rise to concerted lobbying on behalf of Scotland under the aegis of bodies like the Scottish Council (Development and Industry), which brings together government, employers, unions and local government. In general, however, sectional loyalties are more important, with close links between Scottish groups and English groups operating in the same field. They will usually avoid clashing on policy matters for fear of weakening their influence and will often share tasks, with the larger English organisation frequently undertaking much of the necessary research and investigative work.

Interest groups in Scotland have a number of points of access to government. For purely Scottish groups, the most important of these is the Scottish Office which, once convinced, can pursue the matter within Whitehall. Given the absence of ministers and MPs in London for most of the week, interest group contacts, except for the largest and wealthiest groups, tend to be with the Edinburgh civil servants. The smallness of the Scottish political arena means that personal acquaintance is easier and civil servants may be more accessible than their Whitehall counterparts, though this further tilts the balance of influence in government and weakens political control. In the case of groups which deal exclusively with the Scottish Office, there is recurrent frustration at the limitation of its powers and its inability to respond to their demands, especially where extra expenditure is involved. Traditionally, this problem is met by a mixture of firmness (telling the groups that no more is available) and cooption, hinting that Scottish ministers are doing their best but need the support of the interest group to outmanoeuvre Whitehall. In the 1960s and early 1970s, the Scottish Office managed this with considerable success. In the conditions of the late 1980s, it has become increasingly difficult.

The Policy Process

The key question regarding the network centred on the Scottish Office remains the extent to which it is able to make policy itself as opposed simply to adapting the policy initiatives coming from its Whitehall big brothers. As the Scottish Office is part of a unitary system of government, its minister a member of Cabinet and the ruling party, it would be futile to look for Scottish policies in conflict with those emerging from London departments. Yet there may still be scope for some Scottish distinctiveness, reflecting differing pressures within the Scottish policy network.

Policy issues may arise within the UK network or the Scottish network and originate with ministers, political parties, pressure groups or the civil service. At an early stage, other relevant departments will be sounded out through the civil service and the Treasury will be consulted on financial implications. Policy clearance will then be sought from the appropriate Cabinet committee, where negotiation and bargaining may ensue. It may be that opposition from other departments or ministers will kill the policy proposal but if it proceeds it will take one of two modes, which we will describe as *policy autonomy* and *policy leadership*.

Policy autonomy occurs when the Scottish Office (or the Whitehall department) is allowed to proceed on its own, merely keeping the other department informed of developments. Notable examples of this include the Social Work (Scotland) Act of 1968 and the Local Government (Scotland) Act of 1973. Only in certain limited circumstances is it possible for the Scottish Office to proceed on its own like this.

Where it is decided to proceed with a policy for Scotland and the rest of the UK simultaneously, there is policy leadership, in which one department assumes the lead role, preparing the papers and convening joint meetings, with the other department contributing to the development of policy. While a department's assuming the lead role does not imply that it will dominate the process, in practice this does often happen. It is usually the larger Whitehall department which leads, with the Scottish Office making a larger or smaller contribution. On energy matters, for example, the Scottish Office is entitled to be involved in policy development by virture of its electricity responsibilities but these are marginal to the UK energy industry as a whole. In fisheries, by contrast, Scotland has more than half the entire industry and sometimes takes the lead role. The structure and size of the Scottish Office can create further difficulties in joint policy making. A Scottish minister or civil servant with a given range of responsibilities will find that his Whitehall counterpart is more senior or more specialised, putting him at a disadvantage. Another danger for the Scots is being regarded as a mere territorial lobby, concerned only with their own aspect of the issue. Ministers and civil servants have learnt that, to make the maximum impact, they must contribute to the development of the policy as a whole and not confine themselves to the Scottish aspects. Yet, the UK department may have access to better research facilities or have the full attention of a Cabinet minister.

It is difficult to specify policy fields in which Scottish policy autonomy is more likely. Parry (1981) distinguishes three groups of subjects:

1. *The British superstructure* covering defence, foreign affairs, economic and fiscal policy, company and labour law, cash income maintenance;

2. *The Scottish autonomous field* covering education, health, housing, social work, planning, but with reservations in fields like universities and housing finance;

3. *Ambiguous areas* where the framework of policy is required to be integrated but the detailed implementation is not, in industry, agriculture, law and order.

The first and second categories correspond to the allocation of responsibilities between UK departments and the Scottish Office and to our distinction among the spheres of UK exclusive policy-making and Scottish policy autonomy. Defence and foreign affairs clearly fall altogether outwith the Scottish network. Equally clearly, autonomous policy-making is possible only in areas where the Office has the entire administrative responsibility, and there is no overlap with the work of Whitehall departments. This would be the case in non-university education and council housing but not energy or industrial policy. These will also be the areas where the Scottish Office has the staff to engage in policy development. Yet, while this is a necessary condition for policy autonomy, it is not sufficient. The circumstances surrounding an individual proposal are also important. In specialised areas, of interest mainly to professional bodies and interest groups, Cabinet may allow different arrangements in Scotland and England; but on high profile political issues governments will be sensitive to apparent contradictions in their policies. So, the Children Act of 1975, which followed a highly publicised case, had to contain uniform provisions for the protection of children. This applies equally to major items of party policy or ideologically-inspired initiatives, such as comprehensive education in the 1960s and 1970s, the sale of council houses and perhaps the deregulation of urban public transport in the 1980s. Issues which might in some circumstances be regarded as matters of administrative detail will at other times assume great political salience and engage the interest of the Prime Minister or Cabinet. In the mid 1980s, a routine revaluation of property for rating caused a political outcry among Conservative supporters and provoked a prime ministerial intervention which led, eventually, to the introduction of the poll tax. Occasionally, ministers can 'logroll' in Cabinet, agreeing to back colleagues on English and Welsh matters in return for backing on another issue in Scotland. An example of England and Wales going ahead on a matter without Scotland is the privatisation of water supply, though it is not clear just what considerations in Cabinet led to this difference.

One factor inhibiting Scottish policy autonomy is a concern with equity, that people should be treated the same wherever they live in the UK. The problem with this principle, however, is that there is more agreement on its desirability than on its practical definition. Since the war, it has been accepted that cash welfare benefits should be equal throughout the country, though benefits in kind may differ. Policies on council house rents, which have a direct impact on disposable income, have differed both between England and Scotland and among local authorities, though the system of tax relief on mortgages is the same. It seems that the real incidence of inequities is less important than their political salience and effects. So, even where public sector salaries are negotiated separately in Scotland, the Treasury ensures that they do not diverge radically from those in England, fearing that claims for parity will put an upward pressure on both sides of the border. Since the definition of equity is so contentious, it becomes an element in the argument. In the lengthy argument about whether Scotland should be allowed to resume a new towns programme which had been abandoned in England in the 1950s, a lot of time was spent debating which solution was consistent with equity (Keating and Carter, 1987).

Direct cross-border spillovers will also inhibit autonomous Scottish activity and this explains the exclusion of most economic policy-making from the autonomous field. Again, there is an agreed principle, the economic unity of the UK, but continuous argument on what this means in practice. Freedom to offer high industrial subsidies north of the border would have obvious spillover effects in diverting industry from other parts of the UK, but less clear is what effects the Scottish Development Agency's activities might have in England. So the guidelines and funding of the SDA have to be approved inter-departmentally. This can often prove contentious, as when English departments complained that the Scottish inward investment programme disadvantaged the rest of the UK by bringing to Scotland developments which might have gone to England or Wales. After a celebrated battle, the autonomy of the Scottish operation was curtailed. As Scottish Office economic responsibilities expanded in the 1960s, the ambiguous area, in which the extent of spillovers was unclear, was extended. Spillovers exist also in the social policy sphere, in that radically different provision might encourage migration. This is one reason for the centralisation of cash benefits. It was this which is said to have been responsible for the decision to include Scotland in the Housing (Homeless Persons) Act.

Another explanation for areas of policy autonomy is historical. In education and legal organisation there is a history of separate Scottish provision predating the establishment of the Scottish Office and the professions have maintained their independence. In matters like curriculum reform or law reform the interested public can be small and restricted to the professions, who jealously guard their monopoly both from English interests and from the wider pressures of Scottish society. These self-contained policy systems may be self–perpetuating in that proposals will be debated within a restricted elite, cast in the form of Scottish legislation debated only by Scottish MPs and implemented in Scotland by the Scottish Office. Richard Crossman (1977, p.48) recorded his fear of attending the debate on the Social Work (Scotland) Bill as the Scots would resent his presence. There is no doubt that English interventions into such traditionally self-contained policy arenas as education will cause great resentment in Scotland. In other fields, group pressures have ensured uniform UK provision. This is the case in industrial and labour law where both sides of industry, while disagreeing on the merits of political devolution, support uniformity on matters immediately affecting them. It has been pressure from the universities which has kept them out of the Scottish education sphere. In other fields, the received wisdom of the day has diffused through professional and interest group networks to produce similar solutions on both sides of the border.

In recent years, there has been a marked increase in *policy experiment,* a variety of policy autonomy in which Scotland is allowed to proceed on its own, with English departments waiting to see the effects of the policy before comitting themselves. This has been the case with extending liquor licensing hours, the expansion of police powers in the Criminal Justice (Scotland) Act, 1980 and local government finance legislation. As we argue later on, the lack of political control and accountability in Scotland and the Scottish Office, especially where the government lacks a Scottish majority and has little to lose electorally through radical initiatives, encourages this type of policy. On the other hand, in many cases Scotland's going ahead first is due to the accidents of the parliamentary timetable and committee reports.

What all this amounts to is that the Scottish Office does not have its own reserved policy spheres, as opposed to administrative responsibilities but that it may succeed in persuading Cabinet or Cabinet committees to let it pursue a slightly different line tangential to, but not in conflict with, overall policy. Since the Scottish Office is an integral part of Central Government, we should not expect it to have more policy autonomy than other departments and, by and large, it does not. Ross (1981, p.18) notes that 'Scottish administration is distinguished from its English equivalent more by how it does things than by what it does' and it is probably in the field of implementation that we should look for the greatest evidence of Scottish distinctiveness. Policies made jointly with UK departments may be administered separately in Scotland and, given the wide recognition that 'policy will often continue to evolve within what is conventionally described as the implementation stage' (Ham and Hill, 1984, p.11), this may be of substantive importance. Rose (1982) uses the term 'concurrent policies' to describe those policies whose principles are uniform but which are implemented separately. Key Scottish Office responsibilities in policy implementation include the distribution of the Revenue Support Grant and capital allocations to local authorities; allocations to health boards; supervision of the Scottish Development Agency; and deciding on the phasing in of legislation. Given the relatively wide discretion in policy implementation, the Scottish Office will often have an interest in presenting policy proposals as concurrent, a means of achieving common UK ends, rather than as raising policy principles. The case of the designation of Cumbernauld in the 1950s illustrates this well, with the Scottish Office insisting that new towns were merely an efficient and economical way of implementing a common policy on urban overspill and playing down the difference in basic philosophy of the new town approach (Keating and Carter, 1987).

The standing of the Secretary of State and his party's political fortunes also affect the amount of freedom he may be allowed in forging his own policies. Secretaries of State have rarely been senior figures in their own parties, but one who has the confidence of the Prime Minister, as did James Stuart in the 1950s and William Ross in the 1960s, may be given some leeway, as long as the governing party's fortunes in Scotland are maintained. The scope for policy innovation in Scotland is limited by UK policies, leadership from Whitehall departments and the wide demands on the time of a Secretary of State and most of them have been content to function as managers and adaptors of policies. This is particulary true under Conservative governments, which have lacked a substantial political base in Scotland which might have fed demands to ministers. Instead, they have adapted the programme of British Conservatism to Scottish conditions. More recently, as we show below, this has begun to change, with the attempt to rebuild Scottish Conservatism through policy initiative.

The Scottish Lobby

The most prominent role of the Scottish Office is not in making or adapting policy but in lobbying for Scottish interests within central government. As early as 1935, the Gilmour Committee drew attention to the Secretary of State's role as 'Scotland's minister'. with a general brief to promote Scottish interests. Since the Second World War, the role has become ever more prominent as the Scottish Office has emerged as the centre of the most cohesive territorial lobby in the UK. This allows political parties and interest groups, while not sinking their partisan and other differences, to come together behind defined Scottish interests. The cohesion of the Scottish lobby is undoubtedly helped by the existence of separate interest groups within Scotland, and the Scottish office in turn has been known to encourage such groups. So in 1982, the Scottish Office was attempting to heal a split in the Scottish Fishermen's Federation in order to strengthen the Scottish case in European negotiations (Keating and Waters, 1985). The Office has close links with the Scottish Council (Development and Industry), the descendant of an organisation set up by wartime Secretary of State Tom Johnston which brings together representatives from industry, trade unions and local authorities. It lobbies for industrial development in Scotland and in the 1960s and 1970s was used by government to help with economic planning.

The lobbying role has two aspects, ensuring Scotland's share of public expenditure and obtaining favourable decisions on economic and industrial matters. Public expenditure decision—making is discussed in Chapter 4, where the decline in Scottish influence since the 1970s is noted. As far as economic and industrial policies are concerned, the high point of Scottish Office influence was the 1960s and early 1970s. Scotland was critical electorally, swinging against the trend in 1959 and putting Labour into office in 1964 and again in 1974. The rise of nationalism posed a threat to both governing parties and the very state itself, producing a series of material concessions culminating in 1975 in the establishment of the Scottish Development Agency and the designation of the whole country as a development area. The economic climate and assumptions of policymakers, too, were favourable to Scottish demands. The system of diversionary regional policies put in place in the 1960s to steer industry from the south and midlands of England to the development areas was presented as a non-zero-sum game, benefitting the development areas by providing jobs, the prosperous areas by relieving congestion and the national economy by reducing inflationary pressure and bringing into use idle resources. The Scottish Office made the most of these arguments, playing a significant role in developing the system of regional development grants. The growth pole philosophy, by which major developments could be steered to depressed areas to bring jobs and spin off complementary industries to produce self-sustaining growth, was also pressed by the Scottish Office. Interventions by Secretaries of State were critical in bringing north the Ravenscraig steel works, split at the last minute between Scotland and Wales, the Invergordon aluminium smelter, the Post Office Savings Bank in Glasgow and the vehicle plants at Linwood and Bathgate.

The political weight of the Secretary of State is a key factor in the power of the Scottish lobby. We have already observed that they have rarely been important personalities in their party and since the war only one Secretary of State, George Younger, has moved over to a senior Cabinet post (in addition, a former Secretary of State, Michael Noble, served briefly in the Cabinet in a later government). The office of Secretary of State has tended, instead, to mark the culmination of a career. It is significant that no Secretary of State has ever resigned in protest against Cabinet's refusal to accommodate Scottish interests. Some Secretaries of State, however, have had the ear of the Prime Minister or have been at the head of a substantial block of MPs and this has helped in Cabinet or Cabinet committee.

Scotland in the European Community

Since 1973, there has been an additional level in the policy process, the European Community (EC). In some areas, notably agriculture, policy-making is almost exclusively a European function. In others, such as transport, EC responsibilities impinge only indirectly. For Scotland, the most important areas of European policy are the Common Agricultural Policy, which accounts for some two thirds of the Community's budget, fisheries, industrial policy, finance and the special funds such as the Social Fund, the European Regional Development Fund and the European Investment Bank. The main policy making institutions of the Community are:

The Commission appointed by member governments but whose members once appointed owe their loyalties to the Community. It is responsible for the presentation of policy proposals to the Council of Ministers and has a major role in policy implementation. Scottish MPs have twice been appointed commissioners and, while they in no sense represent Scotland, they may be expected to have a sympathetic ear for Scottish concerns.

The Council of Ministers consisting of representatives of national governments. Its membership changes according to the agenda of meetings, member governments sending whichever minister they choose. The Council takes decisions on the proposals of the Commission.

The European Council, which brings together the heads of Governments of member states.

The European Parliament, directly elected but with limited powers.

The Treaty of Rome and the aspirations of its founders contained a commitment to 'supranationalism', the creation of a European level of decision-making superior in its field to national governments and legislatures. In practice the Community's operations have been characterised by bargaining among national governments, with the council of Ministers and the European Council dominating the process. For Scotland, therefore, the Scottish Office, as part of the national government, is the principal avenue to Brussels. It is involved in EC policy making in the same way as in domestic, except that the process is always one of policy leadership, with no scope for policy autonomy. As policy autonomy was in any case rare in the areas covered by the Community, this has not represented a drastic change. The lead in formulating policy and negotiation in the council is usually taken by the appropriate Whitehall department, with the Scottish Office contributing through the inter-departmental network. As it is necessary to allow ministers a certain amount of leeway in negotiations, there is a need to ensure that Scottish interests continue to be represented during the bargaining sessions. This is done in a variety of ways. Where there is an important Scottish interest, a junior Scottish Office Minister will form part of the negotiating team. If the matter is more marginal, there may simply be Scottish Office civil servants attached to the entourage of the UK minister, with provision to refer back to Edinburgh for guidance. Where Scotland has the largest interest in a matter, for instance on fisheries, hill farming or sheep, the Secretary of State has in the past sometimes taken the lead in negotiations, though this is now rare.

For Scottish interest groups, therefore, the best way of approaching the EC is through the Scottish Office and close relations are maintained with the principal groups involved, notably the National Farmers' Union of Scotland. There is an element of mutual support here, as the Scottish Office is able to use pressure and information from interest groups to further the Scottish case. The second channel of access to the EC for Scottish interests is through UK and European interest groupings. The Community maintains an extensive array of consultative committees, on which Scottish groups are represented as part of the UK contingent. These channels, however, are mainly of use for communication and information-gathering. While the Commission encourages direct links with interest groups within states in order to reduce its dependence on national governments for information, the latter jealously guard their decision-making power in the Council of Ministers. So there is no question of by-passing the British government or getting policies directly from Brussels.

On the other hand, dialogue between the Commission and local authorities or other interests may lead to an item being pressed on national governments. So Scottish local authorities have been able occasionally to use their contacts in Brussels to find out what issues are coming up and then to lobby the Scottish Office to pursue the matter through Cabinet to the Council of Ministers. As it has launched its initiative for the free internal market by 1992, the Commission has encouraged such links and in 1988 established a consultative council of regional and local authorities. While Scottish local government is part of this consultative network, the absence of an elected government at the Scottish level has meant that is has no spokesmen of the stature of the presidents of the German Lander, the Spanish autonomous communities or the French regions, themselves often major national figures and active in European associations and lobbying.

In the European Parliament, Scotland has eight members. While this is proportionate to Scotland's share of the UK population, nationalists complain that it compares unfavourably with the fifteen members representing the smaller population of the Republic of Ireland. Members of the European Parliament sit according to party rather than national groups but, like their Westminster counterparts, do have a constituency role. This enables them to raise matters of concern to Scotland and try to gain attention for their own areas but, given the limited powers of the Parliament, is not a major part of the policy process.

Scotland, Wales and Northern Ireland have a further link with the EC in the form of Commission offices in their capitals. This reflects a recognition by the Commission of the special position of the peripheral nations of the United Kingdom, as well as a concern for the level of popular support for the Community there. The Edinburgh Office spends a good deal of time on public relations and also helps interested parties through the maze of EC regulations and grants but does not have a role in the formulation of Community policy.

Much attention is given in Scotland to the various structural funds, notably the European Regional Development Fund and the European Social Fund. These were established to mitigate some of the adverse consequences of free trade within the community, particularly on vulnerable sectors and regions. In practice, the utility of the funds, particularly the regional fund, as policy instruments, has long been undermined by two rules, on quotas and 'non-additionality'. The former means that most regional fund moneys were allocated to member states in fixed proportions, though governments still had to produce projects to justify the expenditure. In recent years, quotas have been relaxed and a larger non-quota element, for which there is genuine competition, introduced. The non-additionality rule is a Treasury regulation which is not recognised officially by the Community but which the Commission is powerless to change. It means that grants under the scheme must not be additional to national expenditures but may replace them. The effect is that, where a private firm is 'awarded' a grant, this merely funds the

grant already made by the national government, which is thus
able to keep the money. Where a regional fund grant is made to
a local authority, the expenditure must still be accommodated
within its existing capital-spending totals. There is some advantage in this case, since part of the expenditure will now be
grant-aided instead of financed by borrowing. While its central
support grant will be reduced to take this into account, the
authority saves on that element of the loan charges financed
from local taxation. The most important effect of the regional
development fund on Scotland was not the impact on its own
spending, which merely offset national spending, but the fact
that, in order to reclaim the money from Brussels, the national
government needed to maintain a national regional policy,
which might otherwise have been abandoned altogether. Most
Social Fund expenditures are undertaken by central government
agencies, notably the Manpower Services Commission and its
successors, and in this case there is no additional spending, the
money being retained by the Treasury in London. In the case of
grants to local government, however, there may be some
additionality and, as there are no rigid national quotas on the
Social Fund, central government encourages local authorities to
apply here. In the 1980s, the British government succeeded in
obtaining 'refunds' from the Community for its disproportio-
nately large contributions to the Community budget. Given the
Community's reluctance to make straightforward rebates, these
took the form of additional grants for regional development. A
great deal of publicity was given to these grants in Scotland but
the non-additionality principle here was applied to the full. The
'grants' were awarded only to central government's own already
committed programmes and the money remained in the Treasurey
in London. This did not prevent the Scottish Office from issuing
press releases announcing that Scotland had gained awards for
financing the A9 trunk road or the Kessock bridge. Such announ-
cements helped build support for the Community in Scotland as
well as boosting the image of Scottish ministers as effective fighters
for Scottish interests.

Over the years, the European Commission has consistently
sought to overcome these fictions, to make the regional fund the
instrument of a genuine community policy and to engage in a
dialogue with regional authorities. In the mid 1980s, what was to
have been a radical reform produced some modest changes.
National quotas were expressed as a range rather than a fixed

amount, a larger non-quota section was instituted and national governments were required to submit regional development programmes in order to be eligible for funding. This was of limited value. In the first round of development programmes, the UK submitted, along with various English, Welsh and Northern Irish items, the whole capital budget of the Scottish Office! The Commission has also encouraged the mounting of integrated development operations, such as that in Strathclyde. These allowed a slightly higher level of funding and a wider range of eligible projects.

As part of the preparation for the free internal market in 1992, another reform of the structural funds was undertaken in 1988–9. The amount available under the regional fund is to be doubled and eligible areas designated according to Community rather than national criteria. Aid will be given on the basis of programmes emphasising entrepreneurship, innovation and technology transfer. The programmes will be managed by new agencies which will have contracts with the Commission. The status of these agencies and their composition will remain a matter for national governments, who remain the dominant actors. It appears that the main beneficiaries of the new regime will be the southern areas of the Community, though parts of Scotland will qualify as declining industrial areas. It is unclear just how well Scotland will do financially but the three-way pattern of communication among Scottish interests, the Commission and the UK government will increase and the question of just how well Scotland is represented will become more salient.

Community membership has thus had little direct impact on the way Scotland is governed but it has extended the network of decision-making and made it necessary to ensure that Scottish influence is exerted there. In the longer term, some people hope for a Europe of small nations and regions, in which the existing states fade away and Scotland could take its place at the council table. The option of Scottish independence within the European Community was the policy of the short-lived Scottish Labour Party in the 1970s and more recently has been adopted by the SNP. There are even people within the Labour Party who, attracted to a more independent Scotland and gradually overcoming their opposition to the Community, see this as a future possibility. On the other hand, popular support for the EC has generally been lower than in other parts of Britain (Keating and

Waters, 1985) and proposing an upward transfer of power as part of a strategy of increasing Scottish autonomy may tend, however consistent, to confuse the electorate.

Political Style

The Secretary of State for Scotland is not a senior member of the Cabinet, yet he faces greater pressures than many of his colleagues. Not only must he manage the administrative side of government over a wide range of functions, but he is the visible centre of government in Scotland. Receiving a degree of public exposure in Scotland second only to the Prime Minister, he must manage the government's political fortunes in an often hostile political climate, reconciling Scotland to London government and Whitehall to Scotland's distinct needs. To do this Secretaries of State have traditionally relied heavily on consultation and consensus-building within Scotland. This style of operation was associated with Tom Johnston during the war and has developed since, encouraged by the small scale of the Scottish political arena and the personal acquaintance of the main actors. So consultation and consensus-building have persisted in Scotland even at times when they have broken down south of the border. During the Trades Union Congress boycott of the National Economic Development Council in the early 1980s, the Scottish TUC and the government continued their dialogue within the Scottish Economic Council. Relations between central and local government have never reached the point of total breakdown. This is not to say that there is a Scottish version of 'corporatism', in which policy is negotiated between the Scottish Office and organised interests. The Scottish Office lacks the power to come to binding agreements of this sort and tends to follow policy leads set elsewhere. The smaller scale of the Scottish arena and the degree of personal acquaintance, however, may permit detailed matters of policy and administration to be resolved in a more consensual mode. This is not merely a question of personal preference. It is a political necessity if the Scottish lobby is to maintain its force that it should be united. It has also proved much easier to secure clearance to proceed on separate policy initiatives where Scottish opinion can be presented as agreed and insistent. So we find Secretaries of State making enormous efforts to secure an agreed line with Scottish interests before approaching Cabinet and Treasury (Keating and Carter, 1987).

Another product of the Scottish Office's role and position is an enhanced role for the civil service as against the politicians. This is partly a consequence of the wide functional spread of the Office, with Ministers at all levels covering a variety of fields. It also reflects the constraints on policy initiative which Scottish ministers have faced; and if most of the originality of the Office's work lies in the modalities of policy implementation, this will put a premium on civil service skills. It was the civil servants who kept alive the idea of regional planning through the 1950s when their political masters had all but abandoned it, maintaining a Scottish tradition which was to be influential into the 1970s. It was civil servants in the SDD who pressed for the two-tier regional form of local government, sold the idea to the Wheatley Commission and successive governments and carried it through under an indifferent Conservative administration in 1973–4 (Keating, 1975). Playing the Scottish card, they were able to persuade Conservative ministers to disregard their party's hostility to the Highlands and Islands Development Board (in 1970) and the Scottish Development Agency (in 1979). In education, SED officials have guarded the distinct Scottish tradition and negotiated change with the profession, with minimum interference from their political masters. As a result, Scotland often gives the appearance of a well-ordered, rationally organised but strangely depoliticised society. The executive is even more powerful in relation to Parliament than in England while within the executive the civil service holds great influence. None of this affects the fact that major items of government policy are pushed through in Scotland as in England, merely that, within the Scottish sphere of influence, political input and control tend to be weak.

The Network under Stress

Scottish territorial management has been dependent on a range of conditions and a set of understandings which we have characterised as 'rules of the game'. For the first twenty years after the Second World War, this system was managed with success. There was such a degree of political consensus as to enable Secretaries of State of both parties to straddle the gap between Scottish demands and Cabinet policies, while stressing the material advantages to Scotland of its peculiar administrative status. The two major parties almost monopolised representation in Scotland as in England and Wales and the practice of alternation in power, as in 1945, 1951 and 1964, providing each with the prospect of unlimited authority, was a strong disincentive to constitutional change. The economic crisis of 1966, followed by the stunning SNP victory at the Hamilton by-election, showed the limits of material promises as the underpinning for centralisation. In 1970, Labour lost power nationally but kept the majority of Scottish seats and was faced for the first time since the war with a government determined on radical change. The Housing (Financial Provisions) (Scotland) Act was a challenge in both partisan and Scottish terms, for it struck at the basis of much of Labour's support in urban Scotland and proposed assimilating Scottish public housing finance to the English model. There was some defiance among Scottish councils, as in England, but Labour was saved a major embarrassment by the failure of the SNP to exploit the issue and the fall of the Heath government in 1974. The advance of the SNP in the two elections of 1974, however, broke the delicate balances of territorial management and forced a more direct response, in the form of an elected Scottish assembly.

This was not so much a replacement for the old system of territorial management as an elaboration of it, since the assembly's powers were tightly circumscribed, excluding most economic matters, and the Secretary of State was to remain, along with the full complement of 71 MPs. The attempt to build a new territorial system incorporating key elements of the old also failed under the weight of the party's internal confusion and the assaults of its opponents. The 1979 General Election did not, however, mark a return to the *status quo ante* 1974. Labour, by adopting devolution, however reluctantly, had stemmed the nationalist tide. At the same time, it had reinforced its own position as a Scottish party of territorial defence. As attention moved back to economic concerns in the 1980s recession and the credibility of the oil issue wore out, it was Labour and not the SNP which was able to pose as the defender of Scottish material interests. In the 1980s, social and economic changes further served to differentiate Scotland from much of England, where the values of individualistic, market-oriented conservatism have had more appeal. As a result, while

Conservative support has fallen steadily to 24 per cent of the vote and 10 seats in 1987, Labour has advanced, taking 50 of the 72 seats. This development ensured that territory would continue to be an important feature of British politics, despite the poor performance of the Nationalist parties (who gained three seats each in 1987).

The year of 1979 posed problems both for the Conservative Government and for the Labour Opposition and hence for the whole governmental arrangement in Scotland. For the Conservatives, the essential problem in 1979 was that of political legitimacy. In the past, this was largely unquestioned, since opposition parties had held fast to the conventions of parliamentary government. In 1979, however, the Conservatives had not only lost support in Scotland but had set aside the result of a referendum in which a majority of voters had supported constitutional change. The discrete compromises of the old system had been blown away in the devolution debate and the issue of Scottish self-government placed firmly on the agenda. At the same time, the English backlash to devolution and the emergence of a raucous group of right-wing Conservative backbenchers meant that Scotland's preferred access to London Government in general, and the Scottish Office budget in particular, was under critical fire.

Under Secretary of State George Younger, territorial management entered a new phase. His strategy was to avoid policy initiatives of his own but to apply the centre's policy to Scotland with the appropriate institutional modifications while acting as a lobby for Scotland in Whitehall, a reversion to the traditional role, but with some important new elements. Government now insisted, against some sceptical comment (see Chapter 5) that a formula determining Scotland's expenditure levels over a wide range of functions gave the Secretary of State absolute discretion to shift spending from one programme to another. This made him both the administrative and political manager of Scotland since, prohibited from coming back to Treasury for more, he had to find money for new demands by cutting back elsewhere. At the same time, he had to manage a considerably weakened Scottish lobby. The nationalist bluff had, in the view of most English ministers and MPs, been called and the threat of nationalist gains was no longer an effective tactic. Nor was Scotland now critical to the electoral fortunes of the governing party, whose base was firmly established in the south of England. Economic circumstances, too, had turned against the

Scottish Office. The collapse of formerly prosperous areas like the English west midlands made it increasingly difficult to argue for diversionary industrial policies and the recession, intensified greatly by the effects of government macroeconomic policy, undermined the major gains of the 1960s, including Bathgate, Linwood, Invergordon and Ravenscraig. There were some successes. The Scottish Office forged a cross-party lobby to save the Ravenscraig steel works, the Scottish Development Agency, Labour's creation of 1975, was spared the Treasury axe and Conservatives supported the fight to keep Scotland's last independent clearing bank in Scottish hands. Within Scotland, Younger's manner ,was conciliatory and, while forcing cuts in the expenditure of Labour local councils, he did not follow his English colleagues in removing the local power bases of the Labour Party through structural reform.

The basic problem for the Secretary of State as territorial manager is that he is expected to calm Scottish discontents without the power and resources to do so. At the same time, Conservative policy, while refusing political devolution, was maintaining Scottish identity and focusing debate around Scottish administrative institutions. The tensions inherent in the system, which could be managed by modest compromises in the 1950s and 1960s, became acute in the 1980s. By late 1985, Younger was locked into battle with local councils over their spending levels, which the Treasury counts against his own totals; with Scottish teachers, traditionally more militant than English but with whom he could not make an independent settlement; and with middle-class ratepayers over a property revaluation. He had been unable to prevent the closure of the Gartcosh steel mill and Ravenscraig was still in danger. The Conservative Party, at 14 per cent, lay fourth in the opinion polls. At this point, Younger was replaced by Malcolm Rifkind, an Edinburgh advocate with an altogether more aggressive style, determined not merely to manage the Scottish Office but to rebuild Conservative fortunes in Scotland through bold policy initiatives. The constraints on him, however, were the same and the major Scottish initiative, inherited from his predecessor, a poll-tax to replace domestic rates, proved an electoral disaster. In June 1987 the Conservatives scored their lowest ever share of the Scottish vote.

1987 brought the 'Doomsday scenario' in which the Conservatives were returned with a safe majority in the UK as a whole but were badly defeated in Scotland. This, it was widely expected, would produce a crisis of legitimacy as well as severe practical difficulties in working the system of administrative devolution which requires a government to have, not a majority of Scottish seats, but enough presentable MPs to form the Scottish administration. In the event, a Scottish Office team was, with some difficulty, assembled though English MPs had to be brought back onto Scottish legislative committees and the select committee on Scottish affairs was abandoned. More serious in the long run was the question of legitimacy and authority in Scotland. The constitutional position, of course, remained quite clear. Government, as long as it possesses an overall parliamentary majority, can govern whatever the territorial distribution of its support. Yet the conventions underpinning the system of territorial management do involve government of the periphery through local elites with some basis in local society. For its part, the opposition, where it is dominant in the periphery, accepts rule by the Westminster majority because, under the system of alternation, its turn will come. In the 1980s, one party is in long-term, if not permanent, control at the centre, while another party enjoys hegemony in the periphery. Under these circumstances, the incentives to play by the old rules of the game are sharply reduced.

It was widely predicted in the aftermath of the 1987 election that the returned Conservative government would have to tread carefully in Scotland, holding back its more ideological measures in view of their rejection by the Scottish electorate and its weak parliamentary position. This betrayed a fundamental misconception of the nature of the parliamentary system. In Britain, governments are restrained not by the Opposition which, by definition, is in the minority but by their own dissident backbenchers, especially when these have backing in the wider party or groups normally supportive of the Government. This factor has served to weaken parliamentary control over the Scottish Office since Scottish MPs alone cannot threaten a government's majority, without mobilising normally uninterested English colleagues. In 1987, paradoxically, the government's Scottish losses strengthened its parliamentary autonomy. Virtually without Scottish backbenchers and with a skeleton of a party in Scotland, it had a largely free hand. Already under George Younger the weakness of Scottish Conservative interests had allowed the Scottish Office to pioneer measures like rate—capping which aroused considerable opposition among

English Conservatives when applied there. In 1987, the parliamentary situation provided the possibilities for a wide-ranging and radical programme to restructure Scottish society and lay the basis for a Conservative revival.

Some Labour radicals, it is true, argued that the Conservatives having lost the election and the referendum, lacked a democratic mandate in Scotland and that direct action to resist government policy would be justified. In the run-up to the 1987 election, this was the basis for the 'Doomsday scenario'. In practice, the argument was impossible to sustain as long as Labour was attached to the doctrine of parliamentary sovereignty and aspired to govern England with Scottish votes. So it was obliged to try and play the game by the old rules. The constitutional tensions which have resulted are discussed later (Chapter 9).

5

Allocating Resources

Does Scotland Get More?

There has been considerable interest over the last twenty years in Scottish public expenditure. Researchers concerned with the economics of Scottish independence (McCrone, 1969; McKay, 1977), the financing of devolution (Heald, 1980a) or the political economy of public expenditure (Cuthbert, 1982; Rose, 1982) have observed the consistently high levels of public expenditure allocated to Scotland by successive governments. The differential became a political issue in the wake of the 1970s debate on devolution, when northern English Labour MPs expressed concern at Scotland's advantage. In the 1980s, it has been southern English Conservatives who have been most vocally concerned about the amounts of money flowing to an area which provides them with so little political support (although some of the most vocal are expatriate Scots such as Michael Fallon and Eric Forth). The growing gap between the power bases of the major parties has thus added a territorial dimension to the old ideological disagreements over the merits of public expenditure.

In this chapter, we address the question of whether Scotland does indeed receive favourable treatment in the distribution of public expenditure and, if so, how the differential might be explained. Comparisons of Scottish public expenditure with that of the rest of the UK usually focus on 'identifiable public expenditure', that is expenditure which can be identified from official records as having been incurred in a particular country. This includes expenditure for which the Secretary of State for

Scotland is responsible together with spending by UK departments such as Social Security and Trade and Industry but
excludes debt interest and expenditure on defence, overseas aid
and overseas services, which is incurred on behalf of the United
Kingdom as a whole.

Parry (1981) records that indentifiable public expenditure per
capita was 109 per cent that of England in 1934–5 and 114 per
cent in 1952–3. King (1973) shows that the differential increased
during the 1960s, from 112 per cent in 1960–1 to 126 per cent in
1969–70 but was reduced briefly under the Heath Government.
Taking a longer perspective, Parry (1982) finds that Scottish
expenditure averaged around 120 per cent of the UK figure
from 1967–8 to 1980–1. This concurs with Heald's (1980b)
memorandum to the Select Committee on Scottish Affairs which
argued that the Scottish/UK 'relative' was 'overall fairly steady
at about 120' and that 'during the past two decades there has
been a major switch of public expenditure in favour of Scotland
and Northern Ireland'. Official data show this continuing into
the 1980s with the differential at 121 per cent in 1983–4 (*Scottish
Abstract of Statistics*, 1988). Heald (1989) uses official figures to
carry this forward to 1987–8, with the same result. Both Heald
and Parry show higher Scottish spending across most services,
though Parry notes that the differential varies, with health,
education and housing in 1980–1 spending respectively 19, 22
and 40 per cent above the UK average.

Problems in Comparing Expenditure Levels

For about twenty years, then, Scottish identifiable public
spending has fluctuated around 120 per cent of the UK figure
per capita and the Conservative Government has maintained the
differential since coming to office. In short, then, Scots have not
been exempt from the general thrust of the expenditure
strategy. The question remains, however, as to how far the
long-term favourable ratio really reflects preferential treatment.
The figures include expenditure for which the Secretary of State
for Scotland is responsible and spending by UK departments
which is incurred in Scotland but on behalf of the UK as a
whole. We cannot always assume the expenditure in the several
nations of the United Kingdom directly benefits the inhabitants
of those nations. (The Treasury and Civil Service Select

Committee (1989) notes some abiguity in government statements on this.) Nor conversely that general UK expenditures do
not have a territorial impact. For example, the figures exclude
defence, yet defence expenditures can have localised benefits. In
contrast to most other services, defence expenditures in Scotland are only about 80 per cent of the UK average *per capita*.
The Ministry of Defence has calculated that in 1986 Scotland
had 6 per cent of expenditure and 9 per cent of employment in
defence procurement; Scotland has 9.03 per cent of UK
population (cited in Treasury and Civil Service Select Committee, 1989).

Some of the differential can be explained by an accounting
convention. The relatively high *per capita* expenditure in
housing (140 per cent of the UK norm) is a reflection of the
high incidence of public-rented housing. By contrast, income-tax
relief on mortgages which, reflecting the higher rate of owner–
occupation, is larger in England, is excluded from the calculation. Government figures showed that in 1984–6, Scotland
received just 7.4 per cent of mortgage interest relief, though
recent changes make the figure impossible to calculate for later
years (*Hansard,* 13 February 1989, col. 81). A serious analysis
of the benefits of public expenditure, however, should take
these 'tax expenditures' into account (Heald, 1983).

Finally, many programmes are based on universal criteria and
any apparent advantage to Scotland reflects a higher incidence
of the social and economic problems at which the programmes
are directed. About 25 per cent of all public spending in
Scotland is on social security, with payments reflecting need as
defined by UK legislation. Scotland's relative 'advantage' is one
which, in the case of the unemployed, many would willingly
forgo.

Determining Scotland's Expenditure

The method of determining the expenditure for which the
Secretary of State for Scotland is responsible has developed
through three phases. In the late nineteenth century, the
'Goschen formula', named after a Chancellor of the Exchequer,
gave Scottish programmes a budget based on the amount of
probate duty raised in the country in 1885. This was 11 per cent
of the UK total, close to the Scottish share of the population.

Initially used for education, it was later extended to other programmes, falling gradually out of use after the Second World War (Kilbrandon Commission, 1973, written evidence, 2). It disappeared finally in education in 1958.

The Goschen formula was replaced by a system in which the Scottish Office bargained for a Scottish share of individual functional programmes. Scottish Office officials liked this system since it placed no advance limit on their budget and allowed them to make a special case for individual services without suffering reductions elsewhere. There was also a limited capacity to retain unallocated funds and divert them into other Scottish programmes, a combination described by Sir Douglas Haddow, permanent secretary of the Scottish Office as a 'very rewarding system' (Select Committee on Scottish Affairs, 19 May 1969). It was indeed this phase which saw large increases in the Scottish share of the budget. Ross (1981) notes that the Scottish Secretary possessed two clear advantages in the process. First, he could concentrate his attention on how much was to be available for one area of the country. Second, because the Scottish population is a small proportion of that of the UK, the sums of money rarely looked large in a UK context. There was a return to a formula basis in the 1970s. This was seen as a means of regulating conflict between the Treasury and the proposed Scottish and Welsh Assemblies. In a period of retrenchment, when the devolution debate had alerted English MPs to Scotland's advantage, it was also welcomed in the Scottish Office as a means of defending its position.

Scottish Office expenditure is now a separate programme in the Government's expenditure plans and falls into two categories. The first consists of expenditures planned on a UK or European basis, such as agriculture, industry and tourism. The second consists of a block of expenditure, within which the Secretary of State is in theory free to reallocate spending among the services. The block itself is increased or cut each year according to changes in the comparable English programmes. Scotland and Wales get respectively 10/85ths and 5/85ths of any increase or decrease in the English programmes (Heald, 1983), a proportion roughly equivalent to population. This approach has three advantages for the Scottish Office. First, the formula applies only to changes in expenditure levels. The base of expenditure within the block is unchanged and reflects the historic Scottish advantage. Second, Scotland has less need for detailed negotiation with the Treasury. Rather, its role is to support the relevant Whitehall departments in their arguments for extra resources. Third, within the resultant total, the Secretary of State is free to reallocate resources between services within the block, an advantage emphasised by the Secretary of State in 1980 (Select committee on Scottish Affairs, 7 July 1980).

Certainly, the formula has allowed Scotland to retain its historic differential at around 120 per cent of identifiable expenditure. On the other hand, some mystery continues to surround the issue. The details of the operation of the formula, including the list of 'comparable' English services, are not published. The Scottish block, governed by the formula, does not correspond exactly to 'identifiable expenditure' (which includes items such as agriculture and industry). So, while the differential in identifiable expenditure has been maintained in the 1980s, we do not know precisely how much of this is due to the formula and how much to changes outside the formula. In the longer run, the operation of the formula is subject to the rate of inflation. Since the mid 1980s, the public expenditure survey has been conducted in cash rather than volume terms. So allocations in cash merely to cover inflation will nevertheless count as increases and come under the operation of the formula. So the higher the rate of inflation, the larger the proportion of Scottish expenditure which comes under the formula and the smaller the value of the inherited base. As the relativities under the formula are less generous to Scotland than those in the historic base, this will lead to an accelerating erosion of Scotland's advantage. With inflation in 1988 running over 8 per cent, the Scottish differential was beginning to be eroded significantly.

The freedom of the Secretary of State to reallocate resources within the block is more questionable. Kellas (1984) argues that priorities work out very similarly across territorial departments because of the integrative force of cabinet and party government. Keating (1985a), examining public expenditure white papers in the mid 1980s, found that most of the details of changing priorities were identical in the Scottish and English programmes. Even the wording used to justify changes in education and social work priorities was identical. This implies that the overall UK policy context is a major constraint on the exercise of the Secretary of State's theoretical ability to switch resources.

It still remains to explain how Scotland managed to establish its relatively favourable position and to maintain it through the device of the formula. Is it because the higher incidence of poverty and deprivation required higher levels of expenditure? Is it because the Scottish Office has had structural advantages in the bargaining process? Or is there some other reason?

The Social Needs Argument

One of the possible explanations of Scotland's high expenditure levels is the higher level of social need there. Unfortunately, 'need' is a notoriously difficult concept to define and measure. A key principle underlying much of British social policy is that Government should provide broadly equal access to services across the country. In 1969 the Scottish Office argued:

> Allocations of Scottish departments are now fixed with reference to Scottish needs within the general principle that there should be common standards and criteria for the provision of services throughout Great Britain; where Scottish circumstances differ from those in England and Wales, the scale of provision differs accordingly.
>
> (Scottish Office, 1969)

So the amounts of provision for the elderly in one region should reflect the numbers of elderly in the population, school provision the number of school-age children. The cost of providing these services, however, can vary from one area to another, so that simply examining expenditure levels does not allow us to make conclusions about levels of provision.

The Treasury Needs Assessment Study recognised this in its attempt to construct indicators of need as a basis for financing of the Scottish Assembly. The aim was to find the levels of expenditure which would allow similar provision for Scotland, Wales and the rest of the UK. Its conclusions were not at all palatable to the Scottish lobby for it suggested that, over six major programmes to be devolved, Scottish expenditure was some 22 per cent above the English level while only 16 per cent could be justified on the basis of need. There are indeed serious flaws in the approach taken. As Ross (1981) pointed out, all that the study showed was that Scotland got more of whatever the Government chose to provide in certain spheres. It did not show that Scotland got what it really needed or, indeed, got it in the form it needed. Parry (1981, p.14) similarly criticised the study for seeking 'to put on objective ground matters which are the subject of political debate and interpretation'. Secretary of State George Younger was careful to play down the importance of the study, telling the Select Committee on Scottish Affairs that it was only one piece of information which the government would take into account in reaching decisions. Heald (1980) too, criticised the methodology, arguing that the distinction made between 'objective' and 'subjective' factors must be treated with caution, as neither of these terms is neutral. The objective factors of demographic and social indicators are so only in the context of a workable theory relating them to needs. Heald compares the Needs Assessment Study's methods in this respect unfavourably with the approach used in distributing grants to local government.

A second problem arises with the notion of common policies when there are well-documented variations of provision in practice (McPherson and Raab, 1988). The Treasury approach was to treat 'policy' as a neutral factor which did not need to be identified and measured; and to assume that it was a constant across the four parts of the United Kingdom.

In short, no objective, agreed measure of Scottish needs exists. While in principle need is the basis for allocating resources to departments, in practice the approach is *ad hoc* and based on individual services, rather than a comprehensive formula. George Younger he told the Select Committee on Scottish Affairs:

> we now have public expenditure programmes made up as they always have been on the basis of a United Kingdom Government which decides on the basis of needs what each part of the UK should get.
>
> (Select Committee on Scottish Affairs, 1980, para. 34)

Yet, under questioning, Treasury officials have conceded that the formula for determining the Scottish block is related not to need but to population (Treasury and Civil Service Select Committee, 1989).

The Political Muscle Argument

We have discussed earlier the role of the Secretary of State as a lobbyist for Scotland, a role emphasised by successive holders of the post. In the 1974, Willie Ross was praised by Harold Wilson at a Scottish election meeting for his constant demand in Cabinet in the 1960s that Scotland should get its fair share 'and more than its fair share' (Keating, 1976). In the 1980s, operating under a different system for allocating expenditure to Scotland, George Younger still described his role as to 'fight the Scottish corner'. Sir Douglas Haddow, permanent secretary to the Scottish Office, responded to a suggestion from the Royal Commission on the Constitution chairman that the (pre-1978) system was designed to make sure that Scotland gets more than its fair share of attention and money, that he would 'regard that as a tribute to the success of my own efforts and that of my colleagues' (Kilbrandon, 1973a, Minutes of Evidence, 24 September 1969).

The effect of Scottish political muscle is difficult to measure and, relying on impressionistic judgements, analysts disagree on its importance. MacPherson and Raab (1988) argue that the Goschen formula was a quiet way for the Scottish Office to do well and that a needs-based system might have brought less money. The Scottish Office, as we have seen, argued that the post-Goschen system was ideal. Since 1978, it has argued that the present system is best. Much of course depends on the political circumstances of the time. In the 1960s, when Scotland was a key consideration in the electoral calculations of both parties and public expenditure programmes were expanding rapidly, the service-by-service bargaining approach may have been appropriate. Later, as the Scottish Office itself argued, a formula was the best way to preserve the historic advantage since 'public expenditure control was getting tighter and the days of table−thumping were ceasing to have their effect' (Select Committee on Scottish Affairs, 1980, para. 50). Pottinger (1979) concurs that much of the impact of any Secretary of State depends on the circumstances and attitudes of British government at the time, rather than the abilities of the individual or the needs of Scotland. Rose (1982) argues that there are strict limits on changing expenditure allocations, whose territorial impact is largely a by-product of functional allocations made at the centre. From this viewpoint, the patronage exercised by territorial ministers is largely illusory.

The picture emerging, then, is rather complex. Scotland has received relatively high levels of public expenditure, justified on the basis of social need and attributed in part to the exercise of political muscle. Yet the measurement of need is problematic and the exercise of muscle depends on a complicated set of political circumstances and may well have been over-rated.

Rose (1982) attempts to calculate the relative importance of these factors in determining territorial expenditures. His approach is to determine how much expenditure can be accounted for simply by population and how much by the additional needs of territories and to attribute the remaining differential to political muscle. The conclusion is that the distribution of public expenditure is 'determined by population', while distinctive territorial needs provide the chief justification for spending advantages' (Rose, 1982, P.139). Political muscle plays a smaller role. In practice, there are problems with all three concepts. Population appears to be straightforward, yet it is not clear that British governments have ever used it as the determining factor in resource allocation. Indeed, for many services, such as roads, it could have only a limited explanatory power. For example, the Highland region of Scotland has a large share of road mileage in relation to its share of population. In the absence of evidence that government actually uses population as a basis for resource allocation, then it cannot be used as the starting point for explaining variations in expenditure. Scotland's relatively high levels of expenditure cannot be analysed by concentrating on that part of the expenditure which exceeds its relative share of population, when population share is not the starting point for resource allocation decisions.

The question of need is, as we have already shown, very problematic. Rose's (1982) approach is to quote the Treasury view that areas are entitled to broadly the same level of service and that expenditure should be allocated according to relative need. This, however, is more a justification for expenditure decisions than an explanation of how they are made. Where it suits its purpose, the Scottish Office has been able to point to specifically Scottish rather than UK-wide criteria for services. For example, it could defend the generous admission to the three year general university degree and the fourth year for honours courses on the ground that these reflected *Scottish* national character (MacPherson and Raab, 1988). Rose's (1982) attempt to measure need relies on the Treasury Needs Assessment Study, while recognising its deficiencies. The excess of spending per head above the assessed 'need', he attributes to the political muscle exercised by the territorial departments. So in 1976-7, £16 per head of Scotland's advantage over England reflects needs and £7 muscle, while Wales does less well because of a historic lack of political muscle. However, the Needs Assessment Study has never formed the basis of public resource allocation. It was, rather, an effort to find a totally new basis for expenditure allocation for a Scottish Assembly. It cannot therefore explain a large part of expenditure variations, particularly as these reflect historic patterns determined before 1979, the year of its compilation, and it has since been quietly buried.

Finally, political muscle is treated as a residual and assumed to be the explanation of those variations which cannot be attributed to population and need. We do not want to abandon this idea altogether, but it must be recognised as a complex combination of institutional advantages, political circumstances and individual relationships. It must also be recognised that its exercise in the short run is limited by the tremendous difficulty in making radical changes, given the nature of the British budgetary process. This leads us to a different explanation of Scotland's expenditure advantage, based on the notion of incrementalism.

An Alternative Explanation: Classical Incrementalism

The British public expenditure process is widely recognised as an incremental one (Heclo and Wildavsky, 1974; Wright, 1977; Walshe, 1987). Decision-making focuses on marginal changes from existing expenditure programmes. By confining themselves to marginal adjustments to existing policies, decision-makers limit their choices. One school of thought, indeed, argues that in the absence of time or any means for a comprehensive assessment of options, this may be the only way in which choices can realistically be made (Lindblom, 1959). Government budgeting is often cited as a classic example of the type of complex decision made manageable by incrementalism (Danziger, 1978). Budgetary choice takes place at or around the existing budget – the base – which is transformed into a new budget through marginal changes to the existing levels of expenditure. The bulk of departmental programmes are thus unscrutinised but simply rolled forward to a new year without serious reconsideration of their necessity.

Political feasibility is central to the logic of incrementalism, for Governments know that drastic changes could have severe political consequences. Wildavsley's (1964) study of US federal budgeting showed that more extensive changes occurred immediately after changes in political control and thereafter the incremental process stabilised. Finally, the simplification of budgeting is assisted by stabilised role relationships, which create patterns of mutual expectations among participants, serving to reduce the burden of calculations for the actors and lending stability and clarity to the process (Danziger, 1978).

In Britain, government spending is planned and controlled through the Public Expenditure Survey (PESC) system. This is an annual review of government expenditure plans, which was introduced in 1961. Although the control mechanisms have been modified over the years, the process has changed little. The survey is prepared by officials in the early part of the year and is based on existing plans and the scope for changes. It is above all an incremental process, in which the Treasury ministers and officials seek to prune estimates and departmental ministers and officials to increase them. This involves agreeing on the base expenditure and then identifying and arguing over options for reductions and listing bids for additional resources (Walshe, 1987). When the Public Expenditure Report reaches Cabinet, it provides a projection of existing policies and Treasury judgement about the scope for further growth or the need for reductions. This Treasury judgement becomes the factor on which final decisions on expenditure levels are based. Ministerial contributions, therefore, come into play rather late in the process, confined to areas of disagreement between officials from Treasury and the spending departments. Heclo and Wildavsky (1974), indeed, see permanent officials as having the dominant role in the process, settling disputes on the basis of their judgements as to what will be acceptable to their respective ministers. With decision-making focussed on the margins and conducted largely through bargaining among officials, ministerial intervention is an exceptional resort when all else has failed. Civil servants, however, do take their cues from ministers, seeking to interpret the minister's mind and reflect ministerial preference.

Cabinet choices are constrained by the situation. Spending on existing policies is affected by socio-economic changes. Rising population or unemployment increase the cost of existing policies and therefore reduce the scope for policy developments. Spending on health and social services has been rising because of the increasing numbers of elderly. European Community and NATO obligations have affected agriculture and defence spending since 1980 (Walshe, 1987). This is not to say that there is no scope for political choice. Political priorities from manifesto commitments also determine expenditure. Increased spending on law and order and reductions in housing subsidies provide examples in the 1980s. Major changes are sometimes possible, especially after an election, when the balance of political forces is suddenly altered. So in the years 1967–70 and again in 1975–7, significant increases in the Scottish budget are visible which can be attributed to political factors. In each case, Scotland formed a critical element in the political base of the Labour government and, especially in the latter case, the SNP posed a serious electoral challenge. In both cases, incrementalism then re-emerged as the succeeding Conservative governments maintained the differential. Since 1979, the differential has largely stabilised, despite fears that the new alignment of political forces might result in radical reduction.

The legacy of the Goschen formula and the incrementalism of budgeting explain a great deal of Scotland's expenditure advantages. The formula was set in the late nineteenth century and was roughly based on population, at a time when Scotland had 11/80ths of the UK population. Since then, Scotland's population share has shrunk to less than one-tenth, but in the absence of any positive decision to alter the expenditure relativities, these have remained largely intact. So Scotland's share of expenditure per head has increased. The task of Scottish Ministers and officials until the 1970s was to resist any threatened reductions as unjust and politically dangerous, while seeking to obtain whatever marginal advantages they could in existing programmes. The whole process was conducted with discretion to avoid arousing the jealousy of English ministers and MPs.

Since the return of a formula-based system in the late 1970s, Scottish officials and ministers have been able to secure extra resources only by supporting the corresponding English departments in their bids. Given the tight constraints on budgeting, theirs will be only one influence in determining the final outcome. The Scottish Office block will increase in so far as the relevant programmes are being expanded on a UK basis and vice/versa.

Public Spending in Scotland in the 1980s

Since 1976, control of public expenditure has been a central element of British government strategy. Under the Labour Government, this represented a response to demands from the International Monetary Fund. Under the Conservatives, however, it has stemmed from an ideological conviction. The new Conservatism sees high government spending, taxation and borrowing as central causes of poor economic performance and advocates strict economy, sound financial management and a return to market forces as the solution. In Scotland, this philosophy has had little electoral appeal, with Conservative support declining. While some observers attribute this to Scottish distaste for the new Conservatism, the diagnosis on the political right is that Conservative failure results from the failure to apply the new rigour in Scotland. Conservative backbenchers in the late 1980s began to intervene regularly in discussions on Scottish public expenditure, portraying the Scots as 'force-fed', with public expenditure and the victims of a 'dependency culture', while the Scottish Office budget is described as a 'slush fund' (Dickson, 1988). The assault is thus two-pronged, an ideological attack on high levels of public spending and territorial attack on the privileges enjoyed by ungrateful Scots.

In practice, their target may have been the style and tactics of the Scottish Office under George Younger rather than any substantive advantages obtained. Younger was a rather traditional Scottish Secretary, avoiding ideological rhetoric and continuing to fight in the Scottish corner. Yet in practice, the

Scottish Office has followed the same public expenditure course as the rest of the United Kingdom.

Part of the problem in resolving the issue is in determining just what the government's overall expenditure strategy is and how consistently it has been pursued. Despite the 1979 promises, in the first four years of the Thatcher government, public borrowing fell but money supply targets were not met and spending and taxation rose. In the 1983 Conservative manifesto, the promise of reductions had been replaced with a commitment to maintain firm control over public spending and borrowing. Later, the promise to reduce spending absolutely was replaced with a pledge to reduce it as a proportion of Gross National Product, and tax cuts, rather than a means of economic growth, were presented as the reward of growth. Public expenditure continued to grow to 1987–8 and the January 1988 White Paper promised a further real growth of 1.25% per annum to 1990–1.

Analysis of the Scottish Office budget shows a similar pattern. In 1980, the targets set for it envisaged cumulative reductions in volume terms of 10.6 per cent by 1983–4. In practice, with the general drift of Government policy, there was a 1.3 per cent increase over the period. In the period 1979–80 to 1987–8, Scottish Office spending had stabilised, with a reduction of just 0.3 per cent while the British government's planning total had increased by 9.4 per cent. While these figures, for overall Scottish Office expenditure, are heavily influenced by fluctuating items such as the capital cost of the Torness nuclear power station, there is no evidence here of Scotland being protected from the fiscal rigour. Questioned about his department's falling share of the UK planning total, Secretary of State George Younger replied that this was the result of government priorities, which saw defence and social security rising, while many of the programmes administered by the Scottish Office were to fall.

There remains the question of how the Scottish Office has used its theoretical discretion in allocating and managing its own expenditure block during the decade of retrenchment. The answer is, very similarly to the rest of the British government. Studies of budgeting under fiscal stress suggest that budgeters will concentrate on short-term strategies such as cutting capital spending, reducing subsidies or selling assets (Elcock and Jordan, 1987). Again the Scottish performance is consistent with government strategy as a whole. By 1988–9, British capital spending had been reduced to such an extent that scope for further savings in that direction had been eliminated (Beaton and Collins, 1898). In Scotland, capital expenditure within the responsibility of the Secretary of State fell by about 18 per cent after adjusting for inflation and, as a share of the Scottish budget, from 24.5 per cent to 20 per cent. Secondly, major reductions in subsidies were achieved, particularly in housing through real increases in rents. Housing subsidies fell by 42 per cent in real terms between 1979–80 and 1985–6, and from 11.3 per cent to 6.6 per cent of the Scottish Office budget. Average annual rents rose from £253.69 in 1979–80 to £761.99 in 1987–8, an increase in real terms of 66 per cent. The borrowing of nationalised industries which, for technical reasons, counts as part of the government deficit, has also been cut, through privatisation, price rises and strict controls on investment. The Scottish Office's share of this fluctuated in the early 1980s because of capital spending on Torness nuclear power station but fell rapidly in 1987–8 and is expected to be in surplus by 1989–90.

In terms of growth, the two biggest increases in the 1980s have been health and social work (from 27.4 per cent to 32.7 per cent of the Scottish Office budget) and law and order (up from 5.4 per cent to 7.6 per cent). One surprise is the marginal growth in education's relative share during a period when the school population has been falling. This is to some extent a confirmation of the incrementalism of the process as well as of the difficulties any government would face in reducing expenditure on universal welfare services (those from which everyone benefits) such as health and education, as opposed to redistributive services (which benefit only some) such as public sector housing. The trends, however, all follow those for the UK as a whole. Analysing allocations in the 1985 spending plans, indeed, one of us found that not only did Scottish Office decisions on the distribution increases and cuts among programmes match those of English department, but the wording used to justify the changes was identical (Keating, 1985b).

The Scottish Office, then, possesses a degree of administrative flexibility in detailed issues of resources allocation. It does not have real policy discretion. If Scotland has not been 'Thatcherite' enough in the last decade, then that reflects the performance of the government as a whole, not the Scottish Office.

Table 5.1 Changing priorities in the Scottish Office budget

percentage shares

The Scottish Block	1979–80	1987–8
Tourism	0.2	0.2
Transport	7.6	7.5
Housing	16.0	8.5
Other Environmental Services	8.6	8.0
Law, Order and Protective Services	5.4	7.6
Education	24.9	25.9
Arts and Libraries	0.8	1.0
Health and Social Work	27.1	32.7
Other Puhblic Services	1.3	1.6
Services Outwith the Block		
Agriculture, Fisheries and Food	2.7	2.4
Industry, Energy, Trade and Employment	2.2	3.1
Nationalised Industries External Financing	3.1	1.6

Source: Scottish Office 1984; 1987

Conclusions

Analysis of public spending in Scotland shows that, while Scotland has done consistently better than the United Kingdom norm, the scale and significance of the advantage is questionable, given the difficulties in defining needs. In particular, Scotland's advantage in domestic public spending programmes is offset by its smaller share of defence procurement and tax expenditures. Nor, given the centralising tendencies of British government, can we be sure that Scottish expenditure is allocated according to Scottish priorities and needs. There is evidence that a fortunate combination of circumstances, including the political situation and the decisions of British government on service developments, allowed the Scottish Office to move ahead in some periods, notably in 1967–70 and 1975–7. This was under Labour Governments with a large political stake in Scotland and threatened by an increase in nationalism. For most of the time, though, budget decisions have been incremental. The readoption of a formula in the late 1970s has protected the relative position of the Scottish Office. Its share of public spending has fallen from 5.6 per cent in 1978–9 to 5.3 per cent in 1985–6, to 5 per cent in 1988–9, but this has reflected changes at the British level, notably the rapid growth of social security spending triggered by the early 1980s recession. On comparable services, the differential has been maintained while in real terms Scottish Office expenditure levels have survived the 'New Right' assault on public expenditure only to the degree that English programmes have.

6

Local Government

Principles of Local Government

The United Kingdom, as we have emphasised, is a unitary state. Parliamentary soveriegnty gives Parliament unlimited legislative competence and there is no entrenched division of powers. Yet, unlike other unitary states in Europe, the UK has never established large centralised bureaucracies to administer the basic public services (defence and social security excepted). Rather, administration has been devolved to local authorities and *ad hoc* agencies. Bulpitt (1983) has described the British tradition of territorial government as a 'dual polity' in which central elites were prepared to hand down the business of 'low politics' to local notables, freeing themselves to concentrate on the 'high politics' of foreign affairs and finance. Many observers, indeed, have seen local government in the unitary state as essentially a branch of national administration, filling in the details of policies decided at the centre.

Others (e.g. Hill, 1974), however, have emphasised the tradition of local self-government. The classic exposition of this viewpoint was that of J.S. Mill who argued that:

'The very effect of having local representation is in order that those who have an interest in common which they do not share with the body of their countrymen may manage that joint interest by themselves.'

(quoted in Sharpe, 1970)

Local government has further been seen as a mechanism for promoting participation and the development of community.

It is indeed the only institution other than the House of Commons to be elected directly by universal suffrage and is vested with a degree of discretion in the exercise of its powers. Summing up the various attributes of local government, Midwinter and Mair (1987) see four organising principles:

1. *The ultra vires principle.* Local government is a creature of Parliament and may act only within the specific powers set by it.

2. *The local discretion principle.* Local government has more than mere administrative discretion and can vary its use of statutory powers on the basis of local choice.

3. *The taxation principle.* Local government has a right to levy a prescribed form of local taxation.

4. *The representative principle.* Local government has statutory powers vested in the council as a corporate whole, whose membership is determined by direct election.

For many years, the tension between local government's role as part of a national administrative system and its role as a mechanism for local self-government was more implicit than real. With the exception of incidents such as the defiance of the Heath government's housing legislation at Clay Cross and elsewhere in the 1970s, relations between centre and locality were collaborative rather than conflictual. A whole school of public administration developed which examined local government in an institutional and procedural fashion largely abstracted from wider social and political conflicts. Attention was focused on administrative procedures while local democracy and accountability were taken for granted rather than critically examined.

In recent years, this approach has been undermined by developments in both the political and academic worlds. The traditional collaborative relationships between central and local government have come under strain from a number of sources. The acceptance of national responsibility for social welfare and economic management after the Second World War made it more difficult than ever to distinguish a field of 'local affairs'.

While national policies were based on service expansion and increasing expenditure, this posed no problems for the relationship with local authorities. Since the 1970s, however, central governments have decided that national priorities require a retrenchement in local expenditures. There has also been fiscal competition between the two levels of government. In the early 1980s, central government sought to transfer the burden of taxation onto the localities to make room for cuts in central taxation. The end of political consensus in the 1980s has further intensified conflict, as local government has increasingly abandoned its apolitical, administrative style for a more politicised one (Gyford, 1985) and the Thatcher government, for its part, has launched a major attack on the collectivist traditions of planning and social provision which are the very basis of contemporary local government.

At the academic level, the old public administration approach has given way to an appreciation of the complexities of urban politics. Local government is now seen as part of a series of political, social and economic networks and scholarship has focused on identifying the power relationships within these and the points at which policies are initiated. The statutory framework of local government is still the starting point of much analysis, which has to recognise its constitutionally subordinate position but the analysis of power is increasingly focused on a series of relationships. The principal ones are:

Relations between central and local government.

Relations between local government and other public agencies.

Relations between local government and private sector interests such as business, trade unions and pressure groups.

Relations between local government and the citizens, whether through direct contacts or mediated by political parties and elections.

Relations within local government between elected members and permanent officials.

By adopting this approach and utilising Rhodes' (1987) concept of networks, we can integrate our examination of local government in Scotland into the territorial politics framework developed in Chapter 1.

Local Government Structure

The importance of local government in Scotland can be gauged from the fact that it delivers most of the services for which the Secretary of State is responsible and accounts for nearly half the expenditure in the Scotland programme (see Chapter 5). It has a long history, with its roots in the royal burghs of the Middle Ages and was one of the items guaranteed in the Treaty of Union. In its modern form, local government is the product of the expansion of government in the late nineteenth century and came into being to administer the enhanced responsibilities of the state in social provision and regulation. There were major reforms in 1889 and again in 1929 but the present structure dates from 1975, when the system was comprehensively reorganised.

The reorganisation was part of an international movement of the 1960s and 1970s, to modernise municipal structures, creating larger units based on the needs of physical, social and economic planning and encouraging the emergence of new, more professional and business-like politicians and officials (Heidenheimer *et al.*, 1983). While in most parts of western Europe and North America, including England, the technocratic drive for reform and consolidation of local governments was frustrated, in whole or in part, by local political interests which saw their power bases threatened, in Scotland the radical reform proposals survived largely intact. This is attributable to the strong role played in the whole process by the civil servants in the Scottish Office and the relatively weak input from politicians. This was particularly true under the Conservative Government of 1970–4 which, without a strong party base in Scottish local government, was content to leave the reform largely in the hands of the officials (Keating, 1975).

The process started with the report of the Wheatley (1969) Commission, itself the culmination of years of dissatisfaction with the previous arrangements. Prior to reorganisation, the principal units of local government in Scotland outside the cities were the county councils. Below the counties were large burghs, with most powers except education, small burghs with very limited powers, and districts with delegated powers from the counties. In the four cities of Glasgow, Edinburgh, Aberdeen and Dundee, there were all-purpose corporations. By the 1960s, the system was widely agreed to be in need of reform. Many authorities, particularly the small burghs, were too small efectively to undertake their responsibilities, producing a fragmentation of services. Boundaries were outmoded, taking little account of the facts of contemporary economic and social geography. Low turnout at elections was taken as a sign of public apathy and it was said to be difficult to attract the right 'calibre' of person to serve as elected councillor or official. One problem which particularly exercised the Scottish Office was the inability of the fragmented local authorities to play their part in planning for economic and industrial development, a process which increasingly cut across local authority boundaries.

Larger authorities were also advocated in the 1960s in the name of efficiency in service provision. The evidence here was much less clear than in the case of physical and economic planning and has been subjected to harsh criticism (Dearlove, 1979). It was widely accepted that the small burghs and smaller counties might have to go. There was less consensus on the proposition that the large cities were unable to run social work and education services.

At the same time, the Scottish Office was engaged in a series of regional planning exercises for the eight 'sub-regions' of Scotland. In central and eastern Scotland, these were based on the major urban centres, taking in the rural hinterland and, in the case of Glasgow, Edinburgh and Dundee, on the major river estuaries, following current planning practice. As a result of this experience, officials in the Scottish Development Department were convinced of the need for regional councils with both planning responsibilities and the powers and resources to implement their plans. These could engage in a dialogue with central government on priorities and programmes, then left to get on with the implementation themselves, freeing the centre from the irksome business of detailed intervention. Local government's role, too, would change from a purely administrative and regulatory one to that of an active promoter of development and change. So the Scottish Office joined in the fashionable cry for 'stronger' local government, obscuring the two very different meanings of the phrase. As a former senior Scottish Office official has indiscretely revealed (Ross, 1980), what the Scottish Office wanted was local authorities better able to carry out central policy, not to pursue their own line in defiance of the centre. In a period of consensus on the priority of development, of bringing industry to Scotland, of planning for the expansion of public services, it was easy to overlook this ambiguity of meaning. In the years which followed it was to become more apparent.

After a false start in 1963, local government reform commenced in earnest with the appointment of the Wheatley Commission by the Labour Government in 1966 and its report in 1969. Wheatley identified five weaknesses in the existing system:

1. *Structure.* There were too many authorities and the fragmentation of the system inhibited coherent planning.

2. *Functions.* Small authorities were inefficient and resources could not always be applied where need was greatest.

3. *Finance.* An equitable spreading of burdens was needed and, with larger authorities, equalisation could be undertaken within local government, eliminating the need for such a high level of central intervention.

4. *Membership and organisation.* Councils were unable to attract the right sorts of people and their organisation encouraged an excessive concentration on administrative detail at the expense of policy.

5. *Relationships with central government.* Functions had been removed from the local government to *ad hoc* agencies and central government was forced to intervene in the details of local affairs with constant guidance and advice.

The requirements of a new system were identified as power, effectiveness, local democracy and local involvement.

In practice, Wheatley was heavily influenced by the Scottish Development Department (SDD) in the Scottish Office and its preference for a solution based on the planning sub-regions. Other Scottish Office departments, including the Scottish Education Department (SED), worried about the excessive size of the regions and the problems of managing services on such a large scale, but it was the planning imperative which prevailed. Scotland should be divided into seven regions which should control all the important local government functions, including housing. Because of the size of the regions and the problems of remoteness and the loss of a sense of community, there should be a second tier of local government, the districts. Here the commission fell into some confusion. If districts were to be established, they argued, they would need important functions, otherwise the best people would be unwilling to serve on or work for them. This, in turn, meant that they would have to be quite large. The problem here is that large districts, particularly when based on large historic cities, could come to see themselves as rivals to the regions, whatever their formal status and could lose their role as essentially local bodies. In a note of dissent, two members of the commission argued for small, local districts without powers of their own but with a 'general competence' role, able to supplement regional services across the board (Harvie Anderson and Johnston, 1969). There would thus be a clear distinction in status between regions and districts while avoiding the problem of dividing up functions. The problem was particularly acute in the Glasgow area. The Wheatley Commission recommended that the whole of west-central Scotland should comprise a single region, based on the Clyde estuary and that Glasgow, expanded to take in the surburban burghs, should form a single district within it.

The Wheatley recommendations were accepted by the Labour Government in 1969 but, before they could be implemented, the Conservatives returned to power. In England, the new adminis-tration largely abandoned the work of the corresponding Redcliffe–Maud Commission but in Scotland they stuck with Wheatley. It is clear that the Conservatives at this time had few fixed views on Scottish local government structure. They were only just beginning to organise seriously in local government in Scotland and there was no council lobby within the party for a particular solution. So ministers took their lead from the civil servants. Some changes to Wheatley were made. In response to pressure from the Borders (the areas south of Edinburgh adjoining England), where local Conservatives hoped to unseat the Liberal MP, a separate Borders region was created. Separate all-purpose authorities were created for the island areas of Orkney, Shetland and the Western Isles, which the majority of the Wheatley Commission had wanted to incorporate in the Highland Region. This in itself was a modest step but the concession of all-purpose status to areas of as little as 17,000 population raises serious questions about the argument that economies of scale required huge authorities on the mainland. The Highland Region was further reduced by trans-ferring Argyll to the west central region (later called Strath-clyde) giving the new region a highland periphery radically different in character from its urban core.

Finally, the government decided to allocate housing policy to the districts. This was ostensibly to give the districts a major function, but political considerations were clearly visible. Hous-ing is (or was until recent legislative changes) one of the few areas in which local government has an effective capacity to redistribute income, by subsidising council rents from the rates. Subsidies to owner-occupiers are paid nationally. If housing were allocated to the regional tier, Labour-controlled regions could use revenues generated in rural and suburban areas of owner occupation (and Conservative electoral support) to subsidise urban council tenants (overwhelmingly Labour voters). By allocating housing to the districts, the government also gave suburban areas an incentive to resist incorporation into city districts.

Two significant changes were made during the parliamentary passage of the bill. After a determined campaign, the county of Fife succeeded in gaining regional status for itself, so upsetting the Wheatley logic of estuarial regions in the east of Scotland. The proposals for the west central region (Strathclyde) faced a strong attack from members who thought that the region would be too large and so unbalance the system for Scotland, as well as from Ayrshire members fearful of Glasgow dominance in the new authority. In the event, though, the Strathclyde proposals survived.

The plan for an expanded Glasgow district was not so successful and most of the suburban areas succeeded in staying out of the new district. The regressive fiscal effect of this, however, was reduced by the fact that most of the high-spending services are allocated to the regional level.

Despite the preference of the SDD for a system in which the regions were predominant, the Local Government (Scotland) Act, 1973 makes it clear that each tier is quite independent of the other, exercising separate responsibilities. The region is responsible for education, except for the universities and some higher educational institutions run directly by the SED. It is responsible for social work, for the police service which, in contrast to England, is not run at one remove through a special authority, and for the fire service. It runs public transport services through the passenger transport executive and is the highway authority except for some trunk (national) roads. It is also responsible for water and sewerage. The district is responsible for council housing and for improvement grants for private housing, as well as for libraries, cleansing, leisure and recreation and a range of licensing functions. Planning, such an important theme in the reorganisation debate, is split. The region has responsibility for the structure plan laying down the basic principles of development policy, while the district is responsible for producing local plans to give this detailed effect and for development control, that is, the issuing of permission to build or change the use of a building. To ensure that its strategic priorities are safeguarded, the region has a 'call-in' power, allowing it to take development control decisions itself.

The result was a system in which the region was the more powerful force in local government, responsible for the great bulk of revenue spending (notably in education, police and social work). It was not, however, the predominant force anticipated by Wheatley as the district accounts for around two thirds of local authority capital spending (notably on housing). Despite the insistence of both Wheatley and the Scottish Office on the separate nature of the two tiers and the absence of a hierarchy between them, it is clear that their responsibilities were highly interdependent. The debate on reorganisation was powerfully influenced by the need for integration and coordination in the framing and implementation of urban policies. An accompanying theme to structural reform was a reform of the decision-making system which, under the heading of 'corporate management', sought to achieve comprehensive solutions to urban problems (see below). Yet two-tier local government, especially in cities which historically have had a unitary system, could be seen as a move away from integration.

A major criticism of the reform was the failure to give new powers and responsibilities to local government. The Wheatley Commission's brief had been to examine the system in relation to its existing functions. Certainly, these included the recently reformed planning system which was intended to give local government a greater strategic role, but no additional powers were conceded to make this a reality. In particular, the planning role remained a purely indicative one, attempting to encourage and steer development but without strong powers of intervention to bring that development about. The establishment of the Scottish Development Agency was to fill this gap to some degree in the years ahead but the Agency's relationship to the new local government system was to pose a problem. The other great weakness of the reform was the failure to consider local government finance, which was to prove the major issue of contention and the pretext for a drastic weakening of local government in the following decade.

Table 6.1 Responsibilities of Scottish local councils

Region	District
Strategic planning, structure plans	Local plans and development
Industrial development	Building control
Highways	Housing
Transport	Leisure and recreation
Water and sewerage	Libraries
Education	Environmental health
Social work	Licensing
Police	
Fire	
Registration of births, deaths and marriages	
Registration of electors	
Consumer protection	

The Performance of the System

Since reorganisation, the new structure of local government in Scotland has been blamed for all manner of ills. Critics have charged that the new system is remote, bureaucratic and expensive. These criticisms are extremely hard to evaluate, being phrased in such vague terms. The complaint of remoteness is usually found in former small burghs, where in the past the provost and councillors were known to everyone but which have now been absorbed into larger districts. However, while the small burghs are an important element of the Scottish myth (Chapter 1), only a small proportion of Scotland's population lived in them; and, however close to the citizenry the old councils were, they were in practice too small to do very much. It is true that reorganisation drastically reduced the number of elected councillors in Scotland but in large parts of the country there is still a shortage of candidates. The growth of bureaucracy after reorganisation was examined by Page and Midwinter (1980) who concluded that the growth in local government manpower was part of a long-term trend which had started before reorganisation. Manpower levels stabilised and were slightly reduced by around 1977. In the 1980s, they grew marginally because of the need to administer new legislation on compulsory tendering, school boards and the community charge. As for local government expenditure, this increased steadily throughout the 1960s and early 1970s as social programmes and public works were expanded but has since fallen somewhat (see Chapter 7).

In contrast to England, the basic structure has, until recently, not been a major subject of partisan debate. The Scottish nationalists have consistently advocated single-tier authorities without being specific about the number involved. Labour supported the Wheatly proposals, though recently it has begun to accept that, were a Scottish Assembly to come about, the two-tier structure will have to be examined. The Conservatives, despite the abolition of the English metropolitan counties, left the Scottish regions intact in the mid 1980s, though in 1988 their Scottish conference approved a motion calling for a fundamental reform of the system. A committee was established to make recommendations which could involve a move to a single-tier system. In part, this stems from local dislike of Labour dominance of the major regions, but it also reflects a view that small-scale local government, in terms of area and functions, is now on the political agenda (Adam Smith Institute, 1989).

Arguments about the system have tended to cut across the party divide, pitting rural against urban areas and the four large city districts against their regions. None of the cities has fully accepted its 'demotion' to second-tier district status and resentment at the change has continued to bedevil relationships between the tiers. Amongst younger councillors and officials, who were not active in the old system, however, there is more acceptance of the reformed system. The working relationships of the two tiers was examined by the Stodart (1981) Committee. Although its remit was narrowly defined to exclude consideration of the basic system, the committee did acknowledge 'the substantial body of opinion – not least among some local authorities – which maintains the belief that only the creation of all – or at least most – purpose authorities through the country will produce a wholly satisfactory system of local government' (Stodart, 1981 p.11). Most of the committee's recommendations involved 'tidying up' functions (Clarke, 1982) to reduce the degree of concurrency (two tiers sharing the same function), interdependence and inter-authority conflict.

In practice, such attempts to eliminate conflict through structural reform may be self-defeating. A large degree of interdependence between the tiers of local government is inevitable, given the complementary nature of their functions. Conflict is due not simply to the existence of two tiers with their organisational boundaries but to differing professional and political judgements about appropriate policies and priorities. If these are suppressed or buried in a single organisation, the opportunity for open debate and negotiation may be lost. Two-tier local government can contribute to pluralism, open up issues to public scrutiny and provide some compensation for the absence of political competition in many areas of Scotland, notably the Glasgow conurbation. Young (1983) even argues that since housing and social work were given to different authorities on reorganisation, relationships among the officials and councillors involved have improved, since differences which in the past were papered over now have to be brought out in the open and negotiated. The critical issue, then, is to ensure that this competition is constructive and not purely negative and destructive.

The other official review of the system, the Montgomery Committee, examined the three areas of Scotland where single-tier local government does exist, the island areas of Orkney, Shetland and the Western Isles. Its report (Montgomery, 1984) found general satisfaction among the people of the islands and recommended no major changes. Radical proposals for special status on the lines of the Faroe islands or the Isle of Man were rejected. Suggestions that the councils could take over the work of the Highlands and Island Development Board or the health boards were also dismissed.

While many of the complaints about reorganisation are thus unfounded, it remains true that the reform has not met some of its wider objectives. Turnout at elections, while increasing slightly at reorganisation, has since fallen (see below). Electoral competition outside the cities is often slight. Strategic planning and its implementation were a key objective of reform but the two-tier division of powers and allocation of key environmental and economic responsibilities to the SDA weakened the regions' strategic role from the outset. Regional reports, intended as corporate planning strategies for the regions, were only called for once by the Scottish Office and the importance of structure plans has been downgraded. In particular, there was never an effective integration of land-use planning with financial planning. In the late 1970s and early 1980s, there was a series of inter-agency ventures in urban regeneration, drawing on the powers and resources of both tiers of local government and the SDA but in the late 1980s the potential for positive planning has diminished (see Chapter 8).

On the other hand, the existence of the regions led until the abolition of domestic rates to a greater degree of fiscal equalisation that would otherwise have existed. The prosperous suburbs with their high rateable base came under the same taxation authority as the deprived city areas and rural peripheries. It is significant, for example, that Argyll District, which argued before the Stodart Committee for the right to secede from Strathclyde, qualified its demand with a request that lost revenue should be made up. To some degree regions have also been able to target resources on priority groups and areas. There are, however, immense practical problems in diverting expenditure and the impact of such strategies has been marginal in terms of councils' overall activities and budgets.

The Organisation of Local Government

Local government grew piecemeal in the twentieth century as new services, staffed by specialised professionals were introduced and formalised. As a result, the professional department, organised according to function, became the basis of the system. At the level of the elected members, the committee system developed in parallel with this to become the principal decision-making arm of the council. The committee system allows members to develop specialisms, get an insight into the practicalities of administration and provides a mechanism to control the bureaucracy. It operates with a considerable degree of informality and consensus. The role of the full council meetings was traditionally restricted to endorsing committee reports and adopting the annual budget, itself the sum of individual committee decisions. Of course, there were variations from one council to another. Where there was partisan political control, as in the large cities, then the party caucus and its leadership were the real focus of power, controlling both full council and the committees. Elsewhere, leadership was more dispersed.

There are strengths to this approach, notably the application of professional expertise to service delivery and operations and the ability to bring both expert and political judgement to bear on issues. Typically, directors of the major services work closely with the chairman of the corresponding committee to develop policy initiatives. Professionals can develop arguments with the chairman as to how the service should develop, while the chairman can identify political priorities and assess likely political reaction to bureaucratic initiatives. This is a more fluid working relationship than might be implied by attempts to distinguish sharply between political and professional roles.

The traditional relationships of departments and committees can be summed up as follows (Leach *et al.*, 1986):

It is the officers' right to draw up the agenda (although the chairman may request to have items included) and to have sole responsibility for the drafting of committee reports and the recommendations contained therein.

Officers should be provided with facilities for briefing a commit-tee chairman (and vice-chairman) shortly before a committee meeting. At this meeting, the officers would normally take the chairman through the agenda, advising him or her how best to deal with each item. At committee, officers would expect to present reports and answer questions on them.

Appointment of officers should be on the basis of professional expertise, ability and experience. Officers would expect to be present at appointment panels, and for their advice to be a major consideration in the appointment. They would expect also to make all appointments below a certain level.

Members should channel their information requests through the chief officer and/or by agreement with him, through specified deputies. Junior officers should have no access to members.

Members should not become involved in the management of the department; that is the responsibility of the chief officer.

Members should concentrate on policy and leave the implementation to officers.

Since the late 1960s, the professional department and specialised committee have increasingly been criticised for fragmenting the work of the authority. They may be well suited to administering services but, according to critics, are less well equipped for the broader *governmental* role, that is assessing priorities among services and developing initiatives which cross service boundaries. It was a growing awareness of the need for councils to define their policy goals more clearly and to make strategic choices across their range of responsibilities that led to the movement of 'corporate management', a reform of the internal organisation of local government, along with the reforms of structure which we have discussed. The corporate approach involves breaking with the traditional fragmented pattern of organisation and putting in place mechanisms for establishing priorities and policies for the council as a whole. Individual service and departmental programmes would then flow from the overall plan. At the same time, the increased scale of local government operations and the extended time-horizon of their major decisions called for modernised management techniques.

Another concern was the role of elected members. While the executive authority of the council was vested in the council as a whole or its committees, there was a tendency for members to interest themselves in administrative detail, rather than broad policy issues. The latter were often left to the permanent officials or a few leading committee chairmen. Reformers have tended to argue for less member involvement in what the Paterson (1973) Committee described as 'routine low level decision-making' but the Widdicombe (1986) Report noted that there is still a tendency in Scotland for members not to delegate such matters to officials. In practice, efforts to keep members away from administrative detail and get them to concentrate on broad issues of policy is likely to be futile since all of them are elected in local wards and see their role largely in terms of dealing with the problems of individual constituents. Indeed, as Leach *et al.* (1986) argue, there are two dimensions to the councillor's role, the *strategic* and the *representative*. Some councillors are primarily concerned with broad policy issues concerning the authority as a whole. Most, however, pursue an 'ideology of localism' (Glassberg, 1981), placing more emphasis on their local representative role, on how to advance the interests of their locality, taking their cues on policy from the officials or their party leaders. A successful reform programme needs to take into account these differing roles and the conditions required to perform each.

Management Reform

The origins of management reform lie in a series of reports in the 1960s advocating a greater degree of planning and coordination in local government services (Buchanan, 1964; Planning Advisory Group, 1965; Dennington, 1966; Plowden, 1967; Seebohm, 1969). All started by examining problems of an individual service and concluded that it must be looked at in a wider perspective. The 1970s saw the publication of two reports by the Central Policy Review Staff (CPRS, 1975, 1977) advocating better central–local linkages and a more corporate approach to service delivery at the local level.

During the same period, officers within local government were expressing similar concerns. In 1972, a group was appointed by the Scottish local authority associations and the Scottish Development Department to recommend reforms in management for the new local authorities to be established in 1975. Their report (Paterson, 1973) began with the now familiar diagnosis of departmentalism, arguing that the formulation of policies and plans was carried out independently within service committees and professional departments, each making separate recommendations to full council. Such coordination as took place was provided by the finance committee but was of limited effectiveness since there were no means of judging whether the budget proposals represented a cohesive programme, no criteria for determining priorities between services and no analysis of the policy, as opposed to the financial implications of the budget proposals. The result was waste of resources and conflict in purposes:

> 'housing developments lacking in community facilities, educa-tion and housing provision out of phase with each other, social work problems created by unilateral action taken elsewhere in the organisation, wasteful duplication of facili-ties.'
>
> (Paterson, 1973, p. 66)

They concluded that the need for a corporate approach was well established. At member level, this required the establishment of a Policy and Resources Committee to guide the council in the formulation of policy objectives and priorities. This would be supported at officer level by a chief officers' management team and a chief executive officer. Also recommended was an executive office, grouping the directors of administration, finance and policy planning and, in the larger regions, a policy planning department.

Finally, the report advocated changes in decision-making procedures, to a rational planning approach, focused on the analysis of needs, objective setting, options analysis, action programmes and performance review. New instruments would include position statements, policy plans, a management infor-mation system and improved budgetary procedures integrating policy analysis with resource allocation. In this way, the implementation of corporate objectives could be ensured by linking them to concrete spending decisions.

By shifting the locus and criteria for decision-making, corp-orate management inevitably involves a change in power relationships within the authority. Paterson recognised this in the proposal for an executive office, to provide support for the chief executive in the face of departmental pressures. At the same time, the committee recognised the strength in the professional/departmental approach to local administration and, rather than abolishing departments, recommended that they should be grouped together on the basis of 'programme areas' of related or linked activities. In this way, it was hoped to reap the benefits both of corporate management and of professional-ism, providing the basis for political choice.

Rhodes and Midwinter's (1980) survey showed that Scottish authorities had generally adopted the basic structural reforms recommended by Paterson. Most had appointed chief executives (some of these doubling as departmental heads), and established management teams and policy and resources committees. Fewer authorities employed policy planning specialists. The two largest regions, Strathclyde and Lothian, did have policy planning departments but by the mid 1980s these had been absorbed by the chief executive's and physical planning departments respectively.

Apart from this, however, traditional organisation structures survived, with the new corporate machinery superimposed on them. Rather than make radical changes in their basic structures, most authorities relied on the chief executive and management team to ensure the corporate approach. Other departments tended to ignore the corporate spirit. Subsequent research (Elcock *et al.*, 1989) has confirmed this. The majority of councils have not actively pursued corporate objectives or changed their ways of thinking. Only a handful emphasise the methodology of policy planning, an interdepartmental approach to key issues and the need for a systematic policy framework for resource allocation. Budgetary decisions continue to be made on an incremental basis, with changes at the margins from year to year and corporate structures at best assisting to clarify these limited choices.

There is considerable variation in in practice as to the roles such mechanisms play in local government. In independent (non-party) councils, policy and resources committees tend to be weak and lacking in prestige. In an urban district council examined by Leach *et al.* (1986) the role of the management team consisted of looking out for potential political embarrassment rather than giving corporate advice. In a rural authority, the management team is described as a 'federation of individuals', each rehearsing his professional opinion rather than seeking an overall approach. Even in partisan councils, the policy and resources committee tends to place more emphasis on resources than policy, a reflection of the need for financial retrenchment during the 1980s. In very few of them does the management team meet regularly and the committees tend to be serviced by the traditional professional officers.

In Labour-controlled councils, the party group rather than the policy and resources committee is the main source of overall strategy, while individual service committees continue to enjoy considerable independence. There is also a tendency in Labour authorities to distrust the device of the management team, seen as a means of allowing officers to set policy. This is especially so in the 'New Left' councils (see below); in Lothian, the Labour group ended the practice of regular meetings with the management team.

On the officers' side, there is a similar variation in experience. While all the new councils appointed chief executives in 1975, a number of the smaller ones have subsequently abolished the position. The reasons have varied from a desire to be rid of an individual to a comprehensive reorganisation of structure. Others have combined the post with that of a major service director, usually administration or finance. In Glasgow and Strathclyde, on the other hand, the position has been strengthened. In Strathclyde, a major reorganisation in the early 1980s resulted in the creation of a substantial chief executive's department (Keating, 1988a). Five deputy chief executives were appointed, three of whom have responsibilities for services grouped on a programme-areas basis (personal social services; protective services; and basic services). This followed criticisms about the lack of corporate working and coordination, the separation of policy formulation from implementation and the dominance of traditional departmental attitudes. In Glasgow, a less ambitious reorganisation strengthened the chief executive by bringing the small corporate planning unit directly under his control.

Elsewhere, the climate of retrenchment in the 1980s has strengthened the role of the chief financial officer, who is concerned both with traditional financial management and with the policy implications of expenditure choices (Berridge and Clark, 1986). Experience with management teams has been similarly varied. Berridge and Clark found that the Tayside management team operated less as a corporate management body than a forum for discussing current issues and helping new staff meet their colleagues. Other authorities have found that, either the management team has had to include all chief officers, at the cost of becoming unwieldy, or has had to exclude some causing resentment among those left out.

Turning from structural changes to procedures, we find a similarly varied picture. In some of the large urban councils, the complexity of policy making and the size of their programmes has dictated modern management techniques and a more corporate approach. This is particularly so for the major expenditure decisions. Among the devices used are:

Environmental analysis: the compilation of data on social, economic and demographic trends.

Corporate frameworks for the making of policy: these may be based on major issues, on the needs of individual services, on the needs of client groups, such as young children or the elderly, or on geographical areas (Skelcher, 1980).

Budget options analysis: this involves changing the budgetary process from one in which departments submit bids to the finance committee to one in which the options derive from policy priorities set by the authority as a whole.

Performance review: a series of selective, in-depth reviews of major issues, services or aspects of services.

While few of these have approached the comprehensiveness required of a fully corporate system, they have enabled authorities to exert some degree of control over changing priorities in accordance with general policy guidelines.

Some councils have tried and failed with more ambitious proposals. In Stirling, the council embarked on a zero-based budgeting system, built on action plans and performance budgets which would clarify members' choices. This approach, however, became bogged down in detail, with a budget document of over 600 pages proving excessive for members. In practice, the action plans became bids for resources rather than mechanisms for management control and the overall strategy was lost. There were some modest gains, though. The chief executive's department did carry out corporate analysis in key areas and could point out to members the consequences of certain budgetary choices (Charlton and Martlew, 1987).

For most councils, though, corporate management gave way in the 1980s to crisis management and the need for budgetary restraint. This is particularly so in the case of smaller authorities. Dyer and Sewel (1987) show how Banff and Buchan District started off in the 1970s accepting the corporate gospel but gradually abandoned it in favour of an emphasis on expenditure restraint. Although Dyer and Sewel (1987) claim that this is in practice more of a corporate approach than that of authorities where 'full-blown Chief Executives and their offices spawn voluminous corporate plans', this is to empty the term of all meaning. Corporate planning is about providing a strategic framework for service developments and expenditure decisions, not merely about limiting spending. The Banff and Buchan approach, with the finance department serving as a clearing house for departmental bids, is characteristic of the unreformed structures. While we are aware of few authorities with 'voluminous plans', those with corporate criteria for decision-making are clearly in a separate category.

In a third group of councils, there has been some progress in management reform, without the overall framework of corporate planning. There have been advances in administrative coordination, using techniques such as network analysis, especially in councils with large capital expenditure programmes, to ensure that projects develop in a complementary manner. At the same time, the traditional system remains intact for most services and initiatives still tend to come from the service departments.

There are a number of reasons for the limited adoption of corporate planning in Scottish local government. First, there are *analytical* constraints. It is notoriously difficult to specify needs and objectives in services or to measure output in local government. Attempts to formulate workable objectives tend to lapse either into over-generality (for example, 'to improve the quality of life') or the over-specific ('to increase the number of teachers'). In the former case, they are useless as a guide to action; in the latter case, they are not so much objectives as means to achieve objectives. The same problems arise in central government's more recent Value-for-Money drive, which involves extending powers to the Accounts Commission to ensure that authorities have made effective arrangements for achieving economy, efficiency and effectiveness. Simpson (1986) explains the Value-for-Money approach as starting with a political decision on the quantity and quality of service desired. Value-for-Money is achieved when this level is secured at minimum cost. Again, there are the same problems in specifying objectives, especially in qualitative terms, and in knowing just when they have been met. In practice, such approaches can rapidly degenerate into exercises in cost-cutting irrespective of the policy implications.

The second constraint on the development of the corporate approach has been the persistence of departmentalism, the pervasiveness of bureaucratic politics and the tepid degree of political commitment. Functional professionals in departments remain sceptical of corporate mechanisms and of the ability of the central bureaucracy to give advice on matters affecting their services. Departmentalism was not greatly touched by the corporate ideology after reorganisation, and professionalism remains a strong countervailing force. Service directors are not passive actors in corporate decision-making. Most believe strongly in the service for which they are responsible and wish to see it further developed and funded. This frequently creates a tension when they are asked to think in corporate terms as members of management teams.

Politicians often fail to see advantages in the corporate approach. Some see it as irrelevant to their main interests in service development or ward representation. In Shetland, twice as many councillors sought membership of the planning committee as of the policy and resources committee (Elcock *et al.*, 1989). Other members are suspicious of corporate management as a device to increase the power of officials. Committee chairmen face a conflict of committee, corporate, party, and local constituency pressures. In both Glasgow and Strathclyde, backbench councillors (those who are not committee chairmen), as well as some service directors, have bridled at the centralisation of power implied in the corporate approach (Keating, 1988a).

While corporate management has failed to live up to all its expectations, however, it has, where realistically applied, served to improve the decision-making process. Rescued from the overelaboration which has characterised such management systems as PPBS (Planning, Programming and Budgeting Systems), and with recognition given to the political realities, it has helped clarify choices and evaluate options. Scottish approaches have generally been more modest and realistic than those in England and consequently there has not been the wholesale retreat from the new approach which has occurred south of the border. There has also been a recognition that different types of authority require different management systems. In councils run by partisan groups with strong ideological convictions, there is little prospect of changing minds through policy analysis. At the other extreme, where there is no partisan control and no desire to produce overall policies, other than perhaps cutting back expenditure, then policy analysis has little to contribute. Its greatest impact is in councils who are between the two, with the party organisation necessary to carry policies and programmes through the council but where minds are not made up in advance.

Politics and Decision-Making

One trend which has accelerated since reorganisation is the growth of party politics. In the pre-1975 system, party politics was confined to the large urban and industrial areas. By 1989, six of the nine regions and 43 of the 53 districts, covering the vast majority of Scotland's population, were organised on a party basis. Although non-partisanship is more common than in England, it is largely confined to the rural, Highland and Island areas. At the same time, the nature of partisanship itself has changed. In the past, party control was a means of recruiting councillors, sustaining leadership and, in many cases, distributing patronage. Nowadays, in imitation of national politics, it is often seen as a device for pursuing specific policies. Parties issue manifestoes and take victory at the polls as a mandate for pursuing them. This tendency, like the growth of partisanship itself, started on the left, particularly in the 'new urban left' councils (Gyford, 1985) but has now affected a number of Conservative groups as well (Widdicombe, 1986). So while Labour may promise higher social spending, low council rents and promotion of minority opportunities, Conservatives will offer the alternative of privatisation and spending cuts. The importance of the manifesto varies. In most council, it consists of general statements of principle but in some of the 'New Left' councils it is presented as a precise blueprint for change, which the officers are expected to implement in its entirety. This is a marked contrast with the traditional model, in which ideas for service development originated mainly from officers, albeit based on their perceptions of what members were looking for (Hill, 1974); Gyford (1985). The more ideological left and right are both relatively weak in urban Scotland compared with England but the Thatcher government's assault on the post-war collectivist consensus has raised the ideological temperature. In attacking both collective social provision and spatial planning, central government has questioned not only municipal Labour but the very *raison d'être* of local government in the post-war era; proposals emerging since the 1987 General Election promise further conflict.

This ideological polarisation has had major implications for the
roles of elected members and permanent officers. In their diagnosis of the system, New Left and New Right have, ironically,
much in common, in particular a dislike of bureaucratic paternalism. The solutions, of course, are different. The left favour
increased spending, collective community action, participation
through decentralisation and greater public control over economic
and social life. The right favour dismantling systems of public
provision, establishing individual rather than collective choice and
enhancing efficiency through competitive market-type provision of
services. Ideological polarisation poses severe problems for permanent officers, brought up in the tradition of consensus politics
focused on the service provision. Officers have always prided
themselves on their political neutrality while seeking maximum
discretion for themselves by defining issues in technical, professional terms. Now they are under attack from ideologues of both
sides who accuse them of conservatism, paternalism or self-serving
empire building. Widdicombe (1986, p.33) found that 59 per cent
of councillors agreed that 'officials have too much influence over
decision-making' and noted a tendency for the politicians to
challenge the traditional frontiers between councillors and officials. Other observers have attacked the committee system itself
for its tendency to depoliticise issues by obscuring them in
professional terms and burying councillors in technical detail
(Young, 1981).

In partisan councils, the main locus of decision-making is the
party group. This is a well-established tradition in Labour-
dominated councils. The trend was also noticeable in the Conservative Party following its entry into Scottish local government in
the late 1960s, though by the late 1980s there were too few
Conservative-controlled councils to be able to generalise. Within
the Labour Party itself the nature of political control has been
changing, with a move away from the authoritarian discipline
characteristic of the old Labour machines, towards a more per-
suasive and participative style (Leach *et al.*, 1986). All this has
enhanced the role of elected members against that of officials.

It would be wrong, however, to place all the emphasis on change
and on political confrontation. The major part of council work
remains consensual, with relatively little friction either between
the political parties or between members and officers. This is
particularly so in the committees through which most local government business is conducted. Most councillors still believe that the

role of the officer is to give neutral, professional advice. Except in the most partisan authorities, indeed, councillors see the giving of recommendations, and not merely a list of options, as part of the officers' job. In contrast to England, there is no evidence of Scottish Labour councils seeking committed party supporters for officer posts. Finally, partisanship is muted by the existence of cross-cutting divisions, such as those between geographical areas. Many councillors see their primary role as that of defending constituency interests and dealing with individual cases. This requires not so much partisanship as the cultivation of good relationships with officers.

Elections in Local Government

Elections are the principal means for ensuring accountability and responsiveness of councils to the citizen. Yet, increasingly, questions are being asked about the efficacy of elections as instruments of public choice (Adam Smith Institute, 1989). Rather than seeing local democracy in terms of collective decision, the new Conservatism looks to direct devolution of power from the local authority to the citizen. The nature and quality of local democracy have thus become a central element in the increasing political divisions in Scotland.

Citizens participate in local politics in three main ways, as individuals, through voting in elections, as members of interest groups which seek to influence local government, and as councillors, elected by and representative of the public. For much of its history, local government was seen rather like a private corporation, in which the local ratepayers were the shareholders. Voting was tied to the ownership of property and payment of rates, with the separate vote for businesses being abolished only in 1948. In the post-Second World War period, the principle of universal suffrage has been largely unchallenged, with local elections seen as the means for the whole community to take decisions on policies, taxation and service levels. Over recent years, however, there have been increasing demands to restore the link between voting and payment of taxes, a principle given effect by the nationalisation of the business rate and the introduction of the community charge. At the same time there have been calls for the introduction of more charges for individual local services, further reducing the scope for collective community decisions on service levels and expenditure.

A major justification given for the attack on local government is the belief that local elections are characterised by low turnout, limited knowledge and general apathy. Some analysts have argued that local government is insulated politically from the electorate (Danziger, 1978; Dunleavy, (1980). The bare figures would appear to support this. In Britain as a whole, turnout in local elections averages about 40 per cent (Miller, 1988). In Scotland, the figure is somewhat higher, though it has fallen in the years since reorganisation, from 50 per cent in 1974, when regional and district elections were held on the same day, to 44.4 per cent and 44.2 per cent for the most recent regional and district elections respectively. The overall figure may be misleading, since there are many uncontested seats in rural areas. While this may itself be taken as a poor reflection on local democracy, it may equally well reflect satisfaction with the incumbent councillors. Where contests do take place in such seats, turnout is only marginally below the Scottish average. Overall turnout, while it compares poorly with that in national elections, remains higher than under the pre-1975 system. This in turn is probably due to the increased involvement of political parties, who recruit candidates, ensure that most seats are contested and encourage the voters to turn out.

Miller (1988) records a rather high level of knowledge among electors, compared with the studies carried out in the late 1960s for the Wheatley Commission. More than 70 per cent of electors could correctly name their local council, more than 60 per cent could name their local councillor and more than 80 per cent knew which party their councillor represented. A survey conducted for Glasgow District Council produced similar findings. Miller (1988) also found high levels of public support for local government as an institution, and high levels of dissatisfaction with central government. Only a minority blamed local government for the financial difficulties of the 1980s, or supported the proposals for a poll tax. Scots also showed high levels of satisfaction with council services. Only 20 per cent had ever complained about services, compared with 26 per cent for the rest of Britain. Widdicombe (1986, p. 40) concluded that local government is 'generally held in good regard by the electorate'. When asked if the replacement of local government with appointed boards would be a good idea, 72 per cent of Scots were opposed, with just 11 per cent in favour.

Citizens have also shown an increasing tendency to participate in local affairs through organised pressure groups. Many of these are short-lived, formed to protest against rates increases or major development proposals. Others, particularly tenants' association and environmental groups, have a more stable existence and have developed considerable skills in negotiating with local officials. There is statutory provision for public participation in the planning process, through public consultation, examinations in public of structure plans, and planning enquiries, but in other fields, formal procedures for public participation are less well-developed. Non-domestic ratepayers now have statutory rights to be consulted about councils' expenditure plans although in most areas the exercise appears largely fruitless (Martlew, 1984; Leach *et al.*, 1986). Ratepayers' groups have also been found to be ineffective, most having a minimal understanding of the intricacies of local government finance but generally believing that council are characterised by large bureaucracies and wasteful spending.

Another vehicle for public expression is community councils, whose statutory remit is to ascertain, coordinate and express the views of small communities to regional and district councils. District councils are obliged to produce a scheme for community councils and to set one up in any area where twenty or more electors request it. By 1983, there were 1,131 community councils, covering 80 per cent of the population of Scotland. Ninety-eight more had been established but folded (SOCRU, 1986). There is no consistent pattern for formation and survival with Glasgow and Dundee having a much fuller coverage than Edinburgh and Aberdeen; nor is it possible to generalise about rural or urban areas. A key factor appears to be the degree of support and encouragement given by district councils. All but one of the district and islands authorities offer general grants to community councils and most offer accommodation and other services. Glasgow has a well-funded Community Councils Resource Centre. Regional councils are no longer permitted to make general grants to community councils though most are willing to contribute to specific community projects.

Community councils have certainly increased involvement in local affairs. While the effect of reorganisation in 1975 was to reduce the number of councillors from 5,400 to 1,600, community councils attract some 10,000 elected members. Provision for election varies from one scheme to another, with some having a

ward system and others using at-large elections. Some allow all
people over 16 to vote and become members and most provide
additional seats for voluntary groups including churches, youth
and senior citizens' organisations, cultural, educational and sport-
ing associations, residents' and tenants' groups, commercial interests and occasionally political parties. On the other hand, this still
represents a tiny percentage of the Scottish population, many
councils have difficulty in filling all the seats and it is questionable
whether they can be considered truly representative of their areas.

Matters raised by community councils are very diverse, but
there is concentration on roads and transport and planning
matters (SOCRU, 1986). Most districts make formal arrangements for community councils to be consulted on major
planning applications. The allocation of housing and licensing
matters are also of some importance. With the ending of the old
veto poll system under which areas of Scotland could vote to
remain 'dry', many community councils began to exercise their
right to object to licensing applications to achieve the same
effect. Other matters raised include policing, environmental
health and cleansing, leisure and recreation and education. A
range of matters is also pursued with other bodies including the
health service, British Telecom, the post office and the
electricity and gas boards.

The attitudes of councils to community participation varies
considerably. While consultation with individual tenants over
housing developments is regarded as legitimate, tenants' associations are often viewed more suspiciously. There are exceptions.
Glasgow District Council, for example goes to considerable
lengths to consult with groups over its budget proposals
(McFadden, 1989) while Stirling has a highly developed community forum (Charlton and Martlew, 1987). Consultations with
public sector trade unions is now normal, particularly in urban
Labour councils and is extremely well-developed in Lothian
(Titterton, 1982). In independent councils, a stress is often
placed on consultation with the community as a fundamental
principle of the representative process, though there is less
support for consultation with pressure groups, who are regarded
as sectional interests (Leach *et al.*, 1986). Most councillors,
particularly at district level, consult their local community
councils on issues and often attend their meetings. Their
attitudes, however, vary. A third of the councillors interviewed
for a Scottish Office study did not see the community council as

an appropriate body to consult on local issues, some because they had never seen the need for a community council at all, others because they doubted its representativeness (SOCRU, 1986). These stressed the existence of competing points of view in the locality and the need to take a broad, overall view. Community councils, for their part, tended to complain about a lack of proper consultation. In general, of course, councillors will be more receptive to representations from groups and individuals who share their own goals and values.

Candidates

There is a long-standing debate about whether political parties have a legitimate role in local government. Supporters of the non-partisan approach argue that national party policies and ideological differences have no relevance to local issues. They also insist that the ability and personality of the individual candidate rather than the party label should be the determining factor in election. Advocates of partisan local government, on the other hand, point to the advantages of party in simplifying electoral choice and letting the elector know what the policy consequences of his vote will be. Party control of local government can also increase accountability, since the individual elector knows who is in charge of the council and who to punish at the polls should its performance not prove satisfactory.

In general, the non-partisan approach characterised rural areas and small towns in the period before reorganisation (Dyer, 1978; Bealey and Sewel, 1981). Since reorganisation, the number of independent candidates has fallen dramatically while the number of party candidates has risen. There were 644 independent candidates in the 1974 district elections, and just 402 in 1984. At regional level, the number of independents fell from 297 in 1974 to 141 in 1986. The number of independent councillors fell from 459 in 1974 to 304 in 1986 and non-partisan politics is now the norm only in the rural and island areas, although the 1988 district elections saw the election of a number of partisan councillors in these areas.

Councillors represent their communities in the political sense but to what extent are they 'representative' of their constituents in terms of their background and experiences? In one sense, they are clearly not. Just 13 per cent of Scottish councillors in

1985 were women (Martlew, 1988), an insignificant increase over the 1960s when they comprised just 10 per cent (France, 1969). Regional councillors spend an average of 44 hours per month attending meetings against 27 hours for district councillors. Regional meetings can be a long distance from the home and regional councillors spend 17 hours per month travelling to them, against 7 hours for district councillors. The demands of work and family thus prove a considerable obstacle for women in local government. Women appear less well-represented in Scotland than in England where they comprise some 19 per cent of councillors (Widdicombe, 1986). Women accounted for just 12 per cent of Strathclyde regional and Glasgow district councillors in the late 1980s, (Keating *et al.*, 1989). This may be due to the heavy time demands of membership of the two councils but must also reflect on the failure of the Labour Party in Glasgow, in which the traditional male-dominated trade unions play a large role, to bring forward women candidates.

In terms of age, it is the young who are under-represented, with 28 per cent of councillors between the ages of 18 and 44, compared with 46 per cent of the population as a whole (Widdicombe, 1986). The number of younger councillors appears to be increasing, but this is likely to reflect the large turnover since the late 1970s which has provided opportunities for younger candidates to be elected. At times of electoral stability, councillors may remain in office for decades, blocking the prospects for younger people (Keating *et al.*, 1989).

Councillors in Britain as a whole are better educated than the population at large, with four times as many proportionately holding a degree or equivalent. In Scotland, this tendency is somewhat less pronounced. There are fewer professionals, managers and employers in Scottish local government than the UK as a whole and more skilled and semi-skilled manual workers. More councillors in Scotland than elsewhere are employed in the public sector (Widdicombe, 1986). These differences reflect differences in Scotland's socio-economic structure as well as Labour's dominance north of the border. In Glasgow, where Labour held all but a handful of seats in the late 1980s, most regional and district councillors were people of working-class backgrounds who had themselves often started their careers in manual occupations in the private sector but who had moved into white-collar public service jobs, usually after a period of higher education (Keating *et al.*, 1989). They were thus representative of their working-class constituents in terms of their origins and early experiences but were upwardly mobile socially. Many of them were employed in education, local government service or with voluntary organisations and trade unions, occupations requiring similar combinations of interests and skills as being a councillor and which provided the flexible hours necessary for council work.

Scottish councillors each represent more people on average than those elsewhere in Britain, 3,100 compared to 2,200 in Britian as a whole. They also work harder, around 120 hours per month against a British average of 74 hours. This reflects the broader interpretation of official duties in Scotland, with greater recognition of the informal aspects of the councillor's role as well as the burden of housing cases in urban authorities. More Scottish than English or Welsh councillors received allowances for preparing for meetings, attending external organisations as council representative, attending party meetings directly related to council business, and holding councillor surgeries and public consultation meetings (Widdicombe 1986).

Electoral Trends

We have noted the increase in partisanship in local government since reorganisation. This is reflected in the increase in electoral contests. The six partisan regions contain around 90 per cent of the Scottish population and even in non-partisan districts, some 30 per cent of wards have at least one major party candidate (Bochel and Denver 1989). Partisanship was first introduced seriously by the Labour Party in the cities in the early part of the century. Their opponents typically grouped themselves in anti-socialist or pro-business coalitions under the label of Progressive or Moderate. From the 1960s, however, the Conservatives began to displace these, forcing Progressive or Moderate candidates to stand under the party banner or face an official Conservative opponent. In the 1980s, however, their support has been in decline and by 1988 they held no regions and just three districts.

In the SNP there was a long debate over the merits of standing in local elections at all, given their apparent irrelevance to the party's goal of Scottish independence, but during the nationalist revivals in the late 1960s and mid 1970s a large number stood and were elected. They took control of the new towns of East Kilbride and Cumbernauld, as well as Falkirk District and held the balance of power in Glasgow. Since the 1980s, they have adopted a policy of standing in as many seats as possible, to maximise the overall share of the Scottish vote and build support and organisation on the ground. In 1984 they took control of Angus District and between 1986 and 1988 shared control of Grampian region. The Liberal and SDP Alliance and their successors, the Democrats, also contested local elections widely in the 1980s, gaining control of North East Fife and Gordon Districts, where they also hold the parliamentary seats, and sharing power in Grampian.

The Labour Party has led the poll in Scottish local elections since reorganisation, though its share of the vote has varied between 32 per cent in 1977, when it suffered heavy losses to the SNP and 48 per cent in 1984. As in parliamentary elections, its vote is heavily concentrated in the central industrial areas, especially in Strathclyde where its dominance of the regional council has never seriously been challenged. By the late 1980s, it controlled four regions and twenty-four districts and the vast majority of Scots lived under Labour-controlled local government.

The vital question, however, is the extent to which these electoral trends reflect the electors' judgement on the performance of local government or merely the national trend. Many observers, commenting on the apparent uniformity of trends, ask whether local elections are really irrelevant (Miller, 1988). It is true that local elections are often seen as a referendum on the performance of the national government in London and that councillors are swept into and out of office for reasons entirely unrelated to their own qualities. So in 1977 there was a clear swing against the incumbent Labour Government, while in 1980 the pendulum moved against the Conservatives. It would be wrong, however, to write off local elections as meaningless. There are local variations, often treated as puzzling by 'bemused commentators' who have difficulty fitting them into a national pattern (Bruce and Lee, 1982). Miller (1988) notes local variations resulting from differences in style and presentation, local media coverage, personalities and the efficiency of party organisations. The ability of the Liberals to organise effectively in several English cities in the 1970s shows the importance of the latter.

Further, it is a mistake to assume that national trends always and only result from the transmission of national political preferences to the local level. Party images are made up of a complex of ideas, issues and experiences, including local ones. Both major parties have adopted platforms on essentially local issues such as rents, rates, council house sales and education which are presented by their representatives at both national and local levels. Bochel and Denver (1989) argue that the poll tax was the central issue in the 1988 local election campaign and that the result can be read as a generous endorsement of the performance of Labour local government. SNP successes in Glasgow in the late 1970s did not occur uniformly but were concentrated in the peripheral housing schemes where discontent with Labour's urban policies was most acute (Keating, 1988a). Several writers have noted the importance of the provision and financing of urban services in moulding electors' choices (Dunleavy, 1980). Electors may not therefore be behaving irrationally by voting consistently at national and local elections. On the contrary, it would be strange to find electors holding generally rightist views voting for leftist candidates because of personality or some local factor.

Specifically local issues do, of course, arise in local government but are usually handled by councillors on an individual or ward basis, through surgeries, public meetings, telephone calls and letters. Despite widespread partisanship, the councillor's party role is only one facet of the job. There is also the local representative role, carried out, unlike elections, on a daily basis. Councillors must represent their communities as spokespersons and advocates when meeting professionals and administrators, and in this partisanship is largely irrelevant.

7

Central–Local Financial Relationships

Central–Local Conflict

Since the 1980s, the role of local government and its relationship with Central Government has become, in Scotland as in England, a major item of political controversy. In the past, there was a large degree of consensus on the role of local government in providing services and regulating urban development. In the post-war years, central government encouraged local councils to increase service and spending levels as part of a series of national programmes in housing, education, social work and other fields. We have noted that the Wheatley philosophy of an active local government engaged in the physical and social planning of the communities for which it was responsible was accepted by both major parties. Both, too, had a place for local government in their political thought. The Labour tradition of 'municipal socialism' emphasised the role of local government in improving living conditions for working people, while traditional Conservatives saw local governemnt as a protection against the over-mighty state.

In the 1980s, however, Conservative thinking changed radically, to present local government as just another 'vested interest', in league with bureaucrats, socialist politicians and trade unions against the interests of individuals and households. This follows the general anti-collectivist stance of the Thatcher government and its emphasis on individual self-help. Even if the government has not targeted local government directly, its policies of reducing the state's role in physical planning and social welfare would have put it on a collision course with councils, since these areas are the very essence of their contemporary role. The new strategy seeks to enhance individual freedom by restraining expenditure and taxation, increasing efficiency through contracting out services, stressing local government's role in 'enabling' rather than in service delivery and increasing consumer choice through such measures as council house sales and parental choice of schools.

Central–local relations in Scotland are in some respects simpler than in England. One central department, the Scottish Office is responsible for grant allocations and expenditure control as well as all the main spending programmes. On the local government side, a small number of councils is responsible for the bulk of spending and there is just one local authority association, the Convention of Scottish Local Authorities. The small scale of the Scottish political arena means that the main actors are personally acquainted and the Scottish Office does not need a system of regional offices between Edinburgh and the localities. This can give a greater cohesiveness to the policy communities and often allows individual problems to be resolved informally, though observers have cast some doubt on whether the Scottish Office itself is able to act in a truly corporate manner in its relations with local government (Page, 1978).

The distinctive administrative arrangements, however, have not modified the central thrust of Conservative policy and there has been increasing conflict, centred on the critical issue of expenditure. Financial planning for Scottish local government is conducted through the Working Party on Local Government Finance. The local authority representation is composed of senior figures on the political and administrative side, council leaders, chief executives and directors of finance. The Working Party is chaired by the Secretary of State and he is serviced by officials from the Finance Division and Central Research Unit of the Scottish Office. This can best be characterised as an *expenditure network,* a looser idea than a policy community which shares a range of values and a concern for a specific service (Elcock *et al.*, 1989). Relationships within this network are complex. At one level, central government faces the local authorities, the former interested in expenditure control, the later in maximising central grant. At the same time, the local authorities are divided among themselves on the distribution of grant. The partisan dimension is important, too. With the decline of the Conservatives who, by 1988, controlled no regions and only three small districts, the governing party has few allies in COSLA which it has on occasion tried to portray as a partisan Labour body. In fact, on many issues, there is a consensus among Labour, Democrats, Nationalists and Independents, representing the great bulk of Scottish voters.

Given central government's determination to have its way, COSLA has consistently expressed misgivings about the value of participation in these meetings and has produced reports critical of developments (COSLA, 1981, 1982). On the other hand, central government is still to some extent dependent on the local authority professions as regards the scope for reductions. While it has often argued that proposed cuts are simply 'efficiency measures' with no implications for services, it does need to take some account of advice on this. At the same time, there is a shared interest in the expenditure network in protecting overall Scottish expenditure levels against the Treasury. With half the Secretary of State's budget accounted for by local government, this provides an incentive for cooperation, despite the almost ritual conflict which surrounds the process.

The Financial Framework

A basic distinction is made in local government finance between capital and revenue expenditure. It is conventional practice to define expenditure where the benefits are used up quickly – usually within a year – as revenue expenditure, while spending on assets with a life of more than a year is capital expenditure. The distinction is not always clear cut and there is a 'grey area' which is sometimes used to effect in 'creative accounting'. Capital expenditure has three distinguishing features;

1. *It creates new assets or increases the value of an existing asset.*

2. *It provides a flow of benefits to the community over a number of years.*

3. *Its cost is high enough to justify spreading the payments over a number of years.*

Council houses, schools and roads are clear examples of capital expenditure. It can be financed from a capital fund, by borrowing, by capital receipts from the sale of assets, or by capital grants from central government or European agencies. The most common method is by borrowing, with repayments made from the revenue budget.

Revenue (or current) expenditure covers, apart from this, the daily costs of services, notably in the form of wages to employees. It is financed from current income in a separate revenue account. Current income is based on central government grant, on charges for some services and on councils' own taxes. Until 1989, local taxes consisted of rates levied on domestic and business properties according to their notional rental value. Rates proved to be a very politically sensitive tax, since, unlike income tax and value added tax, they are highly visible and they do not rise automatically with inflation. So at times of rising prices local councils were forced to increase the rate level. In 1989, domestic rates were replaced by the community charge, a poll tax levied on individuals with the power to set business rates taken over by central government which then distributes the money back to councils according to population. Councils are not permitted to borrow to cover revenue expenditure in their budgets.

Local authorities can incur capital expenditure only with the consent of the Secretary of State. This is obtained through submitting capital expenditure plans which are scrutinised by the Scottish Office in the light of the government's overall expenditure plans. Allocations, that is approvals to spend up to a certain sum, are then given to local authorities in six blocks for regions (education, social work, roads and transport, water and sewerage, police, and general services) and two blocks for districts (housing and general services). At one time, these blocks were rigidly separated but in recent years councils have had flexibility to move allocations between blocks. In practice, this freedom has had little effect and is useful mainly for avoiding underspending in a block at the end of the financial year.

In other ways, the discretion of councils has effectively been reduced. In the early years after reorganisation, there was widespread capital underspending. The reductions in allocations since then have meant that much of an authority's programme is committed to complete projects started in previous years, leaving little scope for new ones. There is also a requirement to negotiate large projects individually with the Scottish Office. Forward planning has also been made difficult by the practice of allowing local authorities to supplement allocations with capital receipts from the sale of properties during the year. In the case of housing, an assumed level of capital receipts has been written into the capital allocations, leaving an element of uncertainty as to their size. On occasion, the Secretary of State has attached conditions to the block allocations, such as limiting the proportion of the general services block which can be spent on leisure and recreation. Lothian Region had its general consent withdrawn altogether during its budgetary conflict with the Secretary of State and had to have all individual projects approved.

Since reorganisation, the Secretary of State has acquired a large armoury of weapons to influence and control revenue expenditure. The most important mechanism is the Revenue Support Grant (formerly Rate Support Grant). In the discussions of the Working Party, the government declares an overall level of local expenditure on which its grant will be based. This level is determined within the framework of the government's expenditure plans as a whole after taking into account the factors which affect the various services, such as population trends or pay settlements. Secondly, the government declares the percentage of this expenditure which it will meet through grant. From 1976–7, when it was 72.5 per cent it fell to 56 per cent in 1989–90. Cuts in central support have been used both to restrain expenditure and to transfer the burden onto the local taxpayer, helping central government to eliminate its own deficit.

The next step is the distribution of grant among councils. At reorganisation, grant was distributed on a formula based largely on the population of each authority with weightings for numbers of children and elderly people and adjustments for factors such as population sparsity, density and decline. This was rather unscientific and the vagueness of the criteria allowed the formula to be manipulated rather easily to produce whatever result was desired politically (Heald, 1980b). Since 1984, grant has been distributed through the 'client group' approach, which the Scottish Office describe as a simple and defensible way of estimating expenditure need. The objective is to estimate what authorities would need to spend in order to provide a similar standard of service with a similar degree of efficiency.

There are two stages in the calculation. First, a 'primary indicator' is defined for each component of a service. A primary indicator is usually the client group for the service in question, for example *school-age children* for education or the *total population* for leisure services. In some instances, it is difficult to define a client group and other factors which explain expenditure are used, for example road mileage as the biggest influence on highways expenditure. The primary indicator is seen as the main determinant of demand for services and is the main determinant of need. Secondly, analysis of past expenditure is carried out to determine any characteristics outside the control of local authorities which have a systematic effect. These 'secondary indicators', which cause local variations in the unit costs of provision or demand for a service, are analysed using *multiple linear regression*. This is a technique for explaining variations in local expenditure. For example, the sparsity of an area may effect its costs of provision, and if it does so, regression analysis will reveal it by correlating a measure of sparsity with past expenditure. Authorities' expenditure needs, as determined by the primary indicator, are then weighted to reflect the incidence of the secondary indicator.

When it was introduced, the client group method was little understood, even by financial specialists in local government, though directors of finance generally regarded it as an improvement technically on the previous method and as good as they were likely to get (Midwinter *et al.*, 1986). Authorities generally supported or opposed the method depending on whether they gained or lost money as a result of it. There were major technical criticisms at the outset, particularly on the inadequacy of evidence used in determining primary indicators, the rationale for identifying secondary indicators, the lack of supporting evidence for these and the failure to disaggregate services (Midwinter *et al.*, 1987). In recent years, there has been considerable progress on these issues. As a result, the Scottish client group method is a considerable advance on the approach used in the past in Scotland and still used for some elements of grant calculation in England (Bramley *et al.*, 1983), which leaves major items to political judgement. It must be stressed, however, that it is a method for allocating a predetermined amount of expenditure, not for determining its overall level. That continues to depend on the political decisions of central government.

Limiting Expenditure

Since the economic crisis of 1976 led the International Monetary Fund to impose public expenditure cuts on the Labour Government, there has been a constant pressure on public expenditure levels. Given the large proportion of public expenditure accounted for by local government, this had led central governments to seek to control local expenditure. The economic justification for this has been widely questioned (Barlow, 1981; Jackman, 1982; Meadows and Jackson, 1986), since local government's revenue expenditure, being financed from taxation rather than borrowing, has no net effect on aggregate demand or the public sector borrowing requirement; capital expenditure is already tightly controlled by the centre. Rates, however, were a politically sensitive tax and ratepayers groups were well organised in some parts of Scotland, notably in Edinburgh, to demand central intervention to curb local spending levels. The Thatcher Government has claimed the right to control local spending by invoking a supposed convention whereby local government always accepted central government's expenditure ceilings. This, too, is highly contentious and, before 1976, there was no serious attempt to control local spending. Since 1976, however, governments have constantly sought new ways of doing so. In the case of the Scottish Office, the need to control it has been imposed by a Treasury convention that the total expenditure of Scottish local authorities counted as part of the Scottish Office spending total as determined in the Public Expenditure Survey (Chapter 5). Any overspending would thus count as a black mark against the Secretary of State. Since 1989, the locally funded element of local expenditure (that is the proportion now funded by the community charge) has been excluded from PESC but the remainder is still part of it.

The first technique of control was to limit the central grant. Until 1977, grant was adjusted automatically to cover all cost increases. In that year, limits were imposed so that if inflation exceeded the prediction, councils had to make compensating cuts in levels of service provision. Next, the government started to withdraw grant across the board where total local government expenditure was above the predetermined total. This was a control at the level of the system as a whole, criticised for penalising 'prudent' as well as 'overspending' councils and was amended to allow selective abatement of grant. The criterion used was a council's spending compared with its 'guideline'. Guidelines had been introduced at reorganisation at the request of COSLA to help councils plan their expenditure. They broke down the planning total of expenditure as determined (in recent years) by the client group method, according to councils and services. Explicitly described as 'indicative' at the outset' they progressively developed into an instrument of control and COSLA turned against them.

Linking grant abatements to guidelines, however, did not deal with those authorities who were well in excess of their guidelines, who were challenging the government politically and where ratepayers groups were calling for central intervention. New powers were accordingly taken in the Local Government (Miscellaneous Provisions) (Scotland) Act 1981 and the Local Government and Planning (Scotland) Act 1982. These allowed the Secretary of State, subject to parliamentary approval, to reduce the amount of grant to any council and order it to reduce its rate poundage where he considered planned expenditure to be 'excessive and unreasonable'. The terms of the legislation leave a great deal of discretion to the Secretary of State who, in making his decision, may have regard:

– *to expenditure or estimated expenses, in that or a preceding year, of other local authorities which the Secretary of State was satisfied were closely comparable (or as closely comparable as is practicable) with the local authority concerned;*

– *to general economic conditions;*

– *to such other financial, economic, demographic, geographic or the like criteria as he considers appropriate.*

Despite the sweeping nature of these powers, the Secretary of State later felt it necessary to assume a general power of rates limitation which allowed him to fix in advance the maximum increase or minimum decrease in rates which councils could make in one year. This power was never used and was removed from the statute book with the introduction of the community charge in 1989.

Housing finance is organised somewhat differently. Revenue expenditure on council housing is financed from three sources: rents; a subsidy from local taxes (known as the rate fund contribution); and a contribution from central government through the housing support grant. Recent government policy has focused on increasing the share of expenditure met by rents and reducing the other two elements. Housing Support Grant is under its control and has been cut back sharply (Chapter 8). Control over the rate fund contribution was initially attempted through a system known as housing expenditure limits (HELs) whereby any excess rate fund contribution over the government-set limit was deducted pound for pound from the council's capital allocation for housing, thus keeping total housing spending within limits (Midwinter, Keating and Taylor, 1983). In 1985, the Secretary of State went further and took power to set the maximum rate fund contribution for each council.

The 1980s thus saw a drastic increase in central control over local government expenditure levels, with new legislation almost every year. Yet by 1986 the Government was still convinced that the system was not working and that a more fundamental reform was necessary. Before examining this, we will consider the way in which councils reacted to the increased central pressures of the preceeding decade.

The Politics of Local Spending

In the ten years before reorganisation, local government spending doubled in real terms, as centre and locality agreed on the need to expand services. From 1975, however, government policy became more restrictive and central grant increases failed to keep pace with rising costs, causing steep rate increases. Real reductions in the level of expenditure were sought in Government and the percentage of expenditure financed by grant fell from 75 per cent to 68.5 per cent by 1978–9. Cash limits on the grant, set at a level below the rate of inflation, intensified the squeeze and local government expenditure levels fell. Particularly large reductions were imposed in capital spending programmes.

In the late 1970s, however, the political climate changed. A radical Labour Administration came to power in Lothian Region in 1978, followed in 1980 by left-wing administrations in Dundee and Stirling. The Labour Government was replaced in 1979 by the right-wing Thatcher administration, pledged to further expenditure cuts. As a result, the level of rhetoric increased so as often to obscure the reality of what was happening on the ground. There was in practice still a great deal of give-and-take between central and local government. In 1980–1, a proposal from the Secretary of State in the Working Party for a 7.5 per cent reduction in revenue estimates was modified to a 2–3 per cent cut, mainly in capital spending. The Secretary of State confessed that he had been impressed with the points made in discussion and had had a good response from the Treasury to the appeals made (Midwinter, 1984). This was the Scottish network operating in its customary fashion, opponents in Scotland but allies against London. In 1984–5, Government made a pretence of being tough by linking grant penalties to guidelines, but proceeded to accommodate the 'overspenders' by increasing the guideline in line with past expenditure levels. The change had little effect on overall spending but reduced the number of councils over guideline. The much-publicised rate-capping powers failed to bring any significant savings, the most achieved in a single year being £30 million.

On the other hand, some of the most dramatic rates increases owed little to local authority decisions. Between 1978 and 1986, Scottish domestic rates doubled in real terms while revenue spending increased by just 2.6 per cent (Keating, 1985a). The reasons were the reductions in central grant and the revaluation of 1986 which shifted the rates burden from business to domestic premises. In cash terms, the increases were even more dramatic, due to high levels of inflation in the early 1980s. In Lothian Region, in 1980 a 2 per cent real increase in spending required a 41 per cent increase in rates. In 1985–6, despite a real cut in spending levels of 3 per cent, rates increases of 20 per cent were common, due to the combined effects of revaluation and grant reduction.

Turning to the effects of the new restrictions on individual local authorities, we again see a varied pattern, depending on the circumstances of the locality, the impact of central decisions on it and the choices made by the council. Three types of reaction to central restrictions can be identified (Midwinter, 1988).

Compliant authorities reached a compromise with central government by adopting budgets unchanged from previous years or close to the guideline figure. They were characterised by an overriding ethic of fiscal prudence and were concerned to minimise rates, maximise grants and avoid penalties. This approach is justified on economic grounds, the argument being that there is little sense in expanding services if the consequent grant loss removes the local economic advantage. They tended to be concerned to maintain service levels and to achieve greater value for money.

Shadow-boxing authorities stressed the protection and development of services rather than the minimisation of rates. Their strategic aim was to maximise expenditure while minimising penalties and avoiding rate-capping. Such authorities have usually achieved modest growth or maintained services, while reducing reported expenditure through various financial adjustments and accounting devices.

A minority of councils adopted *brinkmanship* strategies, expanding services, setting high rate increases and publicly confronting central government. They thus became an obvious target for central government and angered less strident councils (Heald, 1982) which saw them as inviting new punitive measures which could hurt all of local government. Most councils which adopted these tactics reduced their budgets after central government intervention but still managed net increases in expenditure over the whole period. In the end, compromise was reached, with concessions on both sides (Crompton, 1982; Midwinter, Keating and Taylor, 1983; Charlton and Martlew, 1987).

There is a substantial literature on fiscal stress, the combination of increasing costs of maintaining a given level of service with a decline in available resources. Early studies suggested that, in the short term, councils would 'buy time', through short-term, incrementalist strategies. In the long run, retrenchment was predicted to lead to a greater reliance on rational appraisal and strategic choice of priorities, as in the corporate management model (Stewart, 1980). Jordan (1987), by contrast, argued that long-term financial planning was less likely in periods of restraint and uncertainty. The experience of Scottish local government in the 1980s supports this view. Short-term strategies predominated and targets were achieved through increasing charges, creative accounting, efficiency savings and increases in local taxation. Council house rents, the largest charge available, have increased dramatically in recent years. Creative accounting includes such measures as budget transfers, capitalisation of revenue expenditures, rescheduling debts and arranging for heavy expenditures to show up in the accounts of years when less central government penalties are expected. Authorities have also deferred expenditure, made 'efficiency savings across the board' or 'improved productivity', though the real meaning and impact of such measures is seldom made clear. Increases in local taxation have been substantial and only occasionally, as in the case of Lothian in 1982, seem to have carried an electoral cost. In Dundee and Stirling, they do not appear to have affected local election results at all, either because the councils have succeeded in passing the blame back to the centre or because voters have continued to cast their ballots on the basis of national considerations.

The local outcomes of budgetary politics vary with the historic budget levels, community concerns and the values of councillors. Unfortunately, it is extremely difficult to separate out the effect of these factors and give a definite verdict on what determines the final expenditure level. For example, high spending on council housing in urban areas might be the result of Labour control of these councils or of the characteristics of the areas concerned. One method is by regression analysis, which allows the effect of each variable to be assessed. It is still difficult, however, to determine whether higher levels of expenditure reflect higher levels of provision or simply the higher cost of any level of provision in those areas traditionally controlled by Labour councils.

An analysis of a service where there is a large degree of discretion, library expenditures, showed a more complex picture (Mair *et al.*, 1988). The largest changes occurred immediately after a change of political control. So councils where Labour had just assumed control were likely to increase spending while those where Labour had been in control for some time were more likely to maintain or even cut it. Conversely, the Conservatives were more likely to make cuts where they had just taken office, as in Lothian in 1982 (Parry, 1984) than when they had long been in control, as in Tayside before 1986 (Berridge and Clark, 1987; Midwinter, Keating and Taylor, 1983). Independent councils have often been regarded as fiscally conservative (Dyer, 1978; Bealey and Sewell, 1981; Dyer and Sewell, 1987). In fact, there is considerable variation among them. Borders and Dumfries and Galloway are more fiscally conservative than Highland Region or the Islands authorities, all of whom increased expenditure and rates in the decade of retrenchment.

Central government decisions on grants and capital allocations clearly affect the overall budget and rating decisions of local authorities but the distribution of funds among the individual services is the product of another complex of factors in which central and local decision-makers again interact. Some services, such as education, police and fire, are strongly directed by the centre, with the relevant Scottish Office and local authority departments in close consultation. So, while the Secretary of State has been preaching general fiscal restraint, Scottish Office departments, in line with government priorities, have been encouraging increases in expenditure in certain areas, such as law and order. Others, such as roads or sewerage, depend on technological or geographic factors. Yet others, such as social work or leisure and recreation, are discretionary, with a large role for local choice, though demographic trends and national economic conditions may have a major impact. A paper for the Distribution Committee of the Working Party illustrated the enormous variation in provision of parks, swimming pools and theatres across Scotland. Per thousand population, the area of parks varied from 6 to 69 acres. The square footage of swimming pool varied from 30 to 810 and theatre seats varied from 4 to 48. In social work home-help services, the highest level of provision is almost double that of the lowest (Mid-winter, 1984).

Similar variations exist in levels of taxation, depending on Government grants, local spending decisions, estimates of inflation, levels of non-payment and the use of balances or deficits from previous years.

Attempts by the centre to control the level of local expenditure and taxation have thus been frustrated by the combination of lack of clear vision on the part of central government, the capacity of local authorities to evade restrictions and, above all, the complexity of the factors which actually determine local expenditure and taxation. By the mid 1980s, despite a succession of legislative changes, central government continued to believe that local spending was out of control. This became a political priority when the rating revaluation of 1986 led to sharp increases in domestic rates, sparking off a middle-class protest which led to a prime ministerial intervention. At this stage, the government determined on a new approach, relying less on detailed central intervention than on a new form of local accountability.

The Poll Tax – Increased Accountability or Confusion?

In 1986, the Green Paper, *Paying for Local Government* (Cmnd. 9714) announced the abolition of domestic rates and the introduction of a flat-rate community charge (or poll tax) for each adult. Non-domestic rates would become a national tax, set by central government and with the receipts distributed to local authorities on the basis of population. For a transitional period, pending the introduction of a national rate, business rate increases would be pegged to the price index. Although the green paper criticised the rating system for its inequity, the central theme was the need to promote local accountability:

> Effective local accountability must be the cornerstone of successful local government. All too often this accountability is blurred and weakened by the complexities of the national grant system and the fact that differences arise among those who vote for, those who pay for, and those who receive local government services.
>
> (Cmnd. 9714)

The weaknesses of the rating system were threefold:

1. *Non-domestic rates were paid by businesses and public institutions to whom local authorities were not directly accountable.*

2. *Domestic rates were paid by a minority of local electors and varied in a way which had little or no regard to the use made of local authority services; the burden of rates was carried on too few shoulders.*

3. *Central Government grants were calculated in a way which concealed the real costs of local services from the electorate.*

Many of these assertions are contestable and have been criticised as based on superficial evidence (Midwinter and Mair, 1987). Nevertheless, the Government saw its proposals as leading to a position where local accountability can again become the main determinant of local expenditure and priorities at the margin. The assumption is that the real spending 'needs' of councils will be identified and grant-aided through the client group method. Any discretionary spending above this will be financed through the community charge, giving local electors a clear price for the additional spending.

Unfortunately, the client group method has never reached the degree of sophistication required to determine local needs precisely. It seeks to calculate what authorities need to spend to provide an average level of service but average is never defined except on the basis of past expenditure. So authorities with low levels of past provision are assumed to have low needs.

Nor will the new system necessarily increase accountability. As a result of the changeover, 85 per cent of local expenditure will be controlled by central government – the amount financed by the community charge has now been removed from the PESC total of Scottish Office expenditure to emphasise its local nature. However, the new tax in practice is highly inelastic, since large percentage increases will be needed to finance modest improvements in local services. Small changes in government grant can, through the same gearing effect, produce massive variations in the level of the community charge. In practice, the complexity of the system, far from being reduced, has been increased, with thirty-four stages in the grant calculation. Evidence from the first round of community charges illustrates the confusion which still surrounds the issue.

In announcing the new Revenue Support Grant for 1989–90, the Secretary of State decided to release estimates of what the community charge should be, if councils spent according to need. Not only did this immediately breach the principle that the charge was a matter between a council and its electors, it also incorporated dubious assumptions, in particular that the level of exemptions and losses from community charges would be the same as for rates in 1988–9; and that authorities would not increase their expenditure more than 6 per cent, plus additional spending on community charge administration and school boards. The estimates were criticised widely in local government and, in the event, charges were on average 16 per cent higher. Budgets exceeded needs assessment by 6.5 per cent, compared with 3.8 per cent the previous year. In fact, no fewer than 59 of the 65 councils increased their spending by a greater percentage figure than the Government's provision, leading the Government to disown its previous position and argue that the needs assessment figures are not 'recommendations'.

There were several reasons for the excess over the government's predictions. No grant penalties were applied in the first year of the new system, 1989–90 and some authorities took advantage of this to make up lost revenue from previous years, or sanitise accounts subject for years to creative accounting. Some had wrongly assumed that there would be no penalties in the last year of the old system and had had to raise money from the community charge to make up the shortfall. Others found themselves with balances, which could be used to moderate the charge. Those councils which had increased rates the previous year benefitted from the general increase in business rates, since this was calculated on the basis of what each council had levied the previous year. This, of course, will no longer operate after the transitional period, when business rates become a fully nationally set tax.

Variations also result from accounting practices. The grant increase was just 5.5 per cent but directors of finance are required to give their best estimate of inflation for the coming year and many realistically put this higher than the governments prediction. This would push up charges for two reasons, cost increases of services and the shortfall of revenue caused by the pegging of the non-domestic rate at an unrealistically low level. Moreover, finance directors have to make realistic estimates of the level of non-payment and this tended to be higher than the Government's figure.

Variations were also caused by the introduction of 'safety nets' to modify the impact of the new grant system. The main effect of this was to reduce community charges in Strathclyde at the expense of all other regions. Glasgow particularly benefitted, with taxpayers saving £56 per head. By contrast,

Borders, Central and Grampian taxpayers faced increases of between £52 and £85 above what they would otherwise have paid.

An analysis of budgets in the first year of the new system showed as mixed and confusing picture as ever. While Labour councils did tend to spend over their needs assessment, Labour control was not clearly related to budgetary growth. Labour councils in Glasgow and Clydebank increased their budgets by 40 per cent and 38 per cent respectively, while Labour-controlled Falkirk and Lothian kept growth down to 4 per cent and 6 per cent. The relationship between growing needs, as determined by the government's formula, and growing budgets was very weak. Rather, increased budgets were a feature of all councils and those with historically low budgets were able to increase spending and still stay within their needs assessment.

There is no evidence, then, that the new system has increased either central government's capacity rationally to determine the 'needs' of local communities or the accountability of local expenditure decisions to the electorate. Rather, the field remains characterised by complexity and diversity defying attempts at rigid central control.

8

Challenging the Consensus – Scotland and the New Conservatism

Consensus and accommodation have been the distinguishing characteristics of Scottish territorial management for much of this century. As elsewhere in Britain, pronounced partisan conflict has coexisted with an acceptance of parliamentary sovereignty and a recognition of government's right to govern. The starkness of partisan debate, however, masked a broad similarity of policy approaches between Conservative and Labour Governments. These included full employment, acceptance of the role of trade unions, public ownership of basic services, state provision of social welfare requiring high levels of public expenditure and taxation, and a degree of state management of the economy (Kavanagh, 1987). Within the broad consensus on both political procedures and substantive policies, it was possible to accommodate Scottish particularism through the mechanisms of territorial management and accommodation which we have described. Distinct Scottish institutions were retained to deliver UK policies, Scotland was favoured in the distribution of public expenditure and minor policies changes could be made at the discretion of the Scottish Office.

The Conservative Government elected in 1979 deliberately set out to challenge the consensus (Kavanagh, 1987; Jenkins, 1989), with a blend of economic libertarianism and social authoritarianism. High public spending and taxation were seen as hindering economic growth, government intervention as a distortion of market forces, and bureaucratic provision of services as inefficient and unresponsive to consumer demands. The phrases 'nanny state' and 'dependency culture' encapsulated conventional Conservative wisdom about the shortcomings of the welfare state. The Conservative strategy reflected a body of doctrine known as the 'New Right' analysis, which brought together the economic ideas of monetarism associated with Milton Friedman and the critique of public provision developed by the public choice school of political economists in the United States. According to their prescription, public spending needed to be cut to allow a reduction in government borrowing, to create incentives for investment and work and to reduce the power of the public bureaucracy. Under Margaret Thatcher's leadership from 1975, the British Conservative Party came to combine these policies with a demand for increased spending and sterner policies for law and order and defence.

Inevitably this was to produce a series of conflicts with those institutions rooted in the old collectivist welfare consensus, notably trade unions and local authorities, as well as several of the public service professions. The Thatcher Government has also proved particularly intolerant of dissent, criticism and public displays of opposition and this has provoked a series of conflicts with professions and institutions, such as the universities, the BBC and local authorities, steeped in the liberal and pluralist assumptions of the post-war years. The new strategy has placed a severe strain on the mechanisms of governing Scotland. Under the old consensus, the adjustments to be made in policy or the mechanisms for delivering it in Scotland were marginal. Since 1979, a government has sought a radical transformation of Britain's economic and social order. Scotland is critical here in two respects. Firstly, it is widely assumed that support for collectivist provision and public services is stronger than in England, an assumption for which there is some evidence (see Chapter 9). Secondly, the Government elected in 1979 lacked either a parliamentary majority or plurality of the popular vote in Scotland and since then has steadily lost support. While opponents have used this as further evidence of the Government's lack of Scottish mandate, the Conservatives argue that the two are connected in a different way. Scots, they maintain, have become dependent on the 'nanny state' and it is this 'dependency culture' which is preventing them from appreciating the benefits of the new dispensation.

The principal policies to reflect the new approach have been expenditure reductions, privatisation, the promotion of 'consumer choice' in public services and an increased role for the market in allocating resources. While the Heath Government of the early 1970s had started out with similar intent, it failed to translate the broad ideas into action. In contrast, The Thatcher Government was able to develop policy instruments to affect incremental change (Pirie, 1988). Not all the goals of the programme have been met. We have already shown that the expenditure strategy was modified over the 1980s. While the national budget is in surplus, this is due to tax increases and privatisation rather than cuts in overall expenditure, which has continued to grow. Scotland has followed the overall central strategy.

Parry (1986) sees privatisation as a central element of Conservative strategy, seeking to promote private provision and consumption as a means of increasing consumer choice and reducing the load on the public sector. He sees this as a double challenge in Scotland because the ideology may be less acceptable than in England and because of the dominance of the public sector in the Scottish economy. The political right, for their part, see the underdeveloped Scottish private sector as an opportunity to advance their ideas. Parry (1986) also argues, as we have done so often in this book, that this involves applying policies worked out in the English context and, while there have been some minor differences, the question is often 'whether Scottish ministers wish to accelerate or retain an English-derived strategy'. We can identify four main aspects of the privatisation strategy; asset sales, private provision, contracting out, and increasing choice and user charges. None of the main cases of asset sales in the first two Thatcher terms had a particularly Scottish dimension but in the third term the privatisation of the Scottish bus group and the electricity boards have raised the Scottish issue. While the bus group was not privatised in 1986 like its English counterpart this proved to be merely a postponement. Plans were revealed in 1989 to sell it off in 1990 in the form of eleven separate companies. Given the separate organisation of electricity in Scotland, with two boards combining generation and distribution there was some speculation following the Conservatives' 1987 reverses in Scotland that the industry there might remain in public hands. In fact, by late

1989 Scottish electricity privatisation appeared to be going ahead more rapidly than in England. There have also been moves to privatise the National Engineering Laboratory at East Kilbride, which comes under the Department of Trade and Industry. Labour protests that the Government had no right to dispose of these assets in view of its electoral setback in 1987 were of no avail.

There has been increased emphasis on private provision in education, health, housing, social work and public transport. Health has been a main focus for action through the extension of private health insurance and private hospitals which had previously been of no significance in Scotland. Subscriptions to the private health insurance scheme BUPA increased by 49.6 per cent in Scotland between 1979 and 1984 (Donnelly, 1986). The government's proposals for an internal market in the National Health Service have been applied in Scotland as in England. In social work, the thrust has been to increase private residential homes. The new Social Security claims processing computer centre at Livingston has been handed over to a subsidiary of General Motors to run. Urban public transport was deregulated in 1986 as a result of a UK initiative from free marketeer Nicholas Ridley, then Minister of Transport. The legislation followed trials in England but there is no evidence that Scotland's peculiar problems – notably transport in the rural Highlands and the Glasgow conurbation – were taken into account. Rather, the Scottish Office acquiesced in the strategy set by the Department of Transport. The one difference in the application of the scheme in Scotland, the decision not to privatise the Scottish Bus Group, was emphasised by Ministers as evidence of their concern for Scottish conditions but was later reversed.

Contracting out involves using private firms to administer services while the broad policy decision on what services to provide and at what level remains with the public authorities. The intellectual case rests on the supposed greater efficiency of the private sector and the virtues of competition but it remains highly controversial. Studies on the efficiency of contracting out tend to be emotional and politically biased (Hartley, 1987), with examples selectively chosen to fit predetermined conclusions. It has nevertheless become a major element in government strategy.

Contracting out has been widely used by Central Government and its agencies. In the health services, though, progress was slower in Scotland than in England until the appointment, as Minister, of Michael Forsyth who had a political and professional interest in privatisation (Forsyth, 1983). For local government, the first moves began with the Local Government Planning and Land Act of 1980, a UK-wide piece of legislation which required local authority direct – labour activities (for construction and maintenance) to be put out to tender. A major review in 1985 led to the Department of the Environment issuing a consultation paper *Competition in the Provision of Local Authority Services,* which argued for an extension of competitive tendering. Legislation was finally passed in 1988 (Local Government Act, 1988). This contained two key provisions: the requirement on councils to put out a range of services to competitive tender; and restrictions on 'contract compliance' policies. The list of 'defined activities' for tendering were refuse collection, cleaning of buildings, street and other cleaning, catering in schools and elsewhere, ground maintenance and vehicle repair and maintenance. Sport and leisure management were added later. The tendering timetable allowed four years for completion of the process.

Contract compliance is the process whereby authorities limit their list of approved contractors to employers who meet specified standards with regard to employment or other practices. It is a means of using local government's purchasing power to secure policy goals going beyond its statutory functions and has been criticised as an abuse of power and a restriction on free competition. The 1988 Act specifies a list of non-commercial matters which local authorities must *not* take into account, including fair wages, sex equality, opportunities for the disabled, training ratios for apprentices, trade union recognition, use of South African goods and support for a political party.

In practice, Scottish local authorities' own in-house departments did well in the first round of contracts. Only four lost contracts in competition with outside contractors, the most significant being the building cleaning contracts in Tayside and Strathclyde. This certainly reflects a commitment within most councils to try and keep contracts in-house but legal challenges can be expected in the future. It is too early at the time of writing to evaluate the efficiency of the new arrangements.

Previous studies show that cost savings can accrue from contracting out and forcing in-house departments to reduce manning levels in order to compete. Critics, however, charge that much of the saving is at the expense of the workforce in the form of lower employment, reduced pay and fringe benefits; or achieved through a reduction in quality of service. Doubts have been raised about the capacity of slimmed-down local authority workforces to carry out existing levels of work unless dramatic improvements in productivity are made. There are additional bureaucratic costs in setting up arrangements for monitoring performance. Concerns have been expressed about the weakening of control and accountability and the ability of elected members to intervene to correct grievances on the part of their constituents.

In the early stages of privatisation, the Scottish Office was criticised for an excessive use of London-based advertisers and consultants. The increased pace, however, has provided more opportunities for Scottish-based consultants, stockbrokers, advisors and advertisers. While this has served to give a more Scottish flavour to the process and deflected some of the obvious criticisms, it has not, however, affected the basic policy.

The concern to increase consumer choice has been greatest in education and housing. The parents' charter sought to provide choice for parents by relaxing the rigidity of school catchment areas. School boards, with power over budgets and a significant say in staff appointments, are being established. More controversial is the proposal to allow individual schools to 'opt out' of the local authority system. This did not feature in the Conservatives' 1987 Scottish manifesto though it was promised for England. While this was initially seen as an example of Scottish ministers opting for a different approach, the policy was extended to Scotland after the election. Adler *et al.*, (1987) found that the parental choice legislation had severely curtailed the powers of education authorities. Most parents were aware of their new rights, though only a minority of parents, varying from 0 to 15 per cent, exercised the right, mainly in the cities. The main concern was to avoid particular schools rather than a comparison of the competing types of education offered.

The sale of council houses has generated heated conflict between local authorities and the government. Some authorities have sought to hinder the process or to dissuade tenants from purchase. Although in the 1980s there has been a growing bipartisan support for owner-occupation, the parties are divided on the means of achieving this, with the Conservatives committed to the compulsory disposal of council stock. In the latter part of the decade, the Government turned its attention to the management of public sector housing, attempting to break the bureaucratic centralism of the past by alternative forms of management such as cooperatives and housing associations and allowing private companies to take over the management of council housing.

The last element of the strategy is the increased recourse to user charges instead of taxation to finance public services. The argument here is that where services produce a direct benefit to an individual or household then the consumer should pay directly rather than be subsidised through taxation. Increased charges for leisure and recreation, school meals and planning applications have also been a means to relieve pressure on council budgets. Council house rents were forced up by 40 per cent in real terms over ten years in reponse to central government pressures (MacLennan, 1988).

Most of these innovations are too recent to allow serious evaluation of their impact on Scottish politics. There has been little public support for policies such as competitive tendering (Mori, 1985) or allowing schools to opt out of local government control (Scottish Local Government Information Unit, 1988). The response to this from the political right has been that the Government has not gone far enough in weaning the Scots from their dependency culture and that this explains the Conservatives' low standing in the Scottish polls. Their fortunes will only be improved with more of the same medicine. Such an argument is not only paradoxical, it does not fit with the facts. We have shown (Chapter 6) that Scotland has not been exempt from the overall expenditure strategy and this is true of the vast majority of the new reforms.

The professional community in education have seized on the origins of the new initiatives as a focus of opposition, complaining of the 'Englishing' of Scottish education(Scottish Centre for Social and Economic Research, 1989). Yet, previous major reforms such as the introduction of comprehensive schools in the 1960s were also British initiatives (Adler *et al.*, 1987). In both cases, it was the details and implementation of the policy which was Scottish. So Scottish Office minister Alex Fletcher promoted the legislation allowing parental choice of schools more aggressively than his English counterpart and later in the decade Michael Forsyth was more 'upbeat' in promoting the provision to allow schools to opt out of local authority control.

It seems therefore that there has been a whirlwind of legislative change but this should not lead us to believe that the Thatcher revolution is in place. Parry (1986) shows that Scotland continues to fall behind England in the uptake of private services whether in education, health, social services or housing. Ninety-six per cent of Scots still rely on public provision in health and education, a minority of parents have exercised choice in schools and a minority of council tenants have bought their homes. Central government's policies continue to conflict with the collectivist traditions of Scotland. Two policy areas deserve particular attention as they are fields in which Scotland has had distinctive traditions. They are also areas in which the Conservative Government has sought to make radical changes, away from the tradition of public sector dominance and towards the private market. These are housing and urban regeneration.

Housing Policies

Since the Royal Commission on the Housing of the Working Classes in 1917, there has been acceptance in Whitehall that Scotland's housing needs are both qualitatively and quantitatively different from England's. While legislation applying to Scottish housing has generally followed the English pattern, since the 1920s subsidies for building in the public sector have been higher, partly reflecting the additional costs involved and partly reflecting the relatively greater need. This, combined with local authorities subsidising rents from the rates, resulted in a much larger public sector and relatively low rents.

The implications of the large public sector housing stock in Scotland, which has been concentrated into single-tenure estates, has been far-reaching. Psephologists have identified housing tenure as one of the most significant correlates of voting behaviour (Heath, Jowell and Curtice, 1985; Rose and McAllister, 1986). While the causal relationship here is still unclear, this merely confirms what both Conservative and Labour politicians have long believed. During the 1960s and 1970s, Labour MPs would seek to have council estates located in their constituencies to boost their majorities and building council housing generally was seen as a means of consolidating the Labour vote in the cities. The policy of building low-income housing on greenfield sites on the urban periphery increased social segregation, with implications for other services, including education. School-building programmes took second place to house building in the post-war period and, the school intake in urban areas had a limited social mix (MacPherson and Raab, 1988). Economic planning, too, was affected by the siting of the housing schemes on the peripheries of the Scottish cities.

Yet, such was the pressure to build more houses to replace the inner city slums that successive governments, Conservative as well as Labour, relentlessly increased the number of public sector houses. James Stuart in the early 1950s had been a strong supporter of Harold MacMillan's drive, against Treasury wishes, to fund publicly a massive house-building programme. In the early 1960s, high-rise housing was promoted in Scotland as in England, though by the late 1960s the Scottish Office was beginning to turn against the idea. The solution to the housing shortage proved short-term for by the 1970s serious problems of deprivation were identified in the post-war housing estates while the quality of much of the housing itself was revealed as deplorable.

The turning point came with the publication in 1977 of the Labour Government's housing White Paper which optimistically asserted that the standard of housing in Scotland was higher than in England and that there was a decreasing need for public sector building (which had been in decline since 1970). Instead, there should be more emphasis on renovation and improvement. Clearly, the economic environment in which this review had taken place was important. Tony Crosland's warning to English local authorities in 1975 that the 'party's over' and the IMF intervention in 1976 provided an influential backdrop to expenditure on housing and public expenditure generally. The Green Paper made clear Labour's commitment to increase council rents, to encourage home ownership and improve the management of council housing. Commentators ranging from *Shelter* to *The Scotsman* remarked at the time that the proposals involved a major reversal of Labour's traditional position and the policies advocated would find support in the Conservative Party. As the Secretary of State's chief adviser on housing in the late 1970s later stated, the 1977 Green Paper 'might well have formed the basis of a tacitly agreed housing policy, and even if that is now unattainable the Green Paper's factual analysis of need is likely to remain the basis of official advice to Ministers on housing for some years to come' (Gillett, 1983, p.17).

Legislation in 1978 brought the multifarious grants to local authorities into a pooled Housing Support Grant which offered central government greater powers to determine the housing policies of local authorities. Council house sales were permitted in areas of housing surplus, council rents were pushed up and grants to improve the private sector increased. In line with the general move to policy planning, Housing Plans, formulated by councils and approved by the Scottish Office, became a central element of capital expenditure control. The Labour Government's housing policy was based on pragmatism bounded by the severe economic constraints which operated to prevent public expenditure increases. With its large capital element, housing provided an obvious target for a government looking for swift savings (see Chapter 5); a similar pattern followed in the 1980s.

In the early years of the Thatcher government, housing policy was distinguished from previous years by the clear ideological predisposition in favour of the private sector, with the pursuit of council sales as its centrepiece. Sales were encouraged with 'carrots' in the form of discounts and tax relief and 'sticks' in the form of increased rents and cuts in investment. Restrictions on the types of property for which discounts were available were removed and the amount of discount was progressively increased. Housing Support Grant was cut until only a handful of councils received any at all. The amount by which councils could subsidise rents from the rates was restricted, first by financial penalties and then by statute. As a result, council rents were forced up at a rate far higher than the level of inflation. Rents, which had constituted 47 per cent of the Housing Revenue Account in 1979–80 provided 88 per cent by 1987–88, having increased by half in real terms over the period. Cuts in capital expenditure on housing, which had started in 1977, were increased from 1979.

While the sales policy was identical in England and Scotland, it was much less successful in the latter. By 1988, just 5 per cent of the public stock had been sold in Scotland, compared with 15 per cent in England and Wales. Evidence from a Scottish Office survey (SOCRU, 1985) in the early 1980s showed, not surprisingly, that most of the sales were of houses rather than flats and concentrated in the better-off areas, especially the new towns.

Sales were lower in the urban areas of the central belt, in predominantly council estates and in high rise developments. While sales were extending owner-occupation down the social scale, this primarily affected skilled workers rather than un-skilled workers, the low paid or the unemployed. It was clear that, for a large part of Scotland' population, owner-occupation was ruled out because of low incomes, insecurity of employment or the undesirability as an investment of the council flats in which they were living.

By the late 1980s, the state of Scotland's housing was again becoming a major political issue. In 1987, the Convention of Scottish Local Authorities (COSLA) joined with the campaign Shelter to mark the International Year of the Homeless with a Housing Campaign. Under the heading *Scotland's Housing Crisis,* they called for more money for house building, for modernisation and for the special needs of the elderly, home-less, disabled and single. In November 1986, Glasgow District Council made its own contribution to the debate, with the report of the Grieve (1986) Committee on the city's housing, a hard-hitting document aimed as much at the Council's own record as at central government financial stringency. Scottish Office ministers nonetheless continued to defend their own spending record.

Determining just what is happening to Scottish public sector housing is not as easy as it might appear. The conventions of public expenditure accounting often serve to obscure more than they clarify, while creative accounting and other devices used by local authorities to evade central restrictions complicate matters further. An example of this was striking claim by the Secretary of State, when announcing capital spending for 1987–8, that, compared with 1979, total public investment in housing would more than double, from £337 million to £720 million. This total includes investment by local authorities, new towns, the Scottish Special Housing Association and the Housing Corporation covering new house building and renovation and grants to private owners for repairs and modernisation. The problem with the Secretary of State's claim, though, is that it ignores inflation and compares a *gross* expenditure target for 1987–8 with the *net* expenditure figure for 1979. The former is an obvious problem. The latter may need some explanation.

District councils in Scotland are given a 'net' allocation, or spending limit, for the HRA capital account (for council housing) but are permitted to add to this the proceeds from council house sales. This is less generous than it appears. The 'gross expenditure' figure given by the Scottish Office includes a substantial assumed figure for sales; so that councils must make up the difference between the net and the gross figures by meeting their sales targets. As a result of the curious accounting convention governing the disposal of public assets (in which they count as negative spending) it is the net figure which features in the Public Expenditure White Paper. The importance of this distinction becomes obvious when we note that, for 1987–8, the net capital expenditure figure is £548 million, but the gross figure is 'expected to top £720 million'.

An examination of the net expenditure and allocations for the period back to 1975 in constant price terms, shows that by 1987–8 there had been some recovery, to around the level of 1979–80 but that expenditure was running well below the levels of the mid 1970s. It is true, of course, that the gap between the net and the gross figures was less important in the mid 1970s (when council house sales were small) than in the late 1980s but, even if we generously assume that there were *no* capital receipts in before 1980 and that councils manage to meet *all* the Scottish Office target for sales in 1987–8, total public capital spending on housing was still below the 1976–7 levels in real terms. It was, on the other hand, some 20 per cent up on the 1979 figure – a significant increase but well short of the Secretary of State's claim of doubled expenditure.

For spending by local councils alone, there is a more consistent set of data, giving gross allocations back to 1975–6. Again, the late 1980s saw a recovery, with total spending back at the real levels of 1978–9 but well below the levels of the mid 1970s. Investment in council housing remained below the levels inherited by the government in 1979, though recovering from the trough of 1984 (when some councils lost allocations under the penalty system because of unwillingness to put up rents to cut their rate contributions). These gross allocation figures are dependent on councils meeting sales targets and, given the state of council housing in many parts of Scotland, together with problems of unemployment and low incomes, this is a large assumption. So capital spending levels in practice might be lower than planned unless additional allocations are approved by government.

There was in the early 1980s a substantial increase in the allocation of grants to private owners but this tailed off after the

1983 election, reviving somewhat in time for the 1987 election. This reflects government policies of encouraging the private, against the public sector.

House building has fallen away sharply in the Scottish public sector, particularly for local authorities, since the mid 1970s. So, while local authorities were building nearly half of the houses completed in 1976 and the public sector as a whole accounted for over 60 per cent, by 1985 these figures were down to 11 per cent and 21 per cent respectively. Private building, meanwhile, remained steady, recovering from a slight fall in the early 1980s. Together with the sale of council, new town and Scottish Special Housing Association houses, this has had an obvious effect. In December 1985 the Scottish Office was able to announce that, for the first time since the late 1960s, Scotland had more houses in the private sector than in the public, though this was done by counting publicly financed housing association houses in the private sector.

A few innovative policies were perused but not in any comprehensive manner. Parts of Glasgow benefited from government support funded by the Housing Corporation and channelled through housing associations which redeveloped old tenemental properties. The housing association movement never quite took off in other parts of Scotland as it did in Glasgow where community-based Associations assiduously transformed the appearance of many previously depressed areas. Glasgow District Council negotiated with the Scottish Office and Treasury to be able to establish housing cooperatives in some of the most depressed parts of peripheral schemes (Ospina, 1987). These involved transferring ownership of houses collectively to the tenants, who would manage them cooperatively. The motive was both ideological and financial, to promote new forms of tenure, breaking with the bureaucratic centralism of the past, and to allow the tenants to tap the improvement grants available for the private sector. Potentially, this was an idea capable of bridging the ideological divide which had has been such a marked feature of Scottish housing policy. For the Conservative Government, it offered the prospect of demunicipalisation of part of the housing stock. For the left, it could be presented as an alternative to individual house sales and firmly within the socialist tradition of cooperation. In practice, there were many obstacles in the way of the scheme. While some of these originated in the Scottish Office, most were the result of Treasury rules (Keating, 1988a).

A sharp change in Government attitudes to housing and urban affairs became evident towards the end of Mrs Thatcher's second term. In May 1987, the Scottish Development Department published a discussion document, *Scottish Homes: a New Agency for Housing in Scotland*. This was followed in November with the publication of a White Paper, *Housing: The Government's Proposals for Scotland* (November 1987, CM 242). The origins of the proposals are difficult to trace. Mrs Thatcher took an interest in housing and urban affairs following the June 1987 election and was reportedly chairing a Cabinet committee on housing policy in October 1987 (*The Times*, 21 October 1987). Certainly the thrust of the housing policy for England outlined in the English White Paper (November 1987, CM 214) was similar to the Scottish proposals though the institutional arrangements proposed differed and in England emphasis shifted more strongly away from sales. The new slogan became the 'right to rent' referring to the Government's intention to revive the private rented sector. To a large extent this was motivated by recognition that there was little scope for extending home ownership, especially through council house sales, in England (Murie *et al.*, 1988).

Institutionally, the Government proposed the creation of a new body, Scottish Homes, amalgamating the Scottish special Housing Association (SSHA) and the Housing Corporation in Scotland. The SSHA had been established in 1937 as a means by which central government could directly intervene in housing without having to act through local authorities. Initially seen as building working-class housing in special areas, suffering from severe economic malaise (Begg, 1987), it had developed into a substantial landlord with 78,000 houses in January 1989. The Housing Corporation was set up in 1964, with its functions broadened in 1974 and 1980, and was responsible for registering, funding and supervising housing associations throughout Britain. Scottish Homes, which came into being in April 1989, was seen as more than just combining the functions of the two existing organisations in one body. Its wider remit was to act in a strategic capacity overseeing the implementation of the Government's objectives.

Four objectives were set out in the White Paper: to encourage increased home ownership, to revitalise the private rented sector, to diminish the role of public sector landlords and encourage diversified tenure, and to provide the financial framework to increase the role of the private sector. New private tenancies, brought into being under Part II of the Housing (Scotland) Act 1988, are freely negotiated between tenant and landlord and may either offer security of tenure without rent control or contractual lease with some measure of rent control. Fiscal incentives to companies, particularly under the extension of the Business Expansion Scheme to rented properties in the 1988 budget, have encouraged a plethora of companies to become involved in offering 'assured tenancies' (*Scottish Business Insider*, vol.6, no.3, March 1989).

The most controversial of the new arrangements included in the legislative package was provision for transfer of tenancy, which has become known as the 'Pick a Landlord' scheme. This permitted tenants to transfer *en bloc* from the public sector – though not *vice versa*. The operation of this measure has been strongly criticised by tenants groups which note that, in contrast to the English scheme, ballots are not necessary in determining the views of the tenants and that a majority of tenants are not needed in any scheme for it to be transferred. The Secretary of State's refusal to approve transfers will only be applied when he believes that 'a majority of tenants affected oppose the proposal'. This is in line with the English scheme in which tenants abstaining in the ballot are counted as voting for change.

Housing policy over the last decade has undergone a change which can best be described as decremental, involving a slow but steady reduction of the role of local government in housing. This follows British policy lines but the impact on Scotland has been different to that south of the border because of the differing conditions and institutions. A major redistribution in the allocation of public expenditure on housing has resulted from cuts in Housing Support Grant, limitations on capital expenditure, increased subsidies and grants to home-buyers and those in the private sector seeking to improve their homes. The process has been described as residualisation, meaning that such housing is becoming the tenure 'choice' only of those who have no choice, concentrating the least well-off and least powerful sections of the population in the remaining, least desirable stock (Malpass and Murie, 1987). This is a substantial segment of the Scottish population. Even with 150,000 council houses sold between April 1979 and May 1989 and few new houses built the public sector still constitutes over 45 per cent of the total housing stock. Indeed, the great weakness in government strategy is the marginality of the policies in relation to the ambition of the overall goals. It concentrates on the minority of tenants able to buy their own homes at discounted prices, rather than the needs of the majority, while increasing rents and cutting benefits. It is thus further evidence of the increased social and political division in Scotland in the 1980s. The policies are also marginal in terms of the government's objective of a radical change in Scotland's tradition of public ownership of housing.

Urban Regeneration

Urban planning and regeneration policy is one area in which the distinctive Scottish arrangements for policy formulation and implementation have attracted attention. From the Second World War, a number of innovations in planning were pioneered in Scotland so that, by the early 1970s, the machinery was in place for a coordinated governmental attack on the syndrome of urban decline, drawing on the resources and powers of all the agencies involved. Since then, this cohesive approach has progressively disintegrated under the impact of the new Conservatism with its stress on privatisation and selective economic renewal.

For some thirty years after the Second World War, a remarkable degree of consistency in Scottish Office urban and regional planning policy was maintained by a group of civil servants in the Scottish Development Department (before 1962, the Department of Health for Scotland) (Smith and Wannop, 1985; Keating and Carter, 1987). These were committed to publicly-led planning on a regional basis and were preoccupied above all with the problems of Glasgow, which was identified after the War as the worst-housed city in Europe. Policy in practice reflected a tension between this bureaucratic elite and the municipal Labour establishment, particularly in Glasgow. Under Conservative governments, the role of ministers was to arbitrate this conflict and to negotiate with Treasury and, less frequently, other government departments, for the freedom and resources to pursue the Scottish policy line. Labour ministers were more engaged in policy-making but even they tended to be at one remove from the municipal Labour establishment.

Although nearly all Glasgow and a majority of Scottish Labour MPs were former municipal councillors, none of them served as Scottish Office ministers before the late 1970s (Keating *et al.*, 1989). As for the private sector, this was largely absent as a factor in urban policy-making after the decline of Scottish indigenous capitalism following the First World War.

Policy in the post-war years was dominated by the question of housing, especially in Glasgow. Scottish Office strategy, sold to successive Labour and Conservative ministers, was based on the philosophy of the 1946 Clyde Valley Regional Plan's proposals for reducing urban populations through overspill, limiting urban growth by green belts and accommodating the displaced populations in new towns beyond the green belt (CVRPAC, 1946). Industry, too, would be relocated along with population. Glasgow's Labour Administration had initially rejected this philosophy, fearing the loss of population and with it the title of second city of the Empire, as well as rateable value. Glasgow's own initial planning exercise, the Bruce (1946) Plan, insisted that the city's population could be rehoused within existing boundaries, by building at high density and right up to the boundary. By the early 1950s, Glasgow had formally accepted overspill but in practice the tensions continued, as pressure for housing overwhelmed the programme and the city gradually persuaded the Scottish Office to abandon almost the whole of the green belt land within the city boundary. The result was the creation in Glasgow and in other cities of Scotland of huge peripheral housing estates consisting entirely of council housing and in which social amenities and local employment were seriously lacking. Much of the discredited Bruce Plan was, in practice, implemented in Glasgow (Keating, 1988a) and imitated elsewhere. As pressure on the housing supply continued and new building was dominated by local government, allocation of low-rent housing became both a form of collective patronage for the Labour Party and an element of individual patronage by councillors.

By the late 1950s, pressure on house-building was further increased by schemes for urban renewal. The characteristic device, again particularly in Glasgow, was the Comprehensive Development Area (CDA) in which whole neighbourhoods were demolished and rebuilt to plan. The CDA approach was supported by both central and local government with few dissenting voices. By the late 1960s, the Scottish Office, along with the rest of central government, was turning against the idea of high-rise development but it was some years before city governments changed tack.

In the 1970s, the focus of urban regeneration policy in Scotland, as in Britian as a whole (and indeed, other countries), shifted from physical renewal to a concern with social problems summed up in the phrase 'the rediscovery of poverty'. A series of reports (Glasgow, 1972; WCSP, 1974; Strathclyde, 1977) catalogued the extent of multiple deprivation in urban Scotland, showing that it extended well beyond the slum inner-city neighbourhoods scheduled for comprehensive physical redevelopment. Indeed, to the embarrassment of local Labour elites, some of the worst problems were from the start identified in the post-war peripheral housing estates.

At the same time, the Scottish Office was moving into the economic field, with the revival of regional policies in the 1960s and the strengthening of its economic responsibilities. The result was a reassertion of the planning tradition which had been kept alive in the Scottish Office while regional planning in England had declined in the 1950s. The Scottish Office was thus first in the field with the regional plans of the 1960s, the White Paper on Central Scotland (1962) and a series of subregional planning exercises culminating in the West Central Scotland Plan which appeared in 1974. The philosophy reflected current professional thinking about the need for comprehensive regional planning, embracing cities and their hinterlands, for the integration of physical, social and economic regeneration policies, and for the combination of the efforts of central and local government behind agreed development objectives. Accordingly, the subregional plans emphasised combatting poverty, economic development and physical renewal as elements in a single strategy of urban and regional regeneration. Essential to the implementation of this vision, according to officials in the SDD, was a reformed local government system which would encompass the regional dimension and unite urban and rural areas (see Chapter 6).

By the mid 1970s, then, the machinery was in place for a comprehensive, state-directed attack on Scotland's urban problems, in their physical, economic and social manifestations. A single central government department, the Scottish Office, was responsible for physical planning, housing, transport, social work, health, economic development and (jointly with the

Department of Trade and Industry) regional policy. This, it has
been claimed helps eliminate the inter-departmental rivalries
which have bedevilled central government's efforts at urban
renewal in England (Morison, 1987). There were regional
councils with widely drawn boundaries (especially in Strathclyde) and the major functions including education, social work,
police, highways and transport, which were responsible for
producing plans and had large revenue and capital budgets to
give their plans effect. Their widely drawn boundaries and
extensive functions avoided some of the weaknesses of the
English metropolitan counties. Finally, there was the Scottish
Development Agency, with broad powers in environmental
renewal and industrial intervention.

Together with the district councils, whose primary responsibilities were for housing and local planning, the new-town
development corporations and the Scottish Special Housing
Association, these agencies formed the Scottish urban policy
network. It would be a mistake to exaggerate the cohesiveness
of the network or the tidyness of the administrative arrangements. The division of planning powers between region and
district was always a potential source of conflict, as was the
separation of responsibility for housing from strategic planning
and social work. The allocation of land renewal powers to the
SDA removed from regional control an important instrument
for implementing regeneration policies and priorities. The
differing spatial priorities of the various agencies were to be the
cause of some tension over the years. The test of the system
would be whether these differences could be successfully
negotiated to produce workable strategies.

The first such test came in the mid 1970s with a shift in
priorities in urban policy, for Britian as a whole, away from
overspill and new towns, and towards inner-city regeneration.
This policy shift, signalled by the Scottish Office in 1976, was
welcome to urban councils with its promise of extra resources.
On the other hand, in launching its showpiece of inner urban
regeneration, the Glasgow Eastern Area Renewal (GEAR)
project, the Scottish Office by-passed local government, still
distrusting the municipal Labour elite, and gave the task of
coordination to the SDA. The Agency was to lead the project,
with inputs from regional and district councils, the health board,
the Scottish Special Housing Association, the Manpower Services Commission and the Scottish Office itself. Hailed in 1976

as the largest integrated urban renewal project in Europe, this was to be a comprehensive attack on physical, economic, and social decline in the old East End of the inner city.

There is no doubt that the GEAR project resulted in high levels of public spending in the East End, where capital investment per head by all agencies between 1979–80 and 1983–4 was £2415, against a city average of £937. Figures for 1984–5, produced on a slightly different basis, show the GEAR area gaining £1433 per head in investment, against a city average of £492 (Glasgow, 1984). Nairn (1983) found that £48.6 million or 31 per cent of the expenditure in the GEAR project between 1977 and 1982 could be considered 'extra', attributable to the project; in addition, £19 million in private housing investment would not have taken place in its absence. Between 1979 in 1985, the GEAR area, with 6 per cent of the city's population, accounted for 53.2 per cent of public-sector housing expenditure in priority areas. The key role of Government intervention in pulling around the East End is indicated by the fact that, of the total investment of £500 million in the area between 1977 and 1986, three-fifths was from the public sector (Scottish Office, 1988).

On the other hand, there has been criticism that, rather than an integrated project, the GEAR project has amounted simply to a set of spatial spending priorities for the participating agencies. Despite the ambition of a comprehensive, goal-oriented programme, the overall objectives were not produced until four years into the project and were of such generality as to be little use as a guide to action. The lack of linkage of social, economic and spatial priorities is shown in the fact that less than half the new jobs have gone to East End residents and very few to the long-term unemployed or deprived (McArthur, 1987). Community activists in the area attribute this to the centralist, agency-led structure of the initiative, with participation by the local residents reduced to mere tokenism. Although the lack of participation identified by Nelson (1980) may have been remedied to some degree in the later stages of the project (Wannop and Leclerc, 1987), there has been a continued absence of linkage policies to ensure that the benefits of the economic programmes go to the neediest individuals.

It is beyond the scope of this book to evaluate the overall success of the GEAR project (see Donnison and Middleton, 1987; Keating and Boyle, 1985). Any possibility of substantial

improvement in economic and industrial conditions was overwhelmed by the national recession of the 1980s, and progress
tended to take the form of separate programmes for each
participating agency rather than adherence to an overall plan.
Nevertheless, GEAR did represent a major targetting of
resources by public agencies in a selected area and a format for
protecting plans against arbitrary cuts (Keating, 1988a). As a
model for inter-agency comprehensive renewal, it clearly had a
good deal of potential.

GEAR, however, was to represent the high point of integration in urban renewal. Instead of being built on, the model was
to give way to a more functionally disaggregated approach, at
the risk of losing the advantages of integration which the
Scottish administrative structure can potentially offer. The SDA
had been sent into GEAR by the Scottish Office almost
immediately upon its establishment but, by the early 1980s, had
begun to develop its own strategic priorities. These were to
focus on economic and industrial development; in particular, the
Agency wanted to abandon the social policy role which its
leadership in GEAR had obliged it to assume and which it
regarded as a diversion from its main task. So, in parallel with
its sectoral initiatives, the SDA followed two 'task force'
interventions at Glengarnock and Clydebank with a series of
'area projects', joint programmes of economic regeneration
negotiated with regional and district councils. For its part, the
Scottish Office, while approving of the idea in principle, was
able to disengage itself from direct involvement. Another
advantage for the SDA in formalising its area approach in a
forward programme was that it enabled it to resist Scottish
Office pressure to move into any area hit by the wave of
closures in the early 1980s recession.

Area projects were not comprehensive urban policies, limited,
as they were, to the economic sphere, but they did allow a
degree of economic interventionism and spatial planning which
stood in contrast to the avowedly non-interventionist approach
of the post-1979 Conservative government. This was characteristic of the Scottish Office style under George Younger,
implementing in Scotland the broad lines of Conservative policy
but maintaining and extending the specifically Scottish instruments of intervention.

For their part, local councils accepted the area initiative
approach as a mechanism for obtaining SDA resources at a time

of overall cutback. This allowed the Agency considerable policy leverage since, before allocating resources to projects, it could require policy concessions from the regional and district councils. The first of the new-style area projects was at Leith, an area of Edinburgh ripe for gentrification and fairly easily brought back to life. The first area project in Strathclyde was in Motherwell, an area featuring on the regional council's list of economic priority areas and threatened by the possible closure of the Ravenscraig steel plant. With a sense for geographical/ political balance, the SDA next went to Dundee, where it established two projects. One, in the Blackness area, was a small-scale industrial improvement operation. The second, for the waterfront area, soon expanded into a project for the whole city. This had the advantage of allowing the SDA to negotiate on a broad front with both Tayside Region and Dundee District and integrate all efforts to promote the city's economy under its leadership. Dundee District did not see things quite this way and sought to preserve its own economic development effort independent of the project but a project agreement was finally signed in 1982. Projects followed at Coatbridge, Arbroath, Kilmarnock, Wigtown and Denny and Bonnybridge (Keating and Boyle, 1986). While all were based on formal project agreements, each initiative was different, reflecting the peculiar circumstances of each area and the different agencies involved. There were considerable differences in scale, from small industrial improvement projects to efforts to promote whole cities. Leadership, too, varied. In the early projects, the SDA took the lead but ministers were never happy with major managerial responsibilities appearing to rest with public authorities and progressively encouraged the private sector to take the lead.

The negotiation of area projects with local councils was not always harmonious, given the differences in priorities and policies. The resulting tension could, however, be creative, opening up issues which otherwise might not have reached the political agenda. For example, in connection with arrangements for the 1988 Garden Festival, the SDA was able to persuade Glasgow District Council to make a breach in its policy of not disposing of land to private developers. On the other hand, the pattern of Agency intervention meant that structure plans, at one time intended as the basis for comprehensive land-use strategies, were increasingly by-passed and became little more than vehicles for restricting suburban housing development and out-of-town retailing.

There was also an increasing divorce between the social priorities set out in strategies for tackling urban deprivation and priorities for economic regeneration. The tension between urban regeneration as a 'distressed areas policy' aimed at places with the most acute social and economic problems and regeneration as a contribution to national economic recovery, was present from the outset. It is summed up in the dilemma as to whether the SDA should put its resources into areas of greatest need or those of greatest potential. For some time, the issue was side-stepped with a formula that initiatives would be sited in areas where the gap between performance and potential was greatest, allowing both criteria to be used. Increasingly, the criterion of economic potential became dominant as local councils were displaced as privileged partners by the private sector. This was a response to a more hard-headed commercial approach within the SDA itself, as well as the needs of organisational survival in the political climate of the mid-1980s. Under constant pressure from London departments and the Treasury, the Agency had to demonstrate that it was not a mechanism for 'backdoor nationalisation', for propping up lame duck industries or for sustaining areas doomed by the market to decline. By 1986, the Agency, in a management review, was able to demonstrate its hard-headed approach to the satisfaction not only of the Scottish Office but of the Treasury.

The view of contemporary Conservatism regarding the urban problem is that, like other social and economic ills, it is largely caused by too much government intervention and spending. The solution is to relax planning restraints, cut public expenditure and local taxation and generally encourage markets. In the early years of the Thatcher Administration, this philosophy had little impact on urban regeneration in Scotland. Attempts to privatise the investment function having failed, a new body, Scottish Development Finance Ltd., was set up within the Agency to involve businessmen directly in the decisions. New guidelines were issued, removing the requirement to create jobs and substituting that of providing 'stable and productive employment'. Later, the industrial investment function was run down but attempts by Whitehall departments to curtail the independent Scottish effort to attract inward investment were largely unsuccessful. With the continuation of GEAR, the development

of the area approach and a Scottish Office still prepared to fight
in Cabinet to preserve threatened industries, though, there was
no radical break with the past. In the late 1980s, all this
changed. Within the Scottish Office, ministers appeared determined to apply the new market approach to urban renewal
while the SDA had itself been moving in that direction.

The more commercial approach had important sectoral and
spatial implications. It meant a tilt of policy away from
manufacturing industry, seen in the 1980s as a sector in decline,
and towards commercial and service activities; and a tilt away
from distressed communities toward commercial opportunities in
city-centre and waterfront locations, including an extensive role
in property development. This went along with, and was
encouraged by, a degree of privatisation, with a greater business
input to decision-making and a policy, in the later area
initiatives, of encouraging the private sector rather than the
SDA itself to take the lead role. Much of this was consciously
based on American models of urban regeneration in cities such
as Pittsburgh and Baltimore, where there is a tradition of
combining public powers and finance with business objectives in
city-centre revival. Yet, in much of urban Scotland, the
indigenous business community, which might respond to these
initiatives, has been lacking ever since the demise of Scottish
capitalism after the First World War. Even in central Glasgow,
the SDA had itself to invent and fund a business organisation,
Glasgow Action. Most of the resulting initiatives have relied
heavily on public funding.

Local authorities in many English cities had developed
ambitious economic development strategies in the early 1980s.
Scottish local authorities were slower to take up the issue, with
the exception of Strathclyde, which had declared combatting
unemployment as one of its two corporate priorities – along
with combatting urban deprivation – from the beginning. Even
Strathclyde did not attempt the ambitious interventionist strategies such as those found in the West Midlands, Greater London
or Sheffield. There are several reasons for this. Scottish regional
councils, unlike the former metropolitan counties, have heavy
service responsibilities and few spare resources. There was also
a more traditional view of the role of local government and
great caution about risking public money. Perhaps the most
important reason, however, was the existence of the SDA itself,
with its extensive environmental and industrial responsibilities.

In the context of area projects for regeneration, it seemed to make sense of local government to concentrate on its functional responsibilities in service provision and infrastructure and the SDA on its role in economic regeneration and land renewal. So regional and district councils put their efforts into attracting SDA funding and into providing the complementary resources (Keating and Boyle, 1986).

This has meant, however, that, as SDA regeneration priorities have shifted, so have local government's, with an increasing emphasis on city-centre and waterfront commercial development through subsidies to the private business sector. Examples of successful ventures are quite plentiful. In one of the earliest schemes, Leith was revitalised, gentrified and turned into a place for fashionable living. A similar treatment was later given to Glasgow's Merchant City. The Scottish Exhibition and Conference Centre was built in Glasgow in the early 1980s, financed jointly by the SDA, the two local councils and the private sector but with an arrangement whereby most of the public capital is effectively written off while the private sector obtains a dividend on its investment. When the Centre encountered difficulties, the Scottish Office provided a further boost with substantial grant to build a luxury hotel adjacent to it. Over the river was the site of the 1988 Glasgow Garden Festival, intended as a 'shop window' for local business and a means of attracting visitors to the city. This was achieved through large-scale spending by the SDA, as well as the regional and district councils. At the end of the festival, the exhibition was dismantled and the land handed back to the developers from whom it had been acquired. The St Enoch shopping centre in central Glasgow was also sponsored by the SDA and later developed with private capital. Local councils, for their part, have launched campaigns for civic 'boosterism', extolling the quality of life in Glasgow, Edinburgh or Dundee. As a result, there has been a visible improvement in conditions in Scotland's city centres, notably in Glasgow, which is cited internationally as a successful example of urban renaissance (Keating 1988a)

The peripheral housing estates, on the other hand, have suffered severely from the selective cutbacks in public expenditure which we have examined earlier. Consisting almost exclusively of council housing, they have been penalised by policies which reduce council housing subsidies and restrict capital expenditure on improvement, while tax relief for owner oc-

cupiers continues to rise with inflation. As the SDA has
progressively redefined its role, first as purely economic to
exclude social considerations and then as market-led, it has
found good reason not to place its own resources there,
although by the late 1980s it was involved in Government's
assault on municipal housing. Cuts in social security payments,
for their part, have reduced the amount of cash circulating in
the local economies still further. So spatial inequality within
Scotland's cities has increased as policies have impacted une-
venly upon a spatially segregated urban structure. Largely
written off as areas of economic potential, the peripheral
housing schemes and other deprived areas have had to depend
on social policy initiatives aimed at alleviating poverty. Strathclyde Region has a fairly elaborate social strategy which
identifies needy areas and prescribes positive discrimination in
their favour in the allocation of revenue and capital expenditure. Yet, as we have seen earlier, the real scope for
reallocating resources in local government is limited by statutory
commitments, shortage of resources and central restrictions on
local taxation and spending levels. Indeed, Strathclyde's own
review of social strategy showed that little movement in
mainstream provision had occurred, forcing them to rely heavily
on Urban Programme funding to develop their policies. In
addition, there have been efforts to mount new types of
programme, breaking down the barriers between local government professions to address the needs of people in deprived
communities. While these efforts have included the promotion
of 'community business', small scale enterprises trading locally,
they have increasingly been divorced from mainstream economic
interventions.

This pattern of uneven urban development has not become
the major political issue which it might have, given the move
away from the ideal of comprehensive planning and the
reduction of the local government role. There are several
reasons for a reluctance on the part of local government to
criticise the direction of SDA and central government intervention policies. One is that the opportunity cost of SDA
intervention for a particular city is effectively zero, because the
resources otherwise would be spent elsewhere in Scotland.
Therefore any agency intervention is regarded as positive by the
individual local authority. With the fiscal squeeze, councils need
to lever every pound they can from other agencies almost

regardless of the policy concessions needed. (In a parallel case, the Manpower Services Commission, by instituting a competitive bidding for limited funds for a Technical and Vocational Education Initiative, induced several local councils to make inroads into the principle of comprehensive education.) Also, economic and commercial development can, in Scotland as elsewhere, be presented as the interest of the whole city, as a neutral good for which the city is obliged to strive (Peterson, 1981). The distribution of its benefits can, it is argued, be treated as a separate issue, falling within the province of social policy.

Yet serious questions must be posed about the pattern of policy in late 1980s Scotland. Paying public money to subsidise private enterprise in the most buoyant sectors of the economy, while justified by the philosophy of going with markets rather than against them, is in reality quite inconsistent with government's professed aim of restoring market discipline and reducing the role of government in the economy. It also has serious distributional consequences, since taxpayers are being required to subsidise the owners of private business. Another question concerns, the manufacturing base of Scottish cities. Nearly all the regional development measures of the 1960s and 1970s were focused on bringing manufacturing industry to Scotland as the basis for economic regeneration yet, in the recession of the 1980s, most of these ventures were allowed to go under. Central government policy, in so far as a consistent purpose can be discerned, has been based on the assumption that a large manufacturing sector is not necessary and that the UK can survive economically on the basis of service industries. This thinking appears to draw almost exclusively on conditions in the south of England and the assumption that its experience can be replicated elsewhere. Yet, without a substantial local manufacturing base, Scotland's cities, remote from the main centres of Europe, will have nothing to service. The lack of a real indigenous business sector outside a limited range of central city commercial activities raises further problems for a strategy based on privatisation and explains the large public role in financing and organising many of the measures. Most serious of all, there are clear distributional consequences in an urban renewal strategy focused on central city commercial activities. Without positive linkage policies, there is no guarantee that such measures will benefit the long-term unemployed or the inhabitants of the peripheral housing estates. Yet the underlying philosophy of recent policies is that of the 'trickle-down effect', that the benefits of city centre and commercial development will filter through to the needy population.

The transition of urban regeneration policy from comprehensive renewal to downtown business development is a familiar theme of urban politics literature in the United States. Stone (1987) presents a threefold classification of renewal strategies which is relevant to this, as follows:

1. *Use of public authority and resources to further equality*

2. *Reliance on free market transactions*

3. *Use of public authority and resources to subsidise investment*

The first strategy corresponds to an urban renewal strategy based on social objectives aimed at relieving deprivation, such as was pursued in Scotland and other parts of urban Britian in the 1970s. The second refers to a genuine free-market strategy. The third involves a strategy in which business may set the goals of policy but the public sector subsidises it. This last is the strategy which increasingly prevails in Scotland.

The social implications of this are considerable. The limited economic revival of the late 1980s passed large parts of urban Scotland by. While unemployment levels began to fall from 1985, albeit more slowly than in the rest of Britain, in Glasgow's peripheral housing estates it remained static or increased (Keating, 1989a). Policymakers have not abandoned the urban periphery altogether. Joint social and economic initiatives were launched in 1986 by the regional and district councils for the Easterhouse and Drumchapel estates. In principle, these were intended to be comprehensive approaches on the lines of the GEAR project, with a substantial participation by the communities themselves in determining their future. The SDA, however, made it clear that it did not regard the periphery as one of its priorities, given the lack of economic 'potential'. and restricted its input to some small support for community business and some intervention in the property market in demunicipalised housing. The Scottish Office provided input only where it was consistent with its objective of breaking local authority housing monopolies. The regional and district councils themselves were unable to provide any extra resources, because of central government expenditure restrictions, though there was some re-labelling of existing activities. Without a major contribution from central government and its agencies, the emphasis of the initiatives was inevitably pushed towards a purely social one (Keating and Mitchell, 1987), using the powers and resources of the region and the district.

Later, the Scottish Office (1988) published its own document, *New Life for Urban Scotland*, the counterpart to the English *Action for Cities*, which was criticised widely for its failure to offer anything new. *New Life for Urban Scotland* gave a great deal of credit to central government for existing urban initiatives in Scotland, including those of local authorities, but did recognise that the peripheral estates should henceforth figure among urban renewal priorities. Four pilot schemes were proposed in peripheral estates, and these, in language reminiscent of the GEAR project, 'will simultaneously pursue economic, environmental and social objectives' (Scottish Office, 1988, p. 12). There would be extended privatisation of housing and some intervention by a central agency, Scottish Homes, formed from a merger of the Scottish Special Housing Association and the Housing Corporation (responsible for sponsoring cooperative housing associations). In line with current philosophy, the emphasis was placed on the potential of the private sector to accomplish urban regeneration and no new public resources are promised. Again, it seems likely that policy will treat the estates, built as mere dormitories, as discreet social and economic entities, whose problems can be solved within their own boundaries, rather than reintegrating them into the wider regional economic and social system. The emphasis on private sector leadership is particularly unrealistic given the absence of indigenous business or substantial purchasing power in the estates.

Urban regeneration policy has thus moved a long way since the visions of integrated urban renewal, involving central-local partnership and a simultaneous attack on physical, social and economic ills. In the new dispensation, economic development is seen as primarily the task of the private sector, albeit with generous public subsidies, distributed by central government and the SDA or its successor organisation. Its focus is on areas of maximum market potential, mainly commercial and service activities in the urban centres. The problems of deprived communities are now conceptualised as a 'social' issue, to be handled by the social security system and by local authorities, on a strictly limited resource base.

There is nothing specifically Scottish about this. Despite the existence of the Scottish Office and the Scottish Development Agency, policy in Scotland has followed the same broad lines as that in England, albeit with institutional modifications. The tradition of integrated regional planning and public sector leadership in urban development which was characteristic of Scotland for much of the post-Second World War period has largely disappeared in favour of a more fragmented approach and the encouragement of private initiative. This again reflects the influence of the New Conservatism rather than any Scottish factor. The impact of policy, however, differs in Scotland. The weakness of the private business sector has meant that private sector leadership has had to be spurred by public agencies and underwritten with public funds.

Conclusion

This survey of major government policy initiatives since 1979 shows that the central elements of the Conservative programme have been applied in Scotland as in England. Scotland has not been exempt from the new dispensation, nor have Scottish ministers been in the lead in forging new policy lines. Rather, policy leadership from England has continued and, where they have had discretion, Scottish ministers have taken their cues from the general ideological climate in government. While this represents a break from the consensus policies of the past, there is still a significant degree of consensus on the major issues in Scotland. This is because, among the opposition parties which command the large majority of popular support in Scotland, there is a wide consensus on domestic social and economic issues. Labour's return to the centre ground and the SNP's adoption of a social democratic platform has confirmed this. The partisan division between government and opposition is thus reinforced by the Scottish dimension, with a minority government based south of the border opposed by parties which together gained 76 per cent of the vote at the 1987 General Election. This poses further strain on the Union and it is to this question that we turn in our final chapter.

9

A Union Under Stress

Interpretations of Scottish Politics

We noted in the first chapter that Scotland's position within the United Kingdom was difficult to describe using the familiar categories of political science. It is undeniably 'different' in ways which we have explored, yet it remains part of a unitary state and political system. The problem lies in the nature of the British state itself and its gradual evolution over time in response to immediate, pragmatic considerations, together with a traditional British reluctance to debate general principles or frankly address the question of power, its distribution and control. Generations of students have been instructed in the wonders of the 'British Constitution', that unwritten set of understandings and procedures whose flexibility permitted the transition from monarchy to democracy without a violent break. Yet the truth is that in Britain the language of constitutionalism, is the sense of a debate about the distribution and control of power (Pereira Menaut, 1986), is almost unknown. Instead, all such questions have been swept under the rubric of 'parliamentary sovereignty', the ability of the unitary legislature to exercise untrammelled power. The revival of nationalism in the British periphery from the late 1960s raised serious questions about the adequacy of this Westminster interpretation of British politics and stimulated new approaches to understanding the United Kingdom and Scotland's place within it.

The Federal and Political System Approach

Some writers have sought to describe Scottish government using the concepts of federalism, albeit qualified as 'federal tendencies' (Kellas, 1968, p.18) or 'federal elements' (Rokkan and Urwin, 1983, p.78). Federalism is a territorial separation of powers which allows sovereign governments within a state to pursue differing policies. Neither can trespass in areas within the jurisdiction of the other. Since the Westminster Parliament possesses unlimited competence throughout the UK, it is clear that Scotland's position is not federal. The framers of the Treaty of Union, while rejecting federalism (Ferguson, 1968), however, confused matters by inserting provisions guaranteeing legal and other privileges which would have required federalism and/or a written constitution to make them effective. It is these provisions, with their implication that the Union was based on compact theory, together with the existence of Scots law and institutions such as the Scottish Office, which have prompted the federal analogy. The fact remains, however, that the Union of 1707 was an incorporating one and that the resulting state was and is unitary.

Kellas (1989, p.4), examining Scotland's institutional and cultural distinctiveness, argues that only the notion of a political system 'does justice to the scale and nature of the phenomena which are found in Scottish politics'. A political system is defined in Easton's (1963) terms, as a mechanism for the authoritative allocation of values. The components of this system in Scotland are the items safeguarded by the Act of Union such as the legal, education and local government systems; the Secretary of State for Scotland, the Scottish Office and its agencies; the special arrangements for Scottish bills at Westminster; and the plethora of party organisations, pressure groups and advisory bodies. Within this system, decision-making in matters such as Scottish law reform, Scottish education, housing and local government are made (Kellas, 1989). Certainly, Kellas recognises that many policies are not decided within the Scottish system but at the British level, but even here the Scottish political system, while not determining, is able to make its own demands and needs known. Responding to critics (Mackintosh, 1973; Keating and Midwinter, 1983) who have pointed out that the decision-making power over Scottish as well as British matters lies with a unitary Cabinet and Parliament,

Kellas insists that a political system is not defined solely by political institutions but can be supported by other criteria, such as 'national identity', in 'social organisations' such as those of religion and education and through the distinctive Scottish media. Nor is he prepared to see Scotland relegated to the status of sub-system of the British political system, since any unit of local government could be so described. On the other hand, he does admit that his definition of a political system is 'flexible enough to contain any relatively independent political structure or set of political elements which move together in interaction' (Kellas, 1989, p. 17). Thus, it is not incompatible with other organising concepts such as 'Scottish input to the British political system' (Rose, 1982) or 'policy networks' (Keating and Midwinter, 1983).

Kellas' use of the political system model suffers from conceptual inprecision. He regards the definition of a political system as being a matter of opinion, since the categories of political science are not precise enough to distinguish clearly between a system and a sub-system (Kellas, 1989, p. 259). In our view, the definition of a political system is not a matter of 'importance', it is a matter of adequate conceptualisation.

Easton's aim was a science of politics which could illuminate political activities and processes characteristic of all political systems, even though the structural forms might vary. A political system was defined as 'a set of interactions, abstracted from the totality of social behaviour, through which values are authoritatively allocated for a society' (Easton, 1965, p. 57). The essential variables are the 'making and executing of decisions for a society' and 'their relative frequency of acceptance as authoritative and binding by the bulk of society' (Easton, 1965, p. 97). Also identified were key 'linkage variables' between the political system and its environment. These are input variables (demand and support) and output variables (decisions and actions), as shown in Figure 9.1. A political system survives when it displays the capacity to respond to stress through meeting demands. Failure can result in system instability or secession of some members. Systems develop mechanisms to regulate demands, to keep the system functioning and to avoid overload; these include parties, interest groups and opinion leaders, who synthesise and homogenise demands to permit simplified and workable programmes of action. Response to stress can take the form of structural regulation,

Figure 9.1 A simplified model of a political system

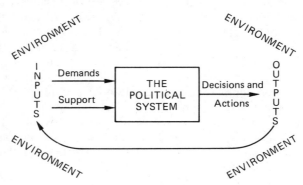

diffuse support and outputs. A regulative response requires the transformation of system goals and structures. The other measures are less radical. Diffuse support binds members by ties of loyalty and affection, imparted through the idea of a common good and political socialisation. Outputs refers to the tangible goods which the system can deliver to people in order to retain their support.

There are critical weaknesses in Kellas' attempt to apply this model to Scotland. First, his treatment is unsystematic. There is no comprehensive discussion of the key analytical concepts, no exposition of the dynamics of the system, no discussion of system responsiveness or feedback. Concepts such as 'demands', 'outputs', and 'authoritative allocation of values' are never properly examined or related to the functioning of the system in terms of the Eastonian model.

Second, much of what Kellas takes to be indicative of a Scottish 'system', we see simply as pieces of a British administrative system. This includes the Scottish Office, quangos and local government. Nor does the existence of a separate legal or education system constitute evidence for a political system, in the absence of mechanisms for the authoritative allocation of values. What matters is the content and substance of laws and policies, not simply the mechanisms through which they are delivered. For example, there are separate Scottish and English laws regarding rate-capping and their detailed mechanisms differ but the purpose and outcomes are the same. We have seen the same effect in other policy fields.

Finally, Kellas consistently presents arguments against his own thesis. Though he is 'an integral part of the Scottish political system and the target of its pressures' (Kellas, 1989, p. 28), 'a Conservative Secretary of State tries to shape Conservative policies for Scottish consumption'. Faced with the evidence of similar policy outputs in Scotland and England, he concludes that this is because the political culture is essentially one with England. Since one of his arguments for a Scottish political system rests precisely on Scottish political culture being distinct in such matters as national identity, religion and education, this in itself weakens the argument. Elsewhere, he concedes that the Secretary of State does not have enough power to be 'Scotland's Prime Minister', that Scotland is subject to a British Cabinet of which the Secretary of State is just a member (Kellas, 1989, p. 28) and that the Scottish and Welsh Offices for most of the time are engaged in the humdrum business of implementing policies decided elsewhere (Kellas and Madgwick, 1982, p.29).

It is clear, then, that Scotland does not constitute a political system in the Eastonian sense. A system model may, however, aid an understanding of Scottish politics, in a different way. There is a *British* political system which is periodically under stress *in* Scotland and which responds through the institutional, socialisation and output mechanisms which we have examined in this book. The Scottish environment and civil society places specific demands on British government, which is forced to produce responses which may be differentiated yet which maintain the integrity of the British system as a whole. The tension runs through all the political institutions in Scotland. The parties must satisfy Scottish demands while doing nothing to undermine their support elsewhere in Britain or the authority of the central government which they aspire to control. The Scottish Office must cater to Scottish demands while remaining part of central government, with its firm rules about unity and collective responsibility. Parliament must pass Scottish legislation while retaining the essentials of a unitary legislature. In none of these cases do we see the 'Scottish' institutions authoritatively allocating values. Rather, the British system allocates in such a way as to secure its own survival against the ever-present threat of its own breakdown in the form of a Scottish seccesion.

200 *Politics and Public Policy in Scotland*

The Territorial Politics Approach

Scottish government can thus be seen as a series of adaptations of the unitary system of government to the distinct political, social and economic environment. Some observers have emphasised the *British* character of government in Scotland as dominant. Rose (1982) emphasises the role of the Scottish Office as part of the British system of government, stressing its role in functional rather than territorial politics. This is a useful corrective for the Scottish political system or quasi-federalist views. The idea of the territorial ministries as simple government departments like any other, however, does not do justice to the role of the Secretary of State for Scotland and the Scottish Office as 'gatekeepers' between the Scottish environment and the UK political system, or as lobbyists for Scottish interests. The latter role is seen by Ross (1981) as the most important feature of the Scottish Office and the one which marks it off most clearly from the functional London-based departments.

Rhodes (1987), too, regards the territorial ministries in Scotland, Wales and Northern Ireland as distinctive, a species of 'sub-central government'. They differ in organisation, being based on territory; in location, being based in the periphery; and in scope, being multi functional. Within government, they articulate both territorial and functional interests and operate within dual political environments, Scottish (or Welsh or Northern Irish) and British. They are simultaneously 'in the centre and for a periphery' (Rhodes, 1987, p. 144). We can thus see the Scottish Office and the other Scottish elements of government serving both a mediating and a management role, maintaining the integrity of the British political system. Bulpitt (1983) has identified 'territorial management' as a historic feature of the British political system, whereby the periphery has been controlled through the collaboration of local elites. Indeed, as long ago as the eighteenth century there was a 'Scottish manager' whose responsibility it was to distribute patronage in Scotland in return for support both for the constitutional order and the government of the day. In this, Scotland bears comparison, not with federal systems, but with those European unitary countries in which territorial intermediaries operate within a unitary state. The key point here is that a *unitary* state is not necessarily *uniform* either in its administrative instruments or in the impact of public policy on the ground in different territories. In France, Italy and, at times, Spain, centrally-appointed territorial administrators and centralist-minded politicians have, while supporting the unitary state, been able to bend the rigidities of central policy to local circumstances and ensure a flow of resources to their territories (Grémion, 1976; Keating, 1988b).

In Scotland, these mechanisms of accommodation and, specifically, the privileged access of territorial representatives and territorial administrators to central resources, have historically been presented as compensation for the lack of real political autonomy. The decision-making powers of the Scottish elements of government are limited but they have influence over the wider decision-making processes of British governments. A self-governing Scotland would have greater latitude in framing its own policies and would, indeed, comprise a political system. On the other hand, it might lose its privileged representation at the centre. This is a central dilemma in Scottish politics and government.

While we have rejected the idea of a Scottish political system, we would maintain that there is a Scottish political 'arena', focused largely on the Scottish Office and the Scottish committees in Parliament. There are distinctive Scottish issues and Scottish aspects of British issues. There are Scottish interest groups, some of which are branches of British organisations while some are independent. There are Scottish newspapers and a strong Scottish dimension to political reporting on television and radio. There is a Scottish legislative process necessitated by the separate legal system. The political parties have Scottish branches which hold conferences at which distinctively Scottish issues are discussed. Scottish local authorities have their own structure and association and deal with the Scottish Office rather than with London. Scottish politicians and the media are aware of a distinction between Scottish and UK affairs; and MPs often consciously choose between a career in Scottish or UK politics (Keating, 1975). This can easily create the illusion of a political system at work until we remember that it all revolves around a unitary Cabinet and Parliament. Yet Scottish politics itself is not an illusion and, running through all the institutions and procedures we examine is a dual identity, Scottish and British. Some political issues are generated at the UK level. Others arise within Scotland and find their way onto the political agenda. Government's response may be a uniform one, the same policy for the whole UK, or a differentiated one, taking account of Scottish demands and circumstances.

British Government has been described in terms of 'policy communities', comprising politicians, officials, professionals and interest groups concerned and particular types of issues, who dominate the policy making and implementation process (Richardson and Jordan, 1979). Most of these are organised along functional lines, revolving around the work of the major government departments and may have considerable scope to develop policy, without conflicting with the overall Cabinet line. There is also a territorial dimension to policy communities, which cross cuts the functional. There is no single 'Scottish policy community', since there is no body in Scotland which can authoritatively determine policies and allocate resources across functional areas. There are, however, functional policy communities which are territorially differentiated or organised separately in Scotland. The Scottish educational policy community's ability to pursue a relatively autonomous line has been well documented (MacPherson and Raab, 1988). Policy communities are characterised, according to Rhodes (1987, p.78) by 'stability of relationships, continuity of highly restrictive membership, vertical interdependence based on shared service delivery responsibilities and insulation from other networks and invariably from the general public'. This catches the Scottish style very well. Territorial politics is conducted largely within the institutions of the unitary state and through functional policy communities. Given the British tradition of secrecy and executive dominance in government, this means that much of the process of territorial bargaining and accommodation is conducted away from the public gaze or smothered in the fictions of Cabinet government. This does not make our task of exploring power relationships any easier; but the vital issue remains that of determining the extent to which the administrative distinctiveness of Scotland allows for real policy differences.

Our survey of Scottish government has indicated that the scope for Scottish innovation is small, tightly constrained by the demands of Cabinet and party government and the unitary state. Yet Scottish demands are increasingly differentiated from those of England. This is placing the mechanisms for managing Scotland within the unitary political system under great strain.

Scotland and the Union

We have argued that Scotland is part of the unitary United Kingdom political system. Yet, while incorporated in 1707, it has neven been fully assimilated. Distinctive civil institutions, issues, political demands and a strong sense of national identity have not only survived but periodically have been strengthened. National identity is not always expressed politically – indeed, it is more easily observed in culture and sport – but the sense of nationhood and the tradition of independence before 1707 have given Scotland an option denied the regions of England, to opt out of the Union. Diehard Unionists who have been calling for a referendum on Scottish independence, assuming that they would win it, have unwittingly conceded this vital principle, that Scots do have the right to resume independence and thus retain an element of sovereignty.

Support for the Union in Scotland, then, is contingent rather than absolute. Part of the reason lies in the failure of the UK state to develop a sense of national identity, in contrast to other European states where nineteenth-century nation-building elites strove to break down old loyalties and mould a new 'national' consciousness (Keating, 1988b). There is not even a name for nationals of the United Kingdom. As Rose (1982, p. 11) puts it 'no-one ever speaks of the "Ukes" as a nation'. In the nineteenth century, the UK was preoccupied with empire building and it was the Empire which became the focus of loyalty and socialisation measures. 'British' citizenship was not even properly defined before 1982 and even now the status of British subject has a bewildering variety of categories. Nor have governments ever sought to define UK nationality in terms of common rights, political equality or economic opportunity. In the 1970s, the Labour Party constantly repeated its commitment to the 'economic and political unity of the UK' without ever really defining what this phrase meant. The failure to develop a sense of national identity is linked to the failure to develop a theory of popular sovereignty, leaving the quaint relic of 'parliamentary sovereignty' as the only firm constitutional principle or test of governmental legitimacy (Jones and Keating, 1985).

The disjuncture between a unitary political system and the absence of a unitary national identity is a source of periodic stress. We can analyse the stresses in the territorial polity by returning to Easton's notion of a political system. Easton identified key linkage variables between the political system and its environment. There are input variables (demand and support) and output variables (decision and actions). A political system survives when it displays the capacity to respond to stress through meeting demands. Failure to meet demands can cause systemn instability:

> 'If demands continue to be thwarted or denied, the disaffection of the members who count might also spill over the regime. Under certain circumstances, part of the membership might even seek to break away from the community in some kind of separatist movement. Output failure, as we might call the result of this willingness or inability to meet demands, would tend in the direction of undermining support for the system, a characteristic kind of stress for a system.'
>
> (Easton, 1965, p. 120)

Political systems develop mechanisms and actors (gatekeepers) for the regulation of political demands, to keep the system functioning and avoid overload. Key roles here are played by parties, interest groups and opinion leaders. Hirschman (1970) has characterised responses to decline in states and organisations in terms of 'exit, voice and loyalty'. That is, individuals can loyally accept their fate, they can seek a voice in changing matters or they can, in certain circumstances, exit. Scotland, unlike other elements of the British political system has always possessed the exit option, that of reassuming its existence as an independent state. It is this which would represent system breakdown in Scotland.

Scotland has long been a stress point in the British political system, given the way in which behaviour, demands and issues differ from those in England. Stress arises to the extent that Scottish political behaviour, demands and issues differ from those in England, testing the ability of a unitary political system to deliver policies which are acceptable in Scotland while within the permissible limits for the UK as a whole. Yet the system has in the past coped with the stress through a series of mechanisms familiar to the Eastonian model. These are the party system; a series of substantive policy outputs, notably in economic matters; and a large measure of diffuse support. More specifically, in the absence of a strong sense of UK national identity, support for the Union has been contingent on the ability of the political parties to integrate Scottish demands with UK priorities; on a perception of the economic benefits derived from the Union; and on a common set of political values between Scotland and England. All are now in question, posing the possibility of system breakdown.

For most of the century since the advent of mass suffrage, Britain has had a balanced two-party system in which the Conservatives have faced, successively, the Liberals and Labour. The competitive, two-party system had three important consequences. Firstly, the parties fought over the vital political centre ground necessary to build a majority, so reducing the potential for extremism. Secondly, a regular alternation of parties in power gave hope to the supporters of both main formations which, in turn, supported state centralisation to maximise their own authority when they achieved office. (It was alternation, indeed, which gave the regime its democratic credentials and reduced demands for constitutional limits on the power of governments or the dispersal of power.) Thirdly, both main formations had some presence in all parts of Britain (excluding Northern Ireland).

Most class, ideological and territorial interests could thus be assured that they would have their turn in power, as part of one of the winning coalitions. At times of turbulence and realignment in the party system, as in the 1880s or the 1920s, this was all called into question and constitutional reform, including territorial devolution and reform of the electoral system, came onto the agenda. In the 1970s, the regime appeared threatened by the rise of Scottish nationalism but this could still be treated as a marginal issue, to be handled by devolutionary devices which left the essentials of the Westminster regime intact. Indeed, it was the explicit hope of the Labour Government that conceding a modest degree of political devolution would lead to the disappearance of the Scottish Nationalists and allow the 'normal' pattern of two-party competition and alternation to resume.

The Thatcher decade has seen a much more fundamental challenge to the party system underlying the regime. The rise of third-party voting has ended the two-party duopoly in the popular vote, though not, given the electoral system, in parliamentary representation. Nor can either of the major parties claim to be truly British in their appeal. This is part of a

206   *Politics and Public Policy in Scotland*

postwar trend which has accelerated in the 1980s. Whereas
Labour won parliamentary majorities in five of the six regions of
the United Kingdom in 1945, it was unable to win in more than
four in all subsequent General Elections in which it won office
(Punnett, 1984). Conservative parliamentary majorities during
the 1950s and in 1970 were dependent upon the party's
predominance in only three of the UK regions. Since 1979, it
has been able to win with the support of only two regions. The
pattern is clear. While Labour support is more widely distributed than that of the Conservatives, both major parties
operate from fewer and narrower regional bases. The 1987
General Election, further emphasised the regional distinctiveness of the two major parties. In England south of the
Severn/Wash line (but excluding London), the opposition parties
could muster only six seats. In Scotland and Wales the
governing Conservatives won just nineteen of 109 seats and
under 30 per cent of the popular vote. The two-party system is
also at its weakest in Scotland and Wales, with only 64.6 per
cent of the vote in Wales and 66.4 per cent in Scotland.

The ability of the major parties to continue to play their
integrative role is thus placed in question. The Scottish media
gave considerable attention to the so-called 'Doomsday scenario'
in the run-up to the 1987 General Election. This suggested that
Scotland would again reject the policies of Thatcherism yet have
them enforced through by an 'English' majority. Labour would
be powerless to prevent the implementation of policies which
the Scots clearly did not want. It was also suggested both by the
Scottish Nationalists and some elements of the Labour Party
that the Conservatives would lack a 'mandate' to govern in
Scotland. In the narrow constitutional sense, there is no
question of the Government's right to govern. The Conservatives have won a UK parliamentary majority and, by custom and
practice, thereby form the Government. There is, though, a
serious question about political legitimacy, whether a government rejected by a large majority of Scots will be able to govern
with the consent which has underlain the British democratic
system.

For the Labour Opposition, the scenario is equally problematic. As its leaders know, it is unable to sustain the 'no
mandate' argument advanced by some within its ranks as long as
it relies on the conventions of parliamentary majorities attained
under the present electoral system to legitimise future Labour

governments. To play the 'nationalist card' would raise doubts about its ability ever to win a British majority again. Yet without challenging the government's legitimacy, Labour cannot effectively respond to nationalist taunts portraying its parliamentary group as the 'Feeble Fifty' (or forty-nine since November 1988). From the other side of the political spectrum, the discrete mechanisms of accommodation by which Scottish interests were managed in the past have been disrupted as some assertive politicians of the English New Right have used their position to intervene regularly in Scottish business.

The economic advantages of the Union have always been a matter of controversy. In the nineteenth century, it opened up imperial markets to Scottish manufacturers but it is arguable that this left Scotland, like the rest of Britian, overly dependent on these. National economic policies of protection in the 1930s have been criticised as damaging to Scotland's export-based industry (Harvie, 1981). In the 1960s, a lively debate took place on the extent to which Scotland was subsidised by the rest of the UK and the economic implications of independence (Simpson, 1970; McCrone, 1969). The major British parties campaigned aggressively on the economic benefits to Scotland of the Union, in particular the disproportionate share of identifiable public expenditure and the national regional policies aimed at sending industries to the development areas. In the 1970s, the focus shifted to North Sea oil, with the nationalist slogan 'Rich Scots or Poor Britons' inviting Scots to keep the benefits to themselves. The British parties found themselves hoist on their own petard, having made the transfer payments from England to Scotland the centrepiece of their defence of the Union. Again, the question is more complicated than might appear at first sight. Oil revenues in themselves might do little to improve the condition of life for the majority of Scots without specific economic and social policies to ensure a proper distribution of the benefits. There is a danger, indeed, that an oil-rich Scotland could suffer further contraction of its manufacturing base as its currency appreciated, with increased social division between the employed and the unemployed.

In the 1980s, the salience of the oil issue greatly diminished, for reasons which are not entirely clear. There has been evidence, nonetheless, that a growing number of Scots now question the economic advantages of the Union. A MORI poll in May 1989 showed 49 per cent of Scots believing that the

Union works against Scottish economic interests. Only 21 per cent believed that economic links with the rest of the UK worked for Scottish interests (*The Scotsman*, 16 May 1989).

The third source of support for the Union has been the broad identity of social and political values between Scots and the English. Some Conservatives have argued that the reason for their electoral failure in Scotland stems from the lack of 'Thatcherism' and see a need for a more vigorous application of the strategy north of the border. As we have shown, however, Scotland has not been exempt from the key elements of the strategy, for the simple reason that the conventions of British government would not allow it. The British political programme was applied, with the Scottish Office refraining from independent policy initiatives, and concentrating on a conventional defence of Scottish interests within the framework of that programme. Other Conservatives have recognised that Scots are less concerned with individualism and more concerned with the values of community than the English. Dalziel (1989) argues that until the Conservative Party can demonstrate that it sees communities as more than simply economic units with a balance sheet and a profit and loss account, and acknowledges them as the heart and soul of Scotland, it will never create a bond with the mass of the people, or recover a significant place in the politics of Scotland. What is the evidence to support this view? Is Scottish anti-Conservatism real in the sense of rejecting Conservative policies, or is it because of the irrationality of voters who benefit from the policies yet vote against the Government for other reasons, as Scottish Ministers regularly suggest?

To answer these questions we have gathered evidence from opinion poll data about Scottish voters' views of government policies. The central features of the New Conservatism concentrate on privatisation, expenditure control, tax reductions and efficiency in the public sector. The emphasis is placed on consumer choice and converting voters from 'collectivism'. Greater individual freedom through markets, less reliance on state welfare and subsidies are purportedly the underlying principles in policies such as the sale of council houses, opting out of schools from local authority control, or reforms in the management of the health service.

A number of problems with opinion polls arise which must be noted at the outset. The wording of the questions considerably affects the responses given. Comparing attitudes over time is not always possible because of the lack of data. Particularly in polls on constitutional reform, the options offered by the pollsters change. The polls also fail to account for the strength of feeling. The listing of 'important' issues may reflect the political agenda set by the media.

The issue of the popularity of Margaret Thatcher is significant for three reasons. Firstly, it is frequently asserted that she is seen as a southern English Scotophobe, which might go some way to explaining her party's lack of support in Scotland (and, if correct, her replacement as Tory leader might aid the Scottish Conservatives). Secondly, she is often seen as dominating her Government and thirdly, she is perceived to personify the values, policies, style and substance of the politics which bear her name. Extreme levels of dissatisfaction with the premiership of Margaret Thatcher have been recorded over the last decade. However, the Prime Minister's personal popularity has generally been greater than that for her Government and not infrequently it has even been greater than support for her party in Scotland. In March 1989, for example, 27 per cent of the Scots expressed satisfaction with the way she was doing her job while 70 per cent were dissatisfied, compared with only 19 per cent who were satisfied with the way the Government was doing its job and 76 per cent who were dissatisfied while the Conservatives were polling only 21 per cent in Scotland (*The Scotsman*, 4 March 1989). This would not suggest that Mrs Thatcher herself is the sole or major cause of the Conservatives' lack of support. It might suggest that her personal style is less unpopular than her policies.

An interesting poll conducted in September 1987 for the *Glasgow Herald* shortly after a highly publicised visit to Scotland strongly suggested that Scots do perceive the Prime Minister as antipathetic to Scottish interests. Respondents were asked how they rated her as Prime Minister for the whole of the United Kingdom and then for Scotland, with 32 per cent considering her to be good as Prime Minister for the UK, but only 9 per cent as good for Scotland. Indeed, 82 per cent felt her performance was poor as Prime Minister for Scotland.

A central element in the Government's education proposals has been allowing parents to take their school out of local education authority control if a majority wish to do so. However, a poll conducted in May 1988 showed 31 per cent supported and 51 per cent opposed. Another significant finding was the response to the question as to whether parents would send their children to a private school if they could afford it – 58 per cent said No and 34 per cent said Yes (*The Scotsman*, 2 May 1988).

The unpopularity in Scotland of certain Government measures is notable. The community charge, or poll tax has been consistently opposed by over 70 per cent of Scots respondents. The depth of feeling is perhaps conveyed by the extent of support for a campaign of non-payment. In December 1988 37 per cent of Scots stated that they supported civil disobedience against the poll tax with 54 per cent against (*The Scotsman*, 12 December 1988).

An attempt to determine whether Scots have a different set of values from southerners by *The Scotsman* in May 1989 con-cluded that they did not though, using the same evidence, presented in Table 9.1, we would reach the opposite conclusion. There is clear evidence here of a more collectivist attitude on the part of Scots.

Table 9.1 Values in Scotland compared with England and Wales, 1989

Which of these comes closest to the ideal country for you and your family?

	percentage	
	Scots	English & Welsh
A country in which private interests and a free market economy are more important	21	30
A country in which public interests and a more managed economy are more important	71	61
A country which emphases the social and collective provision of welfare	60	54
A country in which the individual is encouraged to look after himself/herself	33	38

Source: *The Scotsman*, 6 May 1989.

Evidence on the high proportion of Scots who wish to own a home of their own was cited as evidence of a Thatcherite inclination on the part of the Scots in major articles in both of Scotland's quality papers (*The Scotsman*, 6 May 1989; *Glasgow*

Herald, 21 September 1988). However, this is probably not the essence of Thatcherism for Scots. The desire to own a home is so widespread as to include most supporters of all parties and, while there is evidence that home-owners are more inclined than tenants to vote Conservative, it appears that buying his or her council house does not in itself make an individual more likely to convert to the Conservative Party (Heath *et al.*, 1989).

Response to Stress

The response to stress can take various forms (Easton, 1965, Rudolph and Thompson, 1985). Firstly, there is 'diffuse support', an appeal to an over-arching general good. In Scotland, this takes the form of political parties emphasising the primacy of loyalty to the 'working class' or the 'British nation' rather than to Scotland. This conflicts with the appeal to Scottish particularist interests, necessitated by electoral pressures and the territorial-advocacy roles allocated to Scottish politicians and administrators. Secondly, there are 'output' concessions, that is substantive policy changes, leaving the structures of power intact. The pressures to uniformity entrenched in the unitary system of government and the British political parties make it very difficult for governments to allow other than marginal changes in policy for Scotland. Political demands articulated in Scotland may thus be diverging so sharply from those in England that the limited discretion available in Scottish administration is unable to bridge the gap. More scope is available to adapt policy quantitatively, rather than qualitatively. Scotland has had some success in gaining a larger share from whatever British government is providing and, at times, in moulding the content of British policies to suit Scottish interests. Indeed, pork-barrel politics, the attempt to assuage territorial discontent by material concessions, has a long history in Scotland but is very expensive and has begun to provoke a backlash from other parts of the UK.

A third response to stress is through procedural changes (Rudolph and Thompson, 1985), altering the process of decision-making at the centre, to give greater weight to Scottish interests. There has been a progressive extention of the role of the Scottish Office whose economic functions have expanded steadily since the 1960s. This is a technique of managing territorial tensions but not of eliminating them, since each concession to particularism raises the salience of territory in politics (Keating, 1988b, Miller, 1981). The administrative devolution has served to make the Scottish political arena more self-contained since the Second World War, to present issues increasingly in Scottish terms and to intensify the pressure on Scottish Ministers and officials. This has enhanced the importance of the role of the Secretary of State as a territorial manager, the focus for Scottish demands and discontents and the person held responsible in London for the government's political standing in Scotland. The real decision-making powers of the Scottish Office and its agencies, however, remain tightly constrained. The rule announced in the early 1980s whereby the Secretary of State was given theoretical discretion over the allocation of a large part of his budget is a good example of the problems resulting, since the Secretary of State lacks any power to increase the total. Secretaries of State have thus found themselves with increased responsibility but without significant increases in power, a position which has led more than one Secretary of State to the conclusion that further increased in his responsibilities were not desirable. The danger of political overload is increased. In his role as 'Scotland's minister' and territorial lobbyist, the Secretary of State is the recipient of demands which he can only satisfy by convincing Treasury and Cabinet of his case. The gap between Scottish expectations and his ability to meet them is a constant threat to his integrative and system-maintenance role.

The fourth type of concession to stress is constitutional change, the granting of territorial autonomy. There have been many proposals over the last hundred years for a measure of Scottish Home Rule within the United Kingdom. Yet dividing power by territory is something with which Britain's parliamentary-based regime has found it extremely difficult to cope.

Constitutional Futures

In one sense, the constitutional issue has always been there. Since the advent of scientific opinion polling in the 1930s, tests of opinion have, without exception, shown Scots to be in favour of a degree of self-government, including an elected assembly. Rarely, however, has it been the dominant political issue and Scots have given their votes to parties whose priorities lay at the

UK level. These, in turn, have traditionally diverted Scottish aspirations into a territorial politics which stressed material advantage within the Union rather than constitutional change. It is, as a result, notoriously difficult to measure the strength of Scottish feeling on constitutional change and opinion poll data is of relatively little help here.

It is true, certainly, that, when Scots are asked to list their political priorities, self-government rarely occupies a prominent place. Instead, substantive issues like employment, inflation, housing or the community charge are cited. Opponents of Home Rule have invariably siezed on these responses as evidence that Scots are really indifferent to the issue. Again, the problem lies in the way the question is phrased. Asking people to choose between a substantive policy benefit like employment or good housing and a constitutional change is not only to compare the incomparable, it is to suggest that these are competing objectives. Supporters of Home Rule would argue that, far from competing, they are mutually sustaining. Constitutional change may be a mechanism for changing substantive policies. It is not only Unionists who confuse this link. Nationalists, for their part, often imply that constitutional change in itself will produce material improvements in the lot of Scots, when this in practice will depend on the precise policies pursued under the altered governmental arrangements.

What is notable in the late 1980s is a combination of strong support for Home Rule with large levels of discontent with the substantive policies of the government of the day, a government which has never succeeded in attracting the support of a plurality of Scots at the polls. This poses strains on the British political system which are in some respects more severe than those of the 1970s, when the eruption of support for the SNP was regarded as a marginal issue in British politics. The 1970s devolution formula represented less a dramatic change in constitutional practice than the minimum which the Labour government deemed necessary to preserve the essence of the Westminster Constitution. A directly elected Scottish Assembly was to be established but, sidestepping the old dilemma between access to the centre and autonomy, this was to coexist with a Secretary of State for Scotland and the full complement of Scottish MPs at Westminster. The retention of the old mechanisms of territorial management alongside the Assembly was to reassure both those Scots who feared the loss of the material advantages which came from privileged access to the centre and

Unionists who needed assurance that Scotland would remain tied to the Westminster constitution. Parliamentary sovereignty was explicitly preserved, including the power to overturn Assembly acts and unilaterally to change the terms of the devolution settlement. This attempt to devolve power while retaining it came under scathing criticism from opponents while the maintenance of the mechanisms of privileged access alongside the assembly was the main point of resentment for English MPs who complained that Scotland would enjoy an unfair advantage. From supporters of Home rule, there were criticisms that the Assembly's powers were tightly circumscribed, particularly in the economic field and that it was to depend entirely on revenues transferred from the centre, with no taxation powers of its own. Others criticised the general thrust of the Labour Party strategy, with its emphasis on protecting the party's own position. In particular, the insistence that the Assembly would be elected on the first-past-the-post electoral system virtually guaranteed a Labour majority and raised questions about the scheme as a democratising measure which deserved the support of Scots of all parties (Gunn and Lindley, 1977).

Since 1979, the parties' positions on the devolution issue have changed little. The Conservatives remain adamantly opposed, though the presence of some prominent Home Rulers in the ranks may allow a reconsideration after a change of leadership. Labour's proposals follow the broad lines of the Scotland Act of 1978, though with slightly strengthened economic powers and some taxation powers. They have continued to insist that the fundamental economic and political unity of the UK will be unimpaired, as will parliamentary sovereignty. For most of the 1980s, they also continued to insist that an Assembly could come only from a majority Labour Government at Westminster putting the legislation through as part of its overall programme and would not be negotiated with the other parties. In 1989, they agreed to take part in the deliberations of the constitutional convention organised by the all-party Campaign for a Scottish Assembly, though without a commitment to an all-party approach. The party in Scotland also accepted proportional representation for assembly elections. The Democrats offer a similar system and also strong supporters of the all-party approach.

There is evidence, though, that public opinion has moved on since the devolution debates of the 1970s. Throughout the past decade there has been growing support for some measure of

Scottish Home Rule, with declining support for the status quo. A poll taken in March 1979 showed only 14 per cent favouring independence, 42 per cent supporting an Assembly with substantial powers and 35 per cent for no change with 9 per cent 'don't knows'. By March 1985 a reversal in the support for independence and the status quo had occurred: 33 per cent favoured independence, 47 per cent were for an Assembly with substantial powers and 14 per cent favoured no change with 6 per cent 'don't knows'. Support for independence appears to have come to outstrip support for the status quo sometime early during the second term of Mrs Thatcher's premiership.

The SNP's refined aim of independence in the European Community has added an important dimension to the debate and according to polls commands considerable support. A poll conducted jointly for the Glasgow Herald and BBC Scotland showed that 61 per cent of Scots felt that an independent Scottish Government would best represent Scottish interests in the European Community while only 32 per cent felt this would be best achieved by the UK Government. The same poll found that 55 per cent thought that Scotland would be better off if it was independent in Europe, 23 per cent that it would be worse off, 11 per cent thought neither/no difference and 11 per cent did not know (*Glasgow Herald*, 14 April 1989). The stumbling block for the SNP, however, was that 70 per cent thought it either not very likely or not all likely that Scotland would become an independent member of the EC.

For the UK as a whole Scotland's political alienation remains a marginal issue and there is still a tendency in the major parties to see the solution in *ad hoc* reforms tacked onto the existing constitutional structure, with the essentials of the old regime unchanged. On the other hand, there is an increasing groundswell of support for constitutional reform in other parts of the kingdom. Scotland, indeed, might prove to be the Achilles' heel of the archaic British state, its point of greatest vulnerability. A number of English observers have come to appreciate this and to see the Scottish question as the start of a more general process of constitutional modernisation (Marquand, 1989). It is impossible to do justice to this debate in the space of a few pages, but the major options for reform can be outlined.

One option is the constitutional *status quo*. Contrary to much of what was written in the 1970s, the *status quo* is an option and has been government policy since 1979. Preserving the existing constitutional arrangement, however, is proving possible only by changing its political meaning. Before 1979, Scotland was governed by consent and, on the few occasions on which the government lacked a Scottish majority, the opposition could console themselves with the thought that their turn would come. Since 1979, Scotland has been governed by virture of an English-based majority, with support for the governing party at its lowest point this century. On the only other occasion on which a governing party fell to a quarter of the vote, in 1922, it sparked off a strident Home Rule campaign which was killed off only by the return of a Labour Government (Keating and Bleiman, 1979). It is significant that no-one is prepared to recommend this as a long-term arrangement. The opposition parties call for a Scottish Assembly while the Conservatives, especially since 1986, have set themselves the task of winning the argument on the ground by converting Scots to the new Conservatism. Whether they can do this while setting their face resolutely against an elected assembly must be doubtful. The alternative is not some cataclysmic confrontation but an increasing political alienation in Scotland and a long-term growth in support for separatism.

The second option is devolution. This rather ungainly word, associated with Labour's proposals of the 1970s, has gone out of fashion in recent years. Labour's leadership has begun to use the delphic phrase 'independence in the United Kingdom'. Yet the concept of devolution, the handing-down of prescribed powers to a subordinate assembly within an otherwise unchanged constitution, is central to Labour's thinking. It is the formula which reconciles Scottish self-government with the party's centralist traditions and commitment to parliamentary sovereignty. There are, however, serious problems with the approach as a solution to the impasse of territorial politics in the 1990s. The potential for political conflict between a Conservative UK government and a left-leaning Scotland will be unaffected, while the tight prescription of the Assembly's powers is a recipe for friction and confrontation. Serious doubts must exist about the likelihood of a majority Labour government and about the ability of such a government, should it come about, to get a measure of Scottish devolution through its own parliamentary ranks swollen, as these would be, by English newcomers. Scottish devolution is still seen in the party outside Scotland as an insurance policy against a nationalist resurgence rather than an integral part of the programme. The party's 1989 policy review has, it is true, included constitutional reform but in a piecemeal and half-hearted way. In the absence of a major nationalist presence in Parliament, or evidence of insistent demand in Scotland, devolution is unlikely to feature as a priority.

The programme of the SNP remains that of national independence. This objective appears very clear, yet in practice it is hard to define. In formal terms, a country may be sovereign and independent but its real scope for autonomous action depends on its political, economic and military relationships within the international order of states. The independence enjoyed by Finland or the Republic of Ireland is much more circumscribed, for differing reasons, than that enjoyed by Sweden or France. An independent Scotland in an economic union with England would face severe limits on its independence. Yet nationalists have tended to insist that there would be no customs barriers at Gretna. For some nationalists, this issue is largely irrelevant. The symbolic importance of national independence, with a seat at the United Nations and embassies around the world, is what matters. Others are more concerned with the substance of power and are aware of the need for an international support system for a small independent nation. In the early twentieth century, Scottish nationalists used to argue for Dominion status, which would provide Scotland with the external support system of the Empire while allowing it domestic self-government on the same lines as Canada or Australia. The end of the Empire and the development of the dominions into sovereign states removed this half-way house, leaving only the options of separatism in a dangerous Europe; or of constitutional reform within the UK. The former commanded little popular support while the latter ran up against the refusal of the Westminster Parliament to reform its own constitution. Since the 1970s, however, an external support system has been available in Europe. The option of Scottish independence within the European Community, first floated by the short-lived Scottish Labour Party, has been taken seriously by the SNP only in the 1980s. As we have seen, the option appears to attract considerable popular support, with reservations mainly concerned with its viability. Viability may depend on the political evolution of the EC itself but, with the Conservatives under Mrs. Thatcher turning against their commitment to European unity and Labour and the SNP moving towards it, Scotland may find some common ground. A favourable Scottish disposition to Europe would be a reversal of attitudes at the time of British accession (Keating and Waters, 1985) but would tap more ancient traditions.

The classic solution to the kinds of territorial stress we have described here is a federal system in which central and territorial governments each have their own defined spheres of action, with entrenched powers. In practice, modern federalism is characterised less by a strict separation of powers than by a complex pattern of interaction. Each level of government, however, retains its guaranteed rights and powers, allowing for a negotiation on policy, rather than the central dictation possible under devolution. Federalism is also characterised by symmetry. Since the central government lacks certain powers altogether, there must be territorial governments everywhere to exercise them. This would defuse the notorious 'West Lothian Question' raise in the 1970s, the anomaly that under devolution Scottish MPs could vote on English domestic matters while neither they nor English MPs could vote on Scottish devolved matters. Most federal systems, too, have a second chamber of the central legislature representing territorial interests, allowing further scope for negotiation over territorial politics.

The federal solution has many attractions but its political feasibility in the UK must be in doubt. It would require the Westminster Parliament to accept constitutional limitations on its own powers in order to solve what most MPs still regard as a marginal problem. It would in many ways be easier for Westminster to accept Scottish independence, which would leave its sovereignty and power over the remaining 90 per cent of the United Kingdom unaltered. Federalism would also require England or the English regions to accept a system for which there is no apparent demand.

Principles for Reform

We are not going to present a blueprint for constitutional change. That would be another book in itself. We conclude, instead, with some principles which might guide the search for a constitutional settlement. One is the need to secure a consensus on the system by which Scotland is to be governed so that substantive policy differences can be argued out and resolved democratically. This cannot be done by the classic Westminster device of one party using its parliamentary majority to impose its solution. It must, rather, involve a negotiation among the parties, none of which represents a majority of the Scottish people. It is striking that the British parties have been prepared to concede to Northern Ireland the right to negotiate its on constitutional arrangements – subject to Westminster approval – but have resisted the idea in the case of Scotland where the potential for a creative solution is greater. The process by which Spain re-established self-government for the historic nationalities of Catalonia, Galicia and the Basque Country, followed by the other regions, is a model in this respect. The political forces in the territories themselves took the initiative in framing their statutes of autonomy, which were then negotiated with Madrid. The formation of a Scottish Constitutional Convention at the initiative of the Campaign for a Scottish Assembly represents a move in this direction. While Labour has reversed its stance of seventy years and agreed to participate in the all-party forum, however, the Conservatives have refused. The SNP also declined to participate on the grounds that the Convention would be powerless in the face of the inevitable Westminster veto and that the Convention was a Labour ploy to regain the initiative and outflank the SNP. The history of attempts to gain Scottish Home Rule earlier this century (Keating and Bleiman, 1979) is in danger of repeating itself.

A related concern is that of citizenship and the rights which go with it. One reason why the British parties have been unhappy with the idea of the Scottish people negotiating their own constitutional arrangements is that they have never accepted the sovereignty of the *British* people. Instead, constitutional changes, like substantive policies, have been handed down from a sovereign parliament. Referendums, on Europe in 1975 and devolution in 1979, were brought in not in recognition of popular sovereignty but in order to manage divisions within the Labour Party, and then were qualified as purely 'advisory'. Successive British governments have insisted on parliamentary sovereignty as an effective protection for citizenship rights while allowing differing civil rights in different parts of the kingdom and, in the case of Northern Ireland, tolerating gross breaches of human rights over fifty years. In the 1980s, there was a growing appreciation of the fundamentally undemocratic nature of the British state with its denial of the principle of popular sovereignty and refusal to treat people as other than subjects.

Nairn (1988) insists that only an assertion of republicanism and sweeping away the mystique of monarchy can convert subjects into citizens. Others have queried the Labour Party's resolute refusal to consider the fundamental reforms of the state which democrats elsewhere take for granted (Jones and Keating, 1985). Instead, party spokespersons repeat the old objection that legal citizen rights will merely put power in the hands of reactionary judges. Since Labour proposes to continue to allow these 'reactionary' judges to administer the criminal and civil law, a more logical position might be to reform the system of judicial recruitment and training. Yet is has taken the Thatcher Government to mount an assault on the privileges of the legal profession. In the late 1980s, there was some movement on this. The Democrats, together with a growing element in the Labour Party and a few Conservatives, placed a written charter of rights among their demands and the organisation Charter 88 has gained considerable support among intellectuals and the professional classes disenchanted with the Thatcher Government's use of parliamentary sovereignty to centralise power and attack the autonomous institutions of civil society. A written charter of rights would transform the issue of Scottish self-government, removing much of the justification for central control, and over-ride powers as well as confirming the status of Britons as citizens rather than subjects.

The issue of territorial equity in economic and expenditure policies is likely to become more controversial, whatever constitutional settlement is reached. There will never be an agreed definition of territorial justice, since the matter is essentially political, but greater openness and clarity in expenditure allocations would improve the quality of political debate.

Finally, there is the question of democracy. An elected assembly, while a necessary condition for the improvement of Scottish democracy, is not sufficient. The system of administrative devolution in which major issues are settled in London while Scottish politicians have focused their attention on parochial issues and on pork-barrel politics, has had a debilitating effect on Scottish political life. If this book has focused largely on administrative politics, on the 'inside' view of government, rather than on party politics, the clash of ideologies, social movements, visions and ideals, it is because this is what most of Scottish politics consists of. The capacity to make an authoritative allocation of values being absent, Scottish politics is about how to bend the details of UK policies, how to extract a little bit more, within a framework of values and decisions made elsewhere. Responsibility can always be evaded, since decisions are taken elsewhere. The extension of administrative devolution and the retreat of most Scottish politicians into the Scottish arena (Keating, 1975)) without a corresponding measure of political devolution, has exacerbated this problem since the war.

There are specific measures which would serve to improve the quality of democracy. A move to proportional representation would end the stultifying effect of one-party dominance in many parts of the country. It would allow a Scottish Assembly to be presented as a democratising measure and not a mechanism for permanent one-party control in Scotland. It would confirm the rights of citizens to equal representation. A strengthening of local government would allow communities to take more of the decisions affecting them. More openness in government would improve the quality of information for citizens and encourage more constructive debate. Along with a new parliament these could help a general repoliticisation of Scottish public life, stimulate political competition and open the way to new ideas for confronting Scotland's deep social and economic problems.

References

Adam Smith Institute (1989) *Shedding a Tier* (London, ASI).
Adler, M., A. Petch and J. Tweedie (1987) 'The Parents' Charter in Scotland', in D. McCrone (ed.) *The Scottish Government Yearbook, 1987* (Edinburgh: Unit for the Study of Government in Scotland).
Agnew, J. (1987) *Place and Politics. The Geographical Mediation of State and Society* (London: Allen and Unwin).
Anderson, R. D. (1983) *Education and Opportunity in Victorian Scotland* (Oxford University Press).
—(1985) 'In Search of the Lad o' Pairts: the mythical history of Scottish education: in *History Workshop, 19*.
Balfour (1954) *Royal Commission on Scottish Affairs* Cmd.9212 (Edinburgh: HMSO).
Barlow, J. (1981) *Central – Local Government Financial Relationships and Policy Making in Education and Housing* paper presented to the Political Studies Association Conference, Hull, April.
Bealey, F. and J. Sewel (1981) *The Politics of Independence: A Study of A Scottish Town* (Aberdeen University Press).
Beaton, D. and B. Collins (1988) 'Public Spending' in R. Jackson and F. Terry *Public Domain 1988* (London: Public Finance Foundation).
Beer, S. (1980) 'British Pressure Groups Revisited: Pluralistic Stagnation From The Fifties To The Seventies: in *Public Administration Bulletin* No.32.
Begg, T. (1987) *50 Special Years: A Study in Scottish Housing* (London: Henry Melland).
Berridge, J. and I. Clark (1987) 'Tayside Region', in H. Elcock and A.G. Jordan (eds) *Learning from Local Authority Budgeting* (Aldershot: Avebury Books).
Blondel, J. (1974) *Voters, Parties and Leaders. The Social Fabric of British Politics* (Harmondsworth: Penguin).
Bochel, J. and D. Denver (1984) 'The 1983 General Election in Scotland', in D. McCrone (ed.) *Scottish Government Yearbook, 1984* (Edinburgh: Unit for the Study of Government in Scotland).

——1987) 'Labour Pedominance Reasserted: The Regional Elections of 1986', in D. McCrone (ed.) *Scottish Government Yearbook, 1987* (Edinburgh: Unit for the Study of Government in Scotland).
——(1988) 'The 1987 General Election in Scotland', in McCrone D. (ed.) *Scottish Government Yearbook, 1988* (Edinburgh: Unit for the Study of Government in Scotland).
——(1989) 'The 1988 District Elections', in A. Brown and D. McCrone (eds) *Scottish Government Yearbook 1989* (Edinburgh: Unit for the Study of Government in Scotland).
Bramley, G., A. Evans, P. Leather and C. Lambert (1983) *Grant Related Expenditure: A Review of the System* (Report) (Bristol: School for Advanced Urban Studies).
Brand J. (1978) *The National Movement in Scotland* (London: Routledge & Kegan Paul).
—(1984), 'National Consciousness and Voting in Scotland', in *Strathclyde Papers in Government and Politics,* No.15 (Glasgow: University of Strathclyde).
Brooks, R. (1983) 'Scotland's Health', in K. Ingham and J. Love (eds) *Understanding the Scottish Economy* (Oxford: Martin Robertson).
Brown, C. (1987) *The Social History of Religion in Scotland Since 1730* (London: Methuen).
Brown, G. and R. Cook (eds) (1987) *Scotland: The Real Divide* (Edinburgh: Mainstream).
Bruce, A and G. Lee (1982) 'Local Election Campaigns', in *Political Studies* 30.2.
Bruce, R. (1945) *First Planning Report to the Highways and Planning Committee of the Corporation of the City of Glasgow* (Glasgow: Corporation of Glasgow).
Buchanan (1964), *Traffic in Towns* (Report, HMSO).
Budge, I. and D. Urwin (1966) *Scottish Political Behaviour. A Case Study in British Homogeneity* (London: Longman).
—, J. Brand, M. Margolis and A. Smith (1972) *Political Stratification and Democracy* (London: Macmillan).
Bulpitt, J. (1983) *Territory and Power in the United Kingdom. An Interpretation* (Manchester University Press).
Butler, D. and C. Stokes (1969, 1974) *Political Change in Britain* (1st ed, 2nd ed) (London: Macmillan).
Central Policy Review Staff (1975) *A Joint Approach to Social Policy* (London: HMSO).
—(1977), *Relations Between Central Departments and Local Authorities* (London: HMSO).
Charlton, J. and C. Martlew (1987) 'Stirling District Council', H. Elcock and A.G. Jordan (eds) *Learning from Local Authority Budgeting* (Aldershot: Avebury Books).
City of Glasgow Housing Department (1986) *Public Opinion in Glasgow* (Glasgow: author).
Cmnd. 7308 (1948) *White Paper on Scottish Affairs* (Edinburgh: HMSO).

Cmnd. 9676 (1985) *Future Strategy for Higher Education in Scotland: Report of the Scottish Tertiary Education Advisory Council* (Edinburgh: HMSO).

Clarke, M.G. (1982) 'Stodart and Local Government: Was the Fuss Justified?', in H.M. Drucker and N.L. Drucker (eds) *Scottish Government Yearbook 1982* (Edinburgh: Paul Harris Publishing).

Convention of Scottish Local Authorities (1981), *Government Economic Strategy: The COSLA Critique* (Edinburgh: author).

—(1982), *Central – Local Government Relationships: A Time to Listen – A Time to Speak Out* (Edinburgh: author).

Craig, F. W. S. (1976) *British Electoral Facts, 1885–1975* (London: Macmillan).

Craig, F. W. S. (1989) *British Electoral Facts, 1832–1987* (5th ed) (Aldershot: Gower).

Crewe, I. (1987) 'A New Class of Politics', *Guardian* 15 June

Crompton, P. (1982) 'The Lothian Affair: A Battle of Principles', D. McCrone (ed) *Scottish Government Yearbook 1983* (Edinburgh: Unit for Study of Government in Scotland).

Crossman, R. H. S. (1975) *The Diaries of A Cabinet Minister*, vol. 1 (London: Hamish Hamilton and Jonathan Cape).

—(1976) *The Diaries of a Cabinet Minister*, vol.2 (London: Hamish Hamilton and Jonathan Cape).

Curtice, J. and M. Steed (1988) 'Appendix 2. Analysis', in D. Butler and D. Kavanagh *The British General Election of 1987* (London: Macmillan).

Cuthbert, M. (ed). (1982) *Government Spending in Scotland* (Edinburgh: Paul Harris Publishing).

CVRPAC (1946) Clyde Valley Regional Planning Advisory Committee, *The Clyde Valley Regional Plan* (Edinburgh: HMSO).

Dalziel, I. (1989) 'The Formula for Recovery in Scotland' *Glasgow Herald*, 20 January.

Danziger, J. (1978) *Making Budgets* (London: Sage).

Davie G. E. (1961) *The Democratic Intellect* (Edinburgh University Press).

—(1986) *The Crisis of the Democratic Intellect* (Edinburgh: Polygon).

Davies, T. and A. Sinfield (1987) 'The Unemployed', in G. Brown and R. Cook (eds) *Scotland: The Real Divide* (Edinburgh: Mainstream).

Dawson R. and K. Prewitt (1969) *Political Socialisation* (Boston: Little, Brown).

Dearlove, J. (1979) *The Reorganisation of British Local Government* (Cambridge University Press).

Dennington (1966), *Our Older Homes: A Call for Action* (London: HMSO).

Dickson, A. D. R. (1988) 'The Peculiarities of the Scottish: National Culture and Political Action', in *Political Quarterly, 59.3*

Donnelly, C. (1986) 'Private Health Care in Scotland', in D. McCrone (ed.) *The Scottish Government Yearbook, 1986* (Edinburgh: Unit for the Study of Government in Scotland).

Donnison, A. and A. Middleton (1987) *Regenerating the Inner City. The Glasgow Experience* (London: Routledge & Kegan Paul).

Downs, A. (1957) *An Economic Theory of Democracy* (New York: Harper & Row).

Draper, P. and I. McNicol (1979) 'The New Scottish Input-Output Tables: the Importance of UK and Foreign Trade to Scotland', in *Fraser of Allander Quarterly Economic Commentary*, 4.1.

Dunleavy, P. (1980) *Urban Political Analysis* (London: Macmillan).

Dyer, M. (1978) 'Leadership in a Rural Scottish County', in G. W. Jones and A. Norton (eds) *Political Leadership in Local Government* (Birmingham: Institute for Local Government Studies).

—and J. Sewel (1987) 'Banff and Buchan District Council' in H. Elcock and G. Jordan (eds) *Learning from Local Authority Budgeting* (Aldershot: Avebury Books).

Easton, D. (1953) *The Political System* (New York: Alfred Knopf).

—(1965) *A Framework for Political Analysis* (Englewood Cliffs, NJ: Prentice-Hall, Inc.)

Elcock, H. and G. Jordan (1987) *Learning from Local Authority Budgeting* (Aldershot: Avebury Books).

—, —and A. Midwinter (1989) *Budgeting in Local Government: Managing the Margins* (London: Longman).

Elliott, W. (1932) 'The Scottish Heritage in Politics', in Duke of Atholl *et al. A Scotsman's Heritage* (London: Alexander Maclehose & Co.).

Ferguson, W. (1968) *Scotland. 1689 to the Present* (Edinburgh: Oliver & Boyd).

Finer, S. (1974) *Comparative Government* (Harmondsworth: Penguin).

Forsyth, M. (1980) *Reservicing Britain* (London: Adam Smith Institute).

France G. H. (1969) *Scottish Councillors*, appendix 25 to Royal Commission on Local Government in Scotland, 1966–1969, Cmnd. 4150 (Edinburgh: HMSO).

Franklin, M. (1983) 'The Rise of Issue Voting in British Elections', in *Strathclyde Papers on Government and Politics*, No.3 (Glasgow: University of Strathclyde).

—(1985) *The Decline of Class Voting in Britain* (Oxford University Press).

Fry, M. (1987) *Patronage and Principle. A Political History of Modern Scotland* (Aberdeen University Press).

Gallagher, T. (1987) *Glasgow: the uneasy peace* (Manchester University Press).

Gibson, J. S. (1985) *The Thistle and the Crown: A History of the Scottish Office* (Edinburgh: HMSO).

Gilmour (1937) *Report of the Committee on Scottish Administration* Cmd.5563 (Edinburgh: HMSO).

Gillett, Eric (1983) *Investment in the Environment* (Aberdeen University Press).

Glassberg, A. (1981) *Representation and Urban Community* (London: Macmillan).

226 *References*

Glasgow (1972) *Second Review of the Development Plan. Areas of Need in Glasgow* (Glasgow: Corporation of City of Glasgow, Department of Planning).

Glasgow (1984) City of Glasgow District Council Department of Planning *A Comparative Analysis of Capital Investment in District Council Priority Areas, 1979–80 to 1983–4* (Glasgow: author).

Gray, J., A. F. McPherson, and D. Raffe (1983) *Reconstructions of Secondary Education; theory, myth and practice since the war* (London: Routledge & Kegan Paul).

Grémion P. (1976) *Le Pouvior Périphique. Bureaucrates et notables dans le systéme politique français* (Paris: Seuil).

Grieve, R. (1986) *An Inquiry into Housing in Glasgow* (Glasgow: Glasgow District Council Housing Department).

Grimes, A. (1987) 'Pensioners in Poverty', in G. Brown and R. Cook (eds) *Scotland: The Real Divide* (Edinburgh: Mainstream).

Gunn, L. A. and P. D. Lindley (1977) 'Devolution: Origins, Events and Issues', in *Public Administration Bulletin*, 25.

Gyford, J. (1985) *The Politics of Local Socialism* (London: Allen & Unwin).

—(1985), 'The Politicisation of Local Government', in M. Loughlin, M. D. Gelfand and K. Young (eds) *Half a Century of Municipal Decline* (London; Allen & Unwin).

Hague, R. and M. Harrop (1987) *Comparative Government and Politics* (2nd ed) (London: Macmillan).

Ham, A. and M. Hill (1984) *The Policy Process in the Modern Capitalist State* (Brighton: Harvester).

Hanham, H. J. (1965) 'The Creation of the Scottish Office, 1881–87' in *Juridical Review*

—(1969), 'The Development of the Scottish Office', in J. N. Wolfe, (ed) *Government and Nationalism in Scotland* (Edinburgh University Press).

Hardman (1973), *The Dispersal of Government Work from London*, Cmnd. 5322 (London: HMSO).

Hartley, K. (1987) 'Competitive Tendering' in P. Jackson and F. Terry (eds) *Public Domain 1987* (London: Public Finance Foundation).

Harvie, C. (1977) *Scotland and Nationalism. Society and Politics, 1707–1977* (London: Allen and Unwin).

—(1981), *No Gods and Precious Few Heroes. Scotland, 1914–1980* (London: Edward Arnold).

—(1988a), 'Before the Breakthrough, 1888–1922', in I. Donnachie, C. Harvie and I. S. Wood *Forward! Labour Politics in Scotland 1888–1988* (Edinburgh: Polygon).

—(1988b), 'The Recovery of Scottish Labour, 1939–1951', in I. Donnachie, C. Harvie and I. S. Wood *Forward! Labour Politics in Scotland 1888–1988* (Edinburgh: Polygon).

Harvie Anderson, B and R. Johnston (1969) 'Note of Reservation', in Royal Commission on Local Government in Scotland *Report*, Cmnd. 4150 (Edinburgh: HMSO).

Heald, D. A. (1980a) *Financing Devolution within the United Kingdom* (Canberra: Australian National University).
— (1980b) 'Scotland's Public Expenditure Needs' in H. M. Drucker, and N. L. Drucker (eds) *Scottish Government Yearbook 1981* (Edinburgh: Paul Harris Publishing).
— (1982) 'Public Expenditure in Scotland: memorandum by the specialist adviser', in *Scottish Aspects of the 1982–5 Public Expenditure White Paper,* Committee on Scottish Affairs,1981–2, HC 413 (London: HMSO)
— (1983) *Public Expenditure: Its Defence and Reform* (Oxford: Martin Robertson)
— (1989) 'Territorial Expenditure, Asset Sales and the New Planning Total', memorandum to the Treasury and Civil Service Select Committee, HC 217 (London: HMSO).
Heath, A., R. Jowell and J. Curtice (1985) *How Britain Votes* (Oxford: Pergamon).
— — —and G. Evans (1989) 'The Extension of Popular Capitalism', in *Strathclyde Papers on Government and Politics*, no. 60 (Glasgow: University of Strathclyde).
Hechter, M. (1975) *Internal Colonialism. The Celtic Fringe in British National Development, 1536–1966* (London: Routledge & Kegan Paul).
Heclo, H. and A. Wildavsky (1974) *The Private Government of Public Money* (London: Macmillan).
Heidenheimer, A., H. Heclo and C. T. Adams (1983) *Comparative Public Policy. The Politics of Social Choice in Europe and America* (2nd ed) (New York: St. Martin's Press).
Hill, D. (1974) *Democratic Theory and Local Government* (London: Allen & Unwin).
Hill, M. (1972) *The Sociology of Public Administration* (London: Weidenfeld & Nicolson).
Hirschman, A. (1970) *Exit, Voice and Loyalty. Responses to Decline in Firms, Organizations and States* (Cambridge, Mass.: Harvard University Press).
Hogwood, B. and M. Keating (eds) (1982) *Regional Government in England* (Oxford: Clarendon).
Hood, N. and S. Young (1976) 'US Investment in Scotland – Aspects of the Branch Factory Syndrome', in *Scottish Journal of Political Economy*, Vol. 23
Humes, W. (1986) *The Leadership Class in Scottish Education* (Edinburgh: John Donald).
Hutchison, D. (1987) 'Political Writing in the Scottish Press', in D. McCrone (ed.) *Scottish Government Yearbook, 1987* (Edinburgh: Unit for the Study of Government in Scotland).
Jackman, R. (1981) 'How to Control Local Government Spending' in *Journal of Economic Affairs* 1, 3, April.
Jackman, R. (1982) 'Does Central Government Need to Control the Total of Local Government Spending?' *Local Government Studies*

Vol. 8, No. 3, May–June.

Jenkins, P. (1989) *Mrs. Thatcher's Revolution* (London: Pan).

Johnston, R. J. and C. J. Pattie (1988) 'Changing Voter Allegiances in Great Britain, 1979–87: An Exploration of Regional Patterns', in *Regional Studies*, 22.3.

Johnston, R. J. and C. J. Pattie (1989) 'A Nation Dividing: Economic Wellbeing, Voter Response and the Changing Electoral Geography of Great Britain', in *Parliamentary Affairs* 42.

—— and J. G. Allsop (1988) *A Nation Dividing? The Electoral Map of Great Britain, 1979–87* (London: Longman).

Jones, B. and M. Keating (1985) *Labour and the British State* (Oxford: Clarendon).

——(1988), *Beyond the Doomsday Scenario. Governing Scotland and Wales in the 1980s*. Strathclyde Papers in Government and Politics (Glasgow: University of Strathclyde).

Jordan, G. (1987) 'Budgeting: Changing Expectations' in H. Elcock and G. Jordan (eds) *Learning from Local Authority Budgeting* (Aldershot: Averbury Books).

Kavanagh, D. (1987) *Thatcherism and British Politics. The End of Consensus?* (Oxford: Oxford University Press).

Keating, M. (1975) *The Role of the Scottish MP*. Ph.D. thesis, CNAA

— (1976) 'Administrative Devolution in Practice. The Secretary of State for Scotland and the Scottish Office', in *Public Administration*, 54.2

— (1985a) 'Bureaucracy Devolved', in the *Times Educational Supplement, Scotland*, 5 April.

— (1985b) 'Local Government Spending and Central Control', in *Fraser of Allander Quarterly Economic Commentary*, May.

— (1988a) *The City that Refused to Die. Glasgow: The Politics of Urban Regeneration* (Aberdeen University Press).

— (1988b) *State and Regional Nationalism. Territorial Politics and the European State* (Hemel Hempstead: Harvester–Wheatsheaf).

— (1988c) 'The Labour Party in Scotland, 1951–1964', in I. Donnachie, C. Harvie and I. S. Wood *Forward! Labour Politics in Scotland 1888–1988* (Edinburgh: Polygon).

— (1989a) 'The Disintegration of Urban Policy. Glasgow and the New Britain', in *Urban Affairs Quarterly*, 24.4

— (1989b) 'Local Authorities and Economic Development in Western Europe', in *Entrepreneurship and Regional Development*, 1.

— and D. Bleiman (1979) *Labour and Scottish Nationalism* (London: Macmillan).

— and A. Midwinter (1983) *The Government of Scotland* (Edinburgh: Mainstream).

— and N. Waters, (1985), 'Scotland in the European Community', in M. Keating and B. Jones (eds) *Regions in the European Community* (Oxford: Clarendon).

— and R. Boyle (1986) *Remaking Urban Scotland. Strategies for Local Economic Development* (Edinburgh University Press).

— and C. Carter (1987) 'Policy making in Scottish government. The designation of Cumbernauld New Town', in *Public Administration*, 65.

— and J. Mitchell (1987) 'Glasgow's Neglected Periphery. The Easterhouse and Drumchapel Initiatives', in D. McCrone (ed.) *The Scottish Government Yearbook, 1987* (Edinburgh: Unit for the Study of Government in Scotland).

— R. Levy, J. Geekie and J. Brand (1989) 'Labour Elites in Glasgow', in *Strathclyde Papers in Government and Politics*, 61 (Glasgow: University of Strathclyde).

Kellas J. (1961) *The Liberal Party in Scotland, 1885–1895* Ph.D thesis, London University.

— (1968), *Modern Scotland. The Nation since 1870* (London: Pall Mall).

— (1973, 1989) *The Scottish Political System*, (1st ed and 4th ed) (Cambridge University Press).

— and P. Madgwick (1982) 'Territorial Ministries: the Scottish and Welsh Offices', in P. Madgwick and R. Rose (eds) *The Territorial Dimension in United Kingdom Politics* (London: Macmillan).

Kendrick, S. (1983) 'Social Change in Scotland', in G. Brown and R. Cook (eds) *Scotland: The Real Divide* (Edinbrugh: Mainstream).

Kilbrandon (1973a) Royal Commission on the Constitution, 1969–73, *Report*, Cmnd. 5460 (London: HMSO).

Kilbrandon (1973b) Royal Commission on the Constitution, 1969–73, *Research Paper 7. Devolution and other Aspects of Government: an Attitudes Survey* (London: HMSO).

King D. N. (1973) *Financial and Economic Aspects of Regionalism and Separatism, Commission on the Constitution Research* Paper 10 (London: HMSO)

Lawson, A. (1988) 'Mair nor a rough wind blawin.. .', D. McCrone (ed.) *Scottish Government Yearbook, 1988* (Edinburgh: Unit for the Study of Government in Scotland).

Leach, S., C. Game, J. Gyford and A. Midwinter (1986) 'The Political Organisation of Local Authorities', in *Research Volume 1, Widdicombe Report* Cmnd. 9798 (London: HMSO).

Leruez, J. (1983) *L'Ecosse. Une nation sans état* (Lille: Presses Universitaires de Lille).

Levitt, I. (1983) 'Scottish Poverty: The Historical Background', in G. Brown and R. Cook (eds) *Scotland: The Real Divide* (Edinburgh: Mainstream).

Lindblom, C. E. (1959) 'The Science of Muddling Through', in *Public Administration Review* 19, pp.79–88.

Lindley, P. (1982) 'The Framework of Regional Planning, 1964–1980', in B. Hogwood and M. Keating (eds) *Regional Government in England* (Oxford: Clarendon).

Lock, G. (1989) 'The 1689 Bill of Rights', in *Political Studies*, XXXVII.4.

Lythe, C. and M. Majmudar (1982) *The Renaissance of the Scottish Economy?* (London: Allen & Unwin).

McAllister, I. and R. Rose (1984) *The Nationwide Competition for Votes* (London: Frances Pinter).

McArthur, A. (1987) 'Jobs and Incomes', in D. Donnison and A. Middleton *Regenerating the Inner City. Glasgow's Experience* (London: Routledge & Kegan Paul).

McBeth, A. (1983) 'The Government of Scottish Education; partnership or compromise', in D. McCrone (ed.) *Scottish Government Yearbook, 1984* (Edinburgh: Unit for the Study of Government in Scotland).

MacCormick, N. (1973) review of J. Kellas *The Scottish Political System*, in *Scottish International*, 6.4

McCrone, G. (1969) *Scotland's Future* (London: Oxford University Press).

MacDonnell (1915) *Report of the Royal Commission on the Civil Service* Report 4, Cd.7338 (London: HMSO).

McFadden, J. (1989) 'The Role of the Treasurer', paper presented to ACCA conference on local government finance, Glasgow, September (document never published).

Mackay, A. C. (1986) 'The Deregulation of Local Bus Services in Scotland', in D. McCrone (ed) *The Scottish Government Yearbook, 1986* (Edinburgh: Unit for the Study of Grovernment in Scotland).

McKay, D. (1977) *Scotland 1980: The Economics of Independence* (Edinburgh: Q Press).

Mackintosh, J. (1973) Review of J. Kellas *The Scottish Political System*, in The Political Quarterly, 44.3

McLean, I. (1983) *The Legend of Red Clydeside* (Edinburgh: John Donald)

McLennan, D. (1988) 'Municipal Housing: The Long Goodbye?' *Scottish Government Yearbook 1989* (Edinburgh: Unit for the Study of Government in Scotland).

MacPherson, A. and C. Raab (1988) *Governing Education. A Sociology of Policy since 1945* (Edinburgh: Edinburgh University Press).

Maher, G., (1977) 'The Identity of the Scottish Legal System', in *Juridical Review*.

Mair, C., A. Midwinter and J. Moxen (1988) 'Scottish Library Expenditure in the 1980s: Trends and Variations' in *Library Review*, 37.4.

Malpass, P. and A. Murie (1987) *Housing Policy and Practice*, (2nd ed) (London: Macmillan).

Marquand, D. (1989) 'Now's the Hour', in *New Statesman and Society*, 28 April.

Martlew, C. (1984) 'Consulting Business about the Rates' (report) *Planning Exchange Occasional Paper No. 14* (Glasgow: Planning Exchange).

— (1988), *Local Democracy in Practice* (Aldershot: Avebury).

Meadows, W. and P. Jackson (1986) 'UK Local Government: Alternative Economic Strategies' in M. Goldsmith (ed.) *New Research in Central – Local Relations* (Aldershot: Gower).

Mellors, C. (1977) *The British MP* (Farnborough: Saxon House).

Middleton, K. W. M. (1954) 'New Thoughts on the Union between

England and Scotland', in *Juridical Review*.

Midwinter, A. (1984) *The Politics of Local Spending* (Edinburgh: Mainstream Publishing)

Midwinter, A. (1988) 'Local Budgetary Strategies in a Decade of Retrenchment', in *Public Money and Management*, 8.4

—, M. Keating and P. Taylor (1983) 'Excessive and Unreasonable: The Politics of the Scottish Hit List', in *Political Studies*, 21.3

—, — and — (1984) 'The Politics of Scottish Housing Plans', in *Policy and Politics*, 12.2

Midwinter, A. and C. Mair (1987) *Rates Reform: Issues, Arguments and Evidence* (Edinburgh: Mainstream Publishing).

—, — and C. Ford (1986) 'The Politics of Rate Support Grant Distribution', in D. McCrone (ed) *Scottish Government Yearbook 1986* (Edinburgh: Unit for the Study of Government in Scotland).

—. — and — (1987) 'Regression Analysis and the Assessment of Local Expenditure Need: A Reconsideration' in *Local Government Studies* 13.1

Midwinter, A. and J. Moxen (1991 forthcoming) 'Fiscal Conservatism or Fiscal Prudence? Expenditure in Independent Councils Since Reorganisation', in A. Brown and R. Parry (eds) *Scottish Government Yearbook 1991* (Edinburgh: Unit for the Study of Government in Scotland).

Miller, W. (1981) *The End of British Politics?* (Oxford: Clarendon).

— (1983) 'Testing the Power of Media Consensus', in *Strathclyde Papers on Government and Politics*, 17 (Glasgow: University of Strathclyde).

— (1984) 'There was no Alternative: the British General Election of 1983', in *Parliamentary Affairs*, 37.4

— (1988) *Irrelevant Elections ? The Quality of Local Democracy in Britain* (Oxford: Cherwell Press).

Mitchell, J. (1988) 'Recent Developments in the Scottish National Party', in *Political Quarterly*, 59

— (1989) 'The Gilmour Report and Scottish Central Administration', in *Juridical Review*, December.

— (1990) *The Conservatives and the Union* (Edinburgh University Press).

— (1990) 'Factions, Tendencies and Consensus in the SNP in the 1980s', in A. Brown and R. Parry (eds) *Scottish Government Yearbook, 1990* (Edinburgh: Unit for the Study of Government in Scotland).

Montgomery (1984) *Report of the Committee of Inquiry into the Functions of the Island Councils of Scotland* Cmnd., 9216 (Edinburgh: HMSO).

Morgan, A. (1927) *The Rise and Progress of Scottish Education* (London: Oliver & Boyd).

— (1929) *Makers of Scottish Education* (London: Longman Green).

Morison, H. (1987) *The Regeneration of Local Economies* (Oxford University Press).

232   *References*

Munro, R. (Lord Alness) (1930) *Looking Back: Fugitive Writings and Sayings* (London: Thomas Nelson).

Murie, R. *et al.* (1988) *The Consumer Implications of the Housing Act 1988* (Bristol: School for Advanced Urban Studies).

Nairn, A. (1983) 'GEAR – Comprehensive Redevelopment or Confidence Trick?', in *Fraser of Allender Quarterly Economic Commentary*, 2

Nairn, T. (1981) *The Break-Up of Britain* (2nd ed.) (London: Verso).

— (1988) *The Enchanted Glass* London: Hutchinson).

Nelson, S. (1980) 'Participating in GEAR' (Glasgow: University of Strathclyde, Strathclyde Area Survey).

Norris, G. M. (1983) 'Poverty in Scotland, 1979–83', in G. Brown and R. Cook (eds) *Scotland: The Real Divide* (Edinburgh: Mainstream).

Ospina, J. (1987) *Housing Ourselves* (London: Hilary Shipman).

Page, E. (1978) 'Why Should Central – Local Relations In Scotland Be Different To Those In England?', in *Public Administration Bulletin* No.28

—and Midwinter, A. (1980) 'Remoteness, Efficiency, Cost and the Reorganisation of Scottish Local Government', in *Public Administration*, 58.4

Parry, R. (1980a) 'The Territorial Dimension In United Kingdom Public Employment', in *Studies in Public Policy* No.65 (Glasgow: Centre for the Study of Public Policy).

— (1980) 'The Rise and Fall Of Civil Service Dispersal To Scotland' in H.M. Drucker and N. Drucker (eds), *Scottish Government Yearbook, 1981* (Edinburgh: Paul Harris Publishing).

— (1981) 'Scotland as a Laboratory for Public Administration' Paper presented to PSA UK Politics Group Conference, Glasgow, September.

— (1982) 'Public Expenditure in Scotland', in D. McCrone (ed) *Scottish Government Yearbook, 1983* (Edinburgh: Unit for the Study of Government in Scotland).

— (1984) 'Cutback Management in Lothian Region' (Edinburgh: University of Edinburgh mimeo)

—(1985) 'Britain: Stable Aggregates, Changing Compositon', in R. Rose (ed.) *Public Employment in Western Nations* (Cambridge University Press).

—(1986) 'Privatisation and the Tarnishing of the Scottish Public Sector', in D. McCrone (ed) *The Scottish Government Yearbook 1986* (Edinburgh: Unit for the Study of Government in Scotland).

—(1988) *Scottish Political Facts* (Edinburgh: T. and T. Clark).

Paterson (1973) *The New Scottish Local Authorities: Organisation and Management Structures* (Edinburgh: HMSO).

Payne, G. and G. Ford (1983) 'Inequality and the Occupational Structure', in G. Brown and R. Cook (eds) *Scotland: The Real Divide* (Edinburgh: Mainstream).

Peterson, P. (1981) *City Limits* (Chicago: University of Chicago Press).

References 233

Pereria-Menaut, A-C (1986) *En defensa de la constitución* Pamplona: Ediciones Universidad de Navarra).
Pirie, M. (1988) *Micropolitics* (Aldershot: Wildwood House).
Planning Advisory Group (1965) *The Future of Development Plans* (London: HMSO).
Plowden (1967) *Children and Their Primary Schools* (London: HMSO)
Pottinger, G. (1979) *The Secretaries of State for Scotland, 1926–76* (Edinburgh: Scottish Academic Press).
Pulzer, P. (1967) *Political Representation and Elections in Britain* (London: Allen & Unwin).
Punnett, R. M. (1984) 'Regional Partisanship and the Legitimacy of British Government 1868–1983', in *Parliamentary Affairs*, 37.2
—(1987) *British Government and Politics* (5th ed) (Aldershot: Gower).
Raab, C. (1982) 'Mapping the boundaries of education policy systems; the case of Scotland', in *Public Administration, Bulletin*, 39.
Raab, C. (1983) 'Review of Keating and Midwinter's 'The Government of Scotland', in *Public Administration*, 61.4.
Renton, D. (1975) *Committee on the Preparation of Legislation, Report*, Cmnd. 6053 (London: HMSO).
Rhodes, R. (1981) *Control and Power in Central – Local Relations* (Aldershot: Gower).
Rhodes, R. A. W. (1987) *Beyond Westminster and Whitehall: The Sub-Central Government of Britain* (London: Unwin Hyman).
—and A. Midwinter (1980) 'Corporate Management: The New Conventional Wisdom in British Local Government', in *Studies in Public Policy* No.59, University of Strathclyde, Glasgow.
Richardson, J. J. and A.G. Jordan (1979) *Governing under Pressure* (Oxford: Martin Robertson).
Robertson, D. (1984) *Class and the British Electorate* (Oxford: Blackwell).
Rokkan, S. and D. Urwin (1983) *Economy, Territory, Identity: Politics of West European Peripheries* (London: Sage).
Rose, R. (1970 *The United Kingdom as a Multi-National State* (Glasgow: University of Strathclyde Survey Research Centre, Paper No. 6).
—(1982) *Understanding the United Kingdom* (London: Longman).
—(1985) 'Scotland: British with a Difference', in I. McAllister and R. Rose *The Nationwide Competiton for Votes* (London: Frances Pinter).
—and I. McAllister (1986) *Voters Begin to Choose. From Closed-Class to Open Elections in Britain* (London: Sage).
Ross, J. (1980) 'Local government reform in Scotland. Some subversive reflections', mimeo, Centre for the Study of Public Policy, University of Strathclyde.
—(1981), 'The Secretary of State for Scotland and the Scottish Office', in *Studies in Public Policy, 87* (Glasgow: University of Strathclyde).
Ross, W. (1978) 'Approaching the Archangelic?' in H. M. Drucker

(ed) *Scottish Government Yearbook, 1978* (Edinburgh: Paul Harris Publishing).

RSA (1983) Regional Studies Association, *Report of an Inquiry into Regional Problems in the United Kingdom* (Norwich: Geo).

Rudolph, J. and R. Thompson (1985) 'Ethnoterritorial movements and the policy process', in *Comparative Politics*, 17.3.

Scott, J. and M. Hughes (1980) *The Anatomy of Scottish Capital* (London: Croom Helm).

Scottish Centre for Economic and Social Research (1989) *Scottish Education: A Declaration of Principles, A Joint AdCAS/SCESR Report* (Edinburgh: SCESR)

Scottish Local Government Information Unit (1988), *Opting out and the School Boards (Scotland) Bill* (Glasgow: author).

Scottish Office (1969) *Memorandum to the Select Committee on Scottish Affairs* (Edinburgh: HMSO).

Scottish Office (1984) *Public Expenditure to 1986–87: A Commentary on the Scotland Programme* (Edinburgh: Scottish Office).

—(1987 *Public Expenditure to 1989–90: A Commentary on the Scotland Programme* (Edinburgh: Scottish Office).

—(1988) *New Life for Urban Scotland* (Edinburgh: HMSO).

Sefton, H. R. (1982), 'The Church of Scotland and Scottish Nationhood', in S. Mews, (Ed.) *Religion and National Identity* (Oxford University Press).

Select Committee on Scottish Affairs (1980) *Scottish Aspects of the 1980–84 Public Expenditure White Paper* Parliamentary Paper 689 (London: HMSO).

Session Cases (1953) *MacCormick and Another v. the Lord Advocate.*

Sharpe, L. J. (1970), 'Theories and Values of Local Government', in *Political Studies*, XVIII.2

Simpson, B. (1986) 'The Role of the Accounts Commission in Securing Value for Money' in S. Bailey (ed) *The Role of the Accounts Commission, Centre for Urban and Regional Research Discussion Paper* No. 27, University of Glasgow.

Simpson, D. (1970) 'Independence: the Economic Issues', in N. McCormick (ed.) *The Scottish Debate* (London: Oxford University Press).

Skelcher, C. (1980) 'From Programme Budgeting to Policy Analysis' in *Public Administration*, 58

Skelton, N. (1924) *Constructive Conservatism* (Edinburgh: Blackwood).

Smith, G. (1919) *Scottish Literature: Character and Influence* (London: Macmillan).

Smith, R. and U. Wannop (1985) (eds) *Strategic Planning in Action. The Impact of the Clyde Valley Plan* (Aldershot: Gower).

Smith, T. B. (1957) 'The Union of 1707 as Fundamental Law', in Public Law.

Smout, T. C. (1970) 'Scottish Nationalism, Law and Self-Government', in N. McCormick, (ed.) *The Scottish Debate* (London: Oxford University Press).

—(1986) *A Century of the Scottish People* (London: Collins).
SOCRU (1985) Scottish Office Central Research Unit, *Council House Sales in Scotland* (Edinburgh: Scottish Office).
—(1986) Scottish Office Central Research Unit, *A Review of Community Councils in Scotland, 1983–4* (Edinburgh: Scottish Office).
STEAC (1985) *Future Strategy for Higher Education in Scotland: Report of the Scottish Tertiary Education Advisory Council* Cmnd. 9676, (Edinburgh: HMSO).
Stewart, G. (1927) *The Story of Scottish Education* (London: Pitman).
Stewart, J. D. (1980) 'From Growth to Standstill' in M. Wright (ed) *Public Spending Decisions* (London: Allen & Unwin).
Stodart (1981) *Report of the Committee of Inquiry into Local Government in Scotland* (Cmnd. 8115).
Stone, C. (1987) 'Summing Up', in C. Stone and H. Sanders (eds), *The Politics of Urban Development* (Lawrence: University of Kansas Press).
Strathclyde (1977) *Multiple Deprivation* (Glasgow: Strathclyde Regional Council).
Taylor, P. J. and R. J. Johnston (1979) *Geography of Elections* (Harmondsworth: Penguin).
Titterton, M. (1982) 'Hands Off Lothian! A Study of Militancy and Mobilisation in the Locality' paper prepared for the conference on Local Politics and the State, School for Advanced Urban Studies, Bristol, 24–5 September.
Toothill, J. N. (1961) *Inquiry into the Scottish Economy* (Edinburgh: Scottish Council Development and Industry).
Treasury and Civil Service Select Committee (1989) *Sixth Report. The Presentation of Information on Public Expenditure, HC 217* (London: HMSO).
Twine, F. (1983), 'The Low Paid', in G. Brown and R. Cook (eds) *Scotland: The Real Divide* (Edinburgh: Mainstream).
Walshe, G. (1987) *Planning Public Expenditure in the UK* (London: Macmillan Education).
Widdicombe (1986) *Report of the Committee of Inquiry into the Conduct of Local Authority Business* (HMSO)
Wannop, U. and R. Leclerc (1987) 'The Management of GEAR', in D. Donnison and A. Middleton *Regenerating the Inner City. Glasgow's Experience.* (London: Routledge and Kegan Paul).
Wheatley (1969) Royal Commission on Local Government in Scotland, *Report,* Cmnd. 4150 (Edinburgh: HMSO)
Wildavsky, A. (1964) *The Politics of the Budgetary Process* (Boston: Little, Brown)
Wright, M. (1977) 'Public Expenditure in Britain: The Crisis of Control', in *Public Administration,* 55
WCSP (1974), West Central Scotland Plan Steering Committee, *West Central Scotland Plan – a Programme for Action* (Glasgow: author).
Young, J. (1979) *The Rousing of the Scottish Working Class* (London: Croom Helm).

Young, R. (1981) 'The Management of Political Innovation' *Local Government Studies*, Nov–Dev.

Young, R. (1983) 'Scottish Local Government: What Future?' on D. McCrone (ed) *Scottish Government Yearbook 1984* (Edinburgh: Unit for the Study of Government in Scotland).

Index

237

Index